IBM Maximo Asset Management
The Consultant's Guide
Second Edition

Robert Zientara

2020

ISBN: 978-83-944192-8-8

Proofread by EduLingva Marta Antoszczyszyn

Cover photo: Photo by Crystal Kwok on Unsplash and screenshot from Maximo Preview Site.

Table of Contents

Table of Figures

Glossary

- API—Application Program Interface
- BMS—Building Management System
- BOM—Bill of Material
- BPMN—Business Process Modeling Notation
- CAD—Computer Aided Design
- CIM—Common Information Model (electricity)
- CMMS—Computerized Maintenance Management System
- CPU—Central Processing Unit
- CRM—Customer Relationship Management
- CSS—Cascading Style Sheets
- DB—Database
- DBA—Database Administrator
- DMS—Document Management System
- EAM—Enterprise Asset Management
- EOQ—Economic Order Quantity
- EOS—End of Support
- ERD—Entity Relationship Diagram
- ERP—Enterprise Resource Planning
- ESB—Enterprise Service Bus
- EST—Eastern Standard Time
- ETL—Extract, Transform, Load
- FIFO—First In, First Out
- GIF—Graphics Interchange Format
- GIS—Geographic Information System
- GL—General Ledger
- GMT—Greenwich Mean Time
- GPS—Global Positioning System
- HA—High Availability
- HR—Human Resource Management
- IAS—Item Assembly Structure
- IMAP—Internet Message Access Protocol
- IoT—Internet of Things

- IR—Infrared
- JP—Job Plan
- JPG—Joint Photographic Experts Group
- JVM—Java Virtual Machine
- KPI— Key Performance Indicator
- LAN—Local Area Network
- LDAP—Lightweight Directory Access Protocol
- LIFO—Last In, First Out
- LOTO—Lock-out Tag-out
- MBO—Maximo Business Objects
- MIF—Maximo Integration Framework
- MR—Material Request
- MTBF—Mean Time Between Failure
- M&TE—Measuring and Testing Equipment
- MTTR—Mean Time To Repair
- MUG—Maximo User Group
- OEE—Overall Equipment Effectiveness
- OS—Operating System
- OSHA—Occupational Safety and Health Administration
- PM—Project Management, Project Manager, Preventive Maintenance
- PMP—Project Management Professional
- PMR—Problem Management Record
- PO—Purchase Order
- POP3—Post Office Protocol 3
- PR—Purchase Requisition
- PRINCE2—Projects In Controlled Environments
- QA—Quality Assurance
- QBR—Query Based Report
- RACI—Responsible, Accountable, Consulted, Informed
- RAM—Random-Access Memory
- RDBMS—Relational Database Management System
- REST—Representational State Transfer
- RFC—Request For Change
- RFP—Request For Proposal

- RFQ—Request for Quotation
- RMI—Remote Method Invocation
- ROP—Reorder Point
- ROS—Report Object Structures
- SCADA—Supervisory Control And Data Acquisition
- SLA—Service-Level Agreement
- SMTP—Simple Mail Transfer Protocol
- SR—Service Request
- SSO—Single Sign-on
- UI—User Interface
- UML—Unified Modeling Language
- UNSPSC—United Nations Standard Products and Services Code
- URL—Uniform Resource Locator
- UV—Ultraviolet
- UX—User Experience
- VLAN—Virtual Local Area Network
- VMRS—Vehicle Maintenance Reporting Standards
- VPN—Virtual Private Network
- WAN—Wide Area Network
- WO—Work Order
- XLIFF—XML Localization Interchange File Format
- XML—Extensible Markup Language

Convention Used

ASSETS—module name
Assets—application name
Serial number—field name, button name, tab name, action name
ASSETNUM—database table name
WORKORDER.ASSIGNEDOWNERGROUP—database column
OPERATING—text value
maxadmin—username, security group name, SQL code, Java code, Jython code

In this book, you will find sample SQL statements. They may be preceded with the database indication, e.g., DB2, which means this piece of code is good only for IBM DB2. If there is no database indication, the SQL is generic and can be used with any RDBMS.

I dedicate this book to my wife and sons.

Introduction

Dear Reader,

This is already a second edition of this book, revised and extended. This is not a user's manual but a guide to help you to implement IBM® Maximo® Asset Management. It has been written mainly from the business (functional) perspective. The ideas and concepts are based on my own experience, and they are not a definite knowledge or finished solution but rather some advice and inspiration. I invite you to use whatever you find suitable in this book; you can also modify it to your needs. I have included some technical tips how to improve the system but this only supplements the business side. Fortunately, IBM is producing more and more useful technical articles, so you can easily find the answers to how to create a dialog or prepare a crossover domain there.

One of the goals for this book is to improve Maximo's perception on the market because sometimes users describe it as overcomplicated. This may be the result of the consultants' limited knowledge about the existing functionality. They then try to reinvent the wheel by creating new applications. The result is an unhappy customer and the opinion that Maximo is not good.

This book has been written for the current and future Maximo functional consultants with at least basic knowledge of the system (navigation, structure and configuration); therefore, you will not find many technical examples here (like Java code).

The first part of the book describes the implementation process. It includes some information about its steps and guidelines on how to organize the team. Part II is my explanation of Maximo functionality. This section is structured following Maximo modules and applications, so you can easily find an interesting chapter. In the chapters on applications, you will find chapters titled "Known Issues and Initial Changes" that contain some information about potential limitations of the application and/or suggestions about how to make it better. There are also chapters titled "Saved Queries" with some suggested queries. All other content is specific to the application.

Every feature/query presented in this book has been tested and implemented in real life. The functionality I have described should work in IBM Maximo Asset Management versions 7.5 and 7.6.

Robert Zientara

Part I—Implementation Project

Reminder: a project is a structured effort with a defined goal, budget and timeframe that is supposed to bring the customer some value. The word '**structured**' suggests that your projects should have proper organization and tools—these will be described later in more detail. The last element of the definition, **value,** is not only about issuing an invoice but also about solving issues or improving the customer's operations. The successful implementation will also enrich your experience and increase your value in the job market.

Projects require proper management. The role of the project manager is critically important. This should be an experienced person who has either done Maximo projects or ERP implementations before. Otherwise, they may not understand the challenges you will be facing and which are not trivial. Most of my implementations used a classic waterfall approach, but Maximo, with its quick prototyping features, could also benefit from Agile methodology. If you manage to convince your customers to use Scrum, you will be lucky! But of course, your organization needs to adopt this methodology first.

In the next chapters, I present some indications that should prepare you for your upcoming challenges. If you will follow these guidelines, then your team will be equipped with all the necessary tools and procedures, and there should be no surprises in your next project.

Prerequisites

Your project starts before the offer is even submitted. The first and most important task is to **review and answer ALL the customer's requirements** (I assume that the customer has already asked you to present an offer and presented their expectations). You must know how to address each requirement because this will help you during negotiations. For instance, if you know that some requirements cannot be fulfilled or that you can cover them only partially, you could try to eliminate them or change the scope of the project. Answering the requirement means to prepare time estimations. Try simple categorization.

- The configuration of settings or properties—do not calculate the time;
- Basic configuration—1 day;
- Medium configuration—5 days;
- Heavy configuration—10 days;
- Customization—enter the time manually.

The total number of man-days will give you an overview of how complicated the project is going to be. You can even decide not to bid if you will find that your price will be higher than the customer's budget.
The next task is to gather as much information about the customer and their problems as possible. Here is a list of sample questions you could use; they are divided into the business and technical sections. The answers will help you estimate the scope of the implementation, plan the solution and design the required infrastructure.

Business questions

- What is the official, real and hidden goal of this project? Process automation? Cutting costs? Process standardization? Accountability? Why are there three different goals? Because the official one is usually expressed in the RFP but the real one is in the background. For example, in one of my projects, the customer wanted a solution that would have replicated the functionality of ERP software because ERP licenses were expensive. This hidden goal can be something not explicitly presented in the documentation, such as the protection of the legacy system. You have to identify these goals to address the expectations and mitigate risks.

- Is the customer aware of how Maximo is implemented? This is a typical misunderstanding between vendor and customer. The vendor is offering off-the-shelf product with configuration and customization, while the customer thinks, "I want a 100% customized solution." There should be a clear message for the customer (before the contract is signed): We are offering you ready-to-use functionality, which can be additionally tailored to your needs, but it is not a development platform in which you can require anything.
- What kind of information should be supplied by the new system?
- What kind of equipment will be supported by the system? Core business machines, other equipment?
- What are the expected benefits?
- Who is the sponsor of the project? Is this person high enough in the organization to introduce business changes? If you do not have the upper management's support, then it is very likely that the project will not be successful.
- Who are the influencers? Maybe there is a person who has created the legacy system or signed the order for it—do not expect them to be your friend. You can also find a 'champion' who is a person that knows the processes best and also has a lot of energy. This may be your supporter in the project. Make sure they will be rewarded for their efforts.
- Who are the users of the system? Workers, middle management, or external users, like suppliers?

- Which processes should be supported by the new system: asset management, corrective/preventive maintenance, inventory, purchasing? Are there any existing descriptions of the current processes? If not, then you can expect the processes to be designed during the project, which generates high risk.
- What is the planned integration with other systems: ERP, HR, SCADA, LDAP?
- What is the organizational structure of the company? How complicated is the reporting structure?
- In which locations will the system be used?
- Should the system be used on mobile devices?

IT questions

- How many concurrent users will use the system?
- How many IT environments are planned: production, test, development, QA?
- How reliable is the internal LAN and WAN in terms of speed and availability?
- Will the system be used only in the internal network, through WAN or also via Internet?
- Are there any high availability requirements? This is especially valid when Maximo is the critical system for the organization.
- Should the system be multilingual? Which languages should be installed? This question is closely related to the previous one, because Maximo still has issues on an MS SQL Server that prevent installing languages using different code pages, e.g., Latin-1 and Latin-2.
- What is the preferred operating system: AIX, UNIX, Linux, MS Windows?
- What is the preferred application server: IBM WebSphere, Oracle WebLogic? What is the preferred database system: IBM DB2, Oracle, MS SQL Server? These two questions may affect the price of the project, because in the standard package, the customer gets the

licenses for IBM WebSphere and IBM DB2. If they prefer other software, they need to obtain the licenses separately.

- What is the preferred Internet browser?
- Maximo saves all the attachments in the server folder. Is there a requirement to save them in a different location or integrate them with a document management system?
- Should Maximo be installed in the virtualized environment? What kind of software is used?
- Is there an enterprise service bus used in the company to integrate the systems?
- Is there any specific security policy in the company, for example, blocking some network ports or not allowing the use of Java applications?
- Should Maximo be integrated with LDAP? For authentication only or to load information about user security profiles? Is Single Sign-On functionality required?
- Is it possible to establish VPN access to the servers? This will enable remote configuration and support.
- It is a good idea to present the customer with minimal requirements for the user workstations and determine whether they are compatible with the local policies to avoid issues when the system goes live.
- Ensure that all this information is aligned with Maximo Compatibility Matrix to avoid issues during installation.

To get the answers to these questions, try different sources: ask the customer directly, interview the account managers, check with the colleagues who may have worked for this customer earlier, read the information available on the customer's web page, or review the Internet pages dedicated to the customer's industry. Try to match this information with the requirements—there might be a correlation or you could have addressed some different issues. This will potentially help you during negotiations: you can replace the requirements you cannot fulfill with some new functionalities.

Another important aspect of Maximo implementation is the scope, namely, the number of the business processes being implemented. Of course, it sounds great to implement everything that is possible in one round, but there are a few factors to consider. Everybody (the customer and you) should understand that the implementation of CMMS/EAM system is similar to a small ERP project. It involves different departments, integrates different tools, and requires some organizational and cultural changes. It takes time to understand how the system works, what is missing, what will be not used. Do not forget that the end users must be trained to operate the new user interface and follow the new procedures. My suggestion is always to split the implementation into smaller chunks ("start small") and deliver them process by process, starting with the ones that can bring the biggest positive effects ("quick wins"). Moreover, Maximo has many features that can be added step by step, not in a big bang release.

All of the above factors should be considered before submitting an offer. Proposed budget and schedule need to be realistic (do not assume positive scenarios everywhere) and safe—it should include a contingency for the risk mitigation.

Implementation Steps

Your offer has been successfully submitted and the contract has been signed. It is time to design and implement the solution. Let me explain the steps that make up the project.

- presentations,
- workshops,
- installation,
- configuration,
- data migration,
- training,
- tests,
- go live,
- technical support.

Finally, I will share my 'lessons learned' with you.

Presentations

Each project should start with presenting Maximo's functionality to the customer's implementation team, followed by a short 'sightseeing tour' for you. There is a simple logic behind this:

- you know nothing about the customer's business;
- the customer knows nothing about Maximo, and this issue will constantly arise during the project.

Your presentation (a minimum one-day session—the longer, the better) should cover the topics from system navigation through the purpose of the modules and applications to the built-in features that can help the customer in everyday life. The better you explain how the out-of-the-box features work, the greater the chance is that you can fulfill the customer's requirements using standard Maximo functionality. The presentation must be perfectly prepared, and should be led by your best consultant with broadest knowledge to answer any questions from the audience. After the presentation, the customer should leave with the feeling that they have chosen the best product and the best people to implement it.

Now, your customer should show you how they work and offer you a guided tour. You should see the machinery, procedures and people. These will give you a feel of how they work. Maybe you can find some pain points like poor reporting or the lack of automation, which were not described in the requirements, but may be addressed during the project.

After that, you can sit down together and in series of workshops discuss the best methods to realize the customer's requirements in Maximo.

Work Streams

Many Maximo projects are bigger ventures that will require splitting the work between multiple groups. Here is the list of typical threads or streams.

- workshops and designing the solution,
- installation,
- integrations,
- data migration,
- mobile application,
- reports,
- training,
- testing.

The number of streams is dependent on the project, its scope and complexity, but you should be prepared to lead the project this way (and of course to have enough resources: see chapter 'Implementation Team'). Some team members may participate in different streams, but the streams should be considered different tasks and should be planned separately. Of course, some actions from different streams can be simultaneously, but the project manager and solution architect should always watch the overall progress and quickly react in the case of delays or issues.

Workshops and Design

Before you start meeting with your customer, I would like you to take to heart the statement below.

Maximo has a lot of built-in functionalities. It grew over the years, based on real-life experience, and offers the best practice in maintenance. Please do not create your own solution unless you have determined that Maximo does not offer this kind of functionality. This is the advantage of buying Maximo as an off-the-shelf product with the best practice, predefined data model, security profiles and a strong integration mechanism included. Do not use Maximo as a development framework only; rely on the standard functionality.

Why am I saying this? Because during my career, I have seen too many situations in which the consultant has developed something that already exists, but they did not know about it. I have even seen columns added to the database tables that were copies of the existing ones. It is your responsibility to explain to the customer how the out-of-the-box function works and to discuss with them how their requirements can be fulfilled with it. I know that customers may have their own opinions, but using standard features minimizes the effort during the implementation, support and upgrades. Sometimes, it is worth asking the customer to change their requirement (or maybe even remove some of them) to stay in line with the standard Maximo functions.

Usually, you will organize the workshops in the form of a series of meetings, corresponding to the main Maximo modules:

- Initial configuration,
- Asset management,
- Corrective maintenance,
- Preventive maintenance,
- Inventory and purchasing,

- Contracts,
- Safety,
- Resources.

During the discussions, focus on the maintenance functions of Maximo, talk on how to maximize the reliability of the assets and not on the technical configuration in Maximo!

The paragraph below outlines the topics to be discussed during each workshop.

Initial configuration

- multi-language features e.g. descriptions of Job Plans. Here is the list of the supported languages:
    - Arabic,
    - Chinese Simplified,
    - Chinese Traditional,
    - Croatian,
    - Czech,
    - Danish,
    - Dutch,
    - English,
    - Finnish,
    - French,
    - German,
    - Hebrew,
    - Hungarian,
    - Italian,
    - Japanese,
    - Korean,
    - Norwegian,
    - Polish,
    - Portuguese Brazilian,
    - Russian,
    - Slovenian,
    - Slovakian,

    - Spanish,
    - Swedish,
    - Turkish,
- the company's visual identification (logos on the screen and reports),
- which Maximo skin should be the default one,
- the company's organizational structure (Organizations and sites),
- calendars (holidays, shifts),
- Chart of Accounts,
- currencies and exchange rates,
- taxes,
- measure units,
- fiscal periods,
- Bulletin Board application,
- authentication (LDAP or local),
- email integration:
    - sending notifications,
    - processing incoming emails: workflow and interactions.

Asset management:

- naming convention,
- locations:
    - systems,
    - physical,
    - functional,
    - repair-facility,
- rotating versus non-rotating assets,
- hierarchies,
- meters,
- classifications and parameters,
- failure hierarchies,
- depreciation,
- maps,

- processes:
    - acquiring new assets,
    - moving between locations and sites,
    - decommissioning.

Corrective Maintenance:

- Budget Monitoring application,
- Cost Management application,
- collecting costs (asset/location/GL Account level)? Which costs: material, labor, tools, services? Is the labor cost required or just the labor time?),
- Service Requests application,
- Work Order's phases:
    - planning:
        - deciding who will do the work: the internal or external resources,
        - planning labor, material, tools, services,
        - prioritizing work,
        - Service Addresses,
        - defining SLAs,
    - scheduling:
        - planned dates,
    - dispatching:
        - assigning workers,
    - executing:
        - work permits,
        - reporting labor (work or trip time), materials, tools,
        - approval of labor time,
    - closing:
        - reporting services (invoices),
        - use of Quick Reporting application,
        - Failure Codes entry.

Planned Maintenance:

- equipment covered by preventive actions,

- Job Plans application:
    - conditional plans,
    - nested plans,
    - dynamic plans,
    - Flow Control,
- Preventive Maintenance application:
    - fixed versus floating schedule,
    - time- and meter-based maintenance,
    - Job Plans Sequence,
    - Forecast and Forecast Cost,
- Master PM application,
- Condition Monitoring application.

Inventory Management:

- item sets,
- Item Master application:
    - naming convention,
    - Condition Codes,
    - rotating versus non-rotating,
    - kits,
    - lots,
    - Commodity Codes,
    - relation with the assets (spare parts),
    - item-storeroom relation (cost type: FIFO, LIFO, Average, Standard),
    - vendors information: price, shipment, default vendor,
    - specification: dimensions, weight, etc.
    - printing labels,
    - access rights to storerooms,
- Service Items application,
- Tools application,
- Storerooms and Stocked Tools applications (dedicated rooms, tools, person, car etc.):
    - bins,
    - addresses (Ship To, Bill To),

- Inventory application:
    - reorder,
    - ABC analysis,
    - physical count,
    - reservations (hard/soft/automatic),
- Inventory Usage application:
    - issue,
    - return,
    - transfer,
- Shipment Receiving application,
- Work Order Tracking application,
    - Plans tab (materials, tools, services),
    - Actuals tab (materials, tools),
    - Material Status section.

Purchasing Management:

- company sets,
- Company Master and Companies applications,
- Purchase Requisitions application,
- Desktop Requisitions applications,
- Purchase Orders application,
- Receiving application:
    - materials,
    - services,
- Request for Quotation application,
- Invoices application,
- limits and tolerances in Security Groups.

Contracts:

- Master Contracts application,
- Purchase Contracts application,
- Labor Rate Contracts application,
- Lease/Rental Contracts application,
- Warranty Contracts application,
- Terms and Conditions application.

Safety:

- Hazards application,
- Precautions application,
- LOTO Procedures application,
- Security Plans application.

Resources:

- Crafts application,
- Qualifications application,
- Labor application,
- People application,
    - absences,
- Person Groups application.

Security Groups (roles and responsibilities):

- Sites tab,
- Applications tab,
- Object Structures tab,
- Storerooms tab,
- Labor tab,
- GL Components tab,
- Limits and Tolerances tab,
- Data Restrictions tab (incl. Global Data Restrictions),
- Repair Facilities tab,
- Reports.

Later, you will learn from this book how to prepare for individual sessions and what the necessary details are.

In each workshop, I always include a basic discussion of the topics related to each module that will be then considered in detail in other streams:

- e-Audit,
- e-Signature,
- mobile application,

- integrations,
- data migration (methods, sources, cleansing),
- KPIs,
- reports.

Each business process must be discussed in detail with reference to:
- the roles involved,
- the necessary steps (incl. subprocesses),
- execution on mobile devices,
- notifications,
- integrations,
- escalation path.

A useful tool for a process analysis is RACI (Responsible, Accountable, Consulted, Informed) matrix. It is based on common sense and consists of the list of activities for the process (rows) and the assigned roles (columns):

Activity	Planner	Scheduler	Dispatcher	Engineer
Planning	RA	CI		
Scheduling	C	RA	I	
Dispatching			RA	I
Executing	C	I	I	RA

Figure 1 A sample RACI Matrix

The exercise now is to define the responsibility in each cell. In other words, you will specify:
- who is accountable for this activity (assigns the tasks and approves the results)—only **one** role can be accountable,
- who is responsible (does the work)—at least one role, but not too many,
- who can be consulted—no limitation,
- who should be informed—no limitation.

You can mix the letters in one cell if needed.

Once the matrix is populated, you can analyze it with the customer for correctness: by activity and by role.

An activity analysis:

- there should be only one *A* in a row—this ensures clear decision making,
- there should be minimum one *R* in a row as when there are many *R*s this means the responsibility is not clear,
- no assignment—is the activity really needed?,
- no *C*s—does the responsible role really know everything about the topic?,
- a lot of *I*s—how to ensure that everybody will be informed?.

A role analysis:

- many *R*s in a column—this role is probably overloaded,

no assignments—this role is not needed.

I use the Business Process Model Notation (BPMN 2.0) to describe processes, but you can use any other notation, that works for you and the customer:

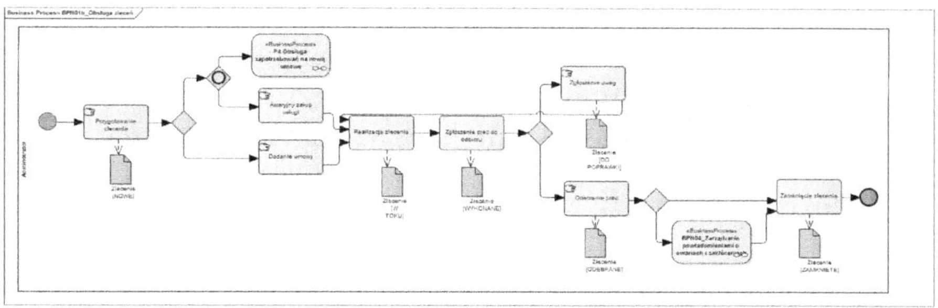

Figure 2 Example of a Business Process Model

Whether you decide to follow my workshop plan or have your own methodology has to be agreed upon with the customer and included in the contract, together with the products described further. This will help the customer organize the team and workshops.

You cannot expect that the above plan can be applied without any adjustments—add/remove some points if needed (especially, when you need to discuss Maximo Add-ons). You should also be prepared for multiple iterations. That means one day you can skip a topic and then come back to it later. There is nothing wrong about it—each project (and workshop) is unique: you will meet different people with different backgrounds and they may ask questions which will change the plan. Over time, the customer will also gradually start to understand the Maximo concepts better and may ask to discuss some previous topics again.
You will only need to make sure that you have covered all the topics during your workshop sessions.

What is the input into your discussions? The lists of requirements, existing processes, use cases, existing reports. Ask the customer to bring anything that can add to the discussion, but also act against extending the scope beyond what has been agreed on in the contract.

Focus on processes, not features. This sounds easy but customers tend to drift away from important topics to discuss the layout of fields or unimportant attributes. You should be the one to remind them that you are here to deliver a working solution that supports processes, not a fancy application. When discussing the processes, try to help solve typical issues, such as:

- unnecessary roles involved,
- too many printouts,
- lack of escalations,
- a lot of different paths in the process,
- missing paths.

This is the moment when you can confirm your additional value by helping improve the processes. You should also show how Maximo could support each process and which functionality will be used, for example: workflow for process automation, escalations for progress monitoring, security groups to define authorization of actions. I repeat: The customer knows nothing about Maximo and probably is wondering if choosing it was a right thing to do. Try to present processes in Maximo live: screens and steps, even without automation. Do not just describe the functionality or show the slides.

CMMS/EAM implementation is only one step forward on the maintenance maturity curve. The concept of the maturity curve means that enterprises have to grow gradually—they cannot become masters of universe over a year.

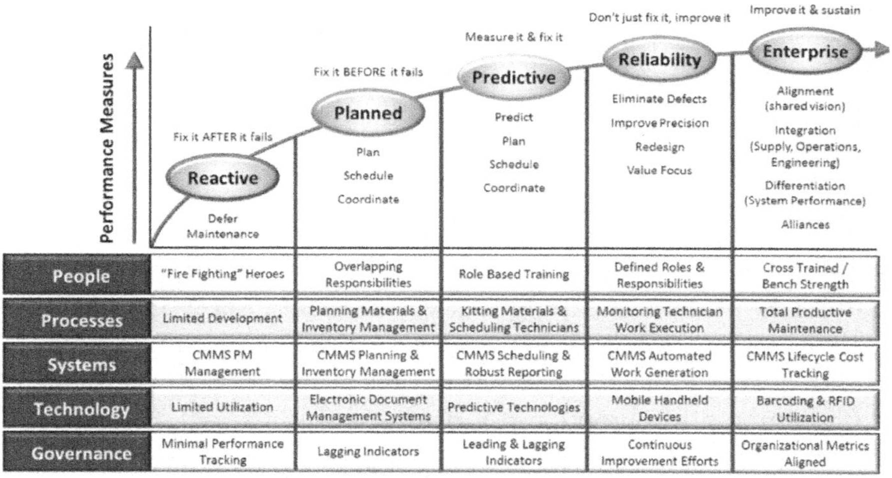

	Reactive	Planned	Predictive	Reliability	Enterprise
	Fix it AFTER it fails	Fix it BEFORE it fails	Measure it & fix it	Don't just fix it, improve it	Improve it & sustain
	Defer Maintenance	Plan, Schedule, Coordinate	Predict, Plan, Schedule, Coordinate	Eliminate Defects, Improve Precision, Redesign, Value Focus	Alignment (shared vision), Integration (Supply, Operations, Engineering), Differentiation (System Performance), Alliances
People	"Fire Fighting" Heroes	Overlapping Responsibilities	Role Based Training	Defined Roles & Responsibilities	Cross Trained / Bench Strength
Processes	Limited Development	Planning Materials & Inventory Management	Kitting Materials & Scheduling Technicians	Monitoring Technician Work Execution	Total Productive Maintenance
Systems	CMMS PM Management	CMMS Planning & Inventory Management	CMMS Scheduling & Robust Reporting	CMMS Automated Work Generation	CMMS Lifecycle Cost Tracking
Technology	Limited Utilization	Electronic Document Management Systems	Predictive Technologies	Mobile Handheld Devices	Barcoding & RFID Utilization
Governance	Minimal Performance Tracking	Lagging Indicators	Leading & Lagging Indicators	Continuous Improvement Efforts	Organizational Metrics Aligned

Performance Measures

Figure 3 Maintenance Maturity Continuum

Matt Midas, Best Practices of Maintenance Planning & Scheduling, accessed 18 April 2020, retrieved from https://inspectioneering.com/journal/2015-04-21/4543/best-practices-of-maintenance-

Too often do clients forget about this and it will be up to you to remind them that one cannot simply jump over one maturity phase but that it takes time to embrace new processes.

There is yet another important pattern: The maintenance process is the same in any conditions. It consists of fixing failures and taking preventive actions, all the while being supported by purchasing and inventory. And all your clients follow this pattern. But they will always tell you that they are very special, and their processes are completely different than the ones of the rest of the world. As I said, this is not true—they execute the same processes. What is different are the procedures, how they are doing it. You should appreciate this fact. The overall processes and the design should reflect this specific issue. Especially, pay attention to the language you use during the workshops and in the documentation. Always use the customer's terms, not the generic wording. This will make the project more user-friendly.

During the discussion, share with the customers your experience from other projects (without divulging sensitive details, of course). Tell the customer how others do the same things. Many customers want to learn something new to improve their own processes and they will appreciate your stories.

Management of Change

I have said before that a Maximo project is similar to ERP implementation, meaning that you not only implement a software solution but also introduce a change in an organization and... its culture. If you want to be successful with the implementation, you cannot overlook this subject. Management of change is a formal process for modifying technology, procedures, and documentation, but also training. The introduction of an EAM solution like Maximo can influence a ot of of these areas. A simple example: before implementing EAM system, a company used to plan for yearly preventive maintenance of equipment in a spreadsheet. The plan was approved as a printout and executed. Maximo works in a different way. First, you create Job Plans, which can be approved by an authorized person (status changed to *ACTIVE*).

Then you create the maintenance schedule in the *Preventive Maintenance* application. Again, this schedule can be approved. Then the Work Orders are created, based on the approved frequency and with an approved list of tasks. This step has no need for approval, because all previous steps have already been confirmed. As you can see, this may require a change in the formal processes, approval paths and documentation (no paper printout is needed to be signed), but finally, people should be trained to understand the new process. This topic is much broader than the discussion suggests. I invite you to learn more about management of change and to prepare for it during the project. You must also get the support for that from the upper management. If you do it correctly, then you increase your chances to have a really successful project.

Homework

My understanding of Maximo implementation is that it is always a joint effort. I encourage each of my customers to participate actively in the project. If you hear from your customer, "the vendor is responsible for doing everything," you are in trouble. Remember there is always a part that lies on the customer's side. I call it 'homework', which is the preparation of data that must be included in the solution.

Below is a sample list of information that customers should provide:

- the list of system languages,
- the list of GL accounts (segments, allowed segment values, allowed segment combinations),
- the list of fiscal periods,
- the list of currencies,
- the list of hazards and precautions,
- the calendar definition with shifts and holidays,
- the list of crafts,
- the list of qualifications,
- the list of employees,

- the list of person groups,
- the list of measure units,
- the list of technical attributes to describe the assets/locations,
- the list of classifications,
- the mapping classification—attributes,
- the list of companies,
- the list of items,
- the list of tools,
- the list of company addresses,
- the logo file to be placed on the log-in page, menu bar, reports, CSS file for the company color scheme, report layout,
- auto numbering prefixes for assets, locations, Job Plans, Work Orders,
- sample data for a data mapping workshop.

To support the customer in doing their homework, you should prepare spreadsheets with mandatory and optional information clearly marked.

Final presentation

After you finish your design and all the documents are ready, you should make a one-day presentation of your products to the customer. You should start with the description of all the products, then explain the structure of the documents (this will make the review and approval easier), and finally, explain the content and description of the solution.

Installation

This is a purely technical step: to install all the environments and make sure the *maxadmin* user can log in to all of them. High Availability (HA) environments will require an experienced specialist on your side to perform the installation.

I strongly suggest that the base language be English, because there are still issues in some places when English names are hard coded (like status name, for example).
Installing a multi-language environment can cause problems. After installation, check all the applications in every language and determine whether there are not any issues. You may find, for example, that the application in a foreign language still contains some English labels, which should be fixed.
International users should check to see if the database has the correct settings for Unicode (*NLS_LENGTH_SEMANTICS* parameter set to *CHAR*), because otherwise, you will have some issues with the local character set. This is part of the standard Maximo installation procedure but if someone else is preparing it for you, this might be forgotten.
All the system elements should be properly secured. Especially, it should not be possible to access the attachments using direct links:

https://server:port/ATTACHMENTS/filename.ext

One more setting is often overlooked: please make sure that all servers synchronize their clocks. This is important, among others, for debugging, because time stamps, for example, in Service Requests, are taken from the database server, while the time in log files comes from the application server. This should be always the same moment in time.

Reporting and KPIs

The presentation of information, analysis and printouts are on the output side of the system and can really bring value to the customer.

Reporting is more than just BIRT/Cognos reports; in Maximo, we have other options to present the data for the users:

- Start Centers, especially result sets in the text or chart format,

- tables in applications, which can be filtered and sorted, and then exported to MS Excel,
- bookmarks can be considered simple report too,
- saved queries are also a form of a report,
- KPIs (they have trend charts and list of values to be exported),
- exporting data to an external data warehouse,
- custom reporting mechanism: one of my customers abandoned the standard reports and used custom export mechanism (to text files) instead, which was directly downloading content from the database tables.

Preparing reports may be time-consuming; you can achieve the same goal using other mechanisms. For example, the customer may want a report with all the delayed Work Orders. A better option will be to prepare a KPI that will show the percent of the delayed Work Orders. If this indicator shows a value above the agreed-upon threshold, the manager can open the ***Work Order Tracking*** application and run saved query: *Delayed WOs*. Then he can check the details of each Work Order.

When talking about a report, you should gather as much information about the content as possible:

- What should be in the report and in what form: table, graph, both?
- How should this information be filtered?
- What are the report parameters?
- Should the report accept the Where Clause from Maximo or run independently? NOTE: In the latter case, the security profile of the user will be bypassed.
- Are there any special printouts, like labels required (for tagging the machines or printing badges for workers)? Does it require barcode printing?
- Should the report do specific calculations? Attach the algorithm.

- In which application should the report be available? NOTE: The report that accesses the assets table can be available also from the ***Work Order Tracking*** application if that's required.
- Should the report be available in multiple languages? NOTE: This requires skilled Report Writer.
- Should the report be available as a button on the toolbar? NOTE: Only reports without parameters can be run from the toolbar.
- Which Security Group should be allowed to run the reports?
- You should discuss with the customer who (which Security Group) should have an access to ad-hoc reporting (QBR—Query Based Report.) Usually I do not give the access to this feature to anyone, or I give it only to advanced users after they have been trained. What is the danger? I remember one client who allowed all users to create their own reports. Then they were bringing them to meetings, and they could never compare them because they had different columns or different filter conditions. On the other hand, QBR offers an interesting option to help users to export ALL the fields from the current application to the spreadsheet. By default, you can export only visible columns from the **List** tab. QBR allows the users to quickly select all columns, run the report preview and export the data in the selected format.

The visual side of the report also counts. Ask if there are any special requests regarding the layout, colors and logos.

Data Model

This is the one of the most important topics that should be thoroughly **discussed**, **documented** and **agreed upon** during the workshops: How will the customer's equipment be mapped to Maximo objects?

What does this mean exactly?

A data model creates a connection between the real and virtual worlds, and should answer at least three questions:

- Which objects will be defined in the database?
    - Only production equipment, or maybe fleet and computers too?
- How will the infrastructure be represented in Maximo? Think about the available options and map the customer's infrastructure accordingly:
    - assets (rotating and non-rotating),
    - locations,
        - systems,
        - physical,
        - functional,
        - repair facilities,
    - classifications and attributes,
    - collections,
    - relationships,
    - routes,
    - meters,
    - items (rotating and non-rotating),
    - storerooms,
    - configuration items,
- How will the objects be defined in the database? For example, the license plate information can be presented as a new field on the asset record or as a classification attribute. Which option is better? The answer depends on the needs: if this information is searchable on the **List** tab, then it should be defined as asset field. Also, if the information is required to be in a specific format like a date, then it should be a field because classification attributes can be only either textual or numeric.
- What is the level of detail to be kept in the database?
    - How would you decompose the machine? Into components, parts?

- If there are multiple levels of detail, who will be responsible for updating the database? How much will it cost?
- What is the business value of having the lowest level of detail?

The data setup will affect all the further work: Work Orders, the supply chain, controlling costs. Make sure you did it right. A **data visualization workshop** can help. I emphasize this because it is a very important step in the project. It is about presenting the results of importing (or manually entering) sample customer data in the system. This will prove that your data mapping is correct. You should remember (this is my mantra) that the customer does not know Maximo and cannot imagine how exactly their data will be presented in the system data structures. Even if you will draw your very best diagrams on a flipchart, they may not understand it. Only a live demonstration can resolve their doubts. Please plan in your project schedule a few days for this activity. This visualization should happen as early as possible because if your initial mapping does not fit the customer's expectations, you will have to re-design the concept. The sooner you present your concept, the better and higher the customer's confidence will be in Maximo.

Configuration

This phase should materialize all the customer's requirements in the form of a configured Maximo system. Please try to embed these suggestions and make sure the work is performed according to the schedule and is properly documented.

Calibration Session

During the configuration phase I always plan at least one day for a 'calibration session'. It is meant to be a presentation for the customer on the current level of the configuration process, especially some screens. This is done to make sure implementing goes into the right direction and also, to ensure the customer's progress in the configuration and (most importantly) that their requirements are implemented.

Development Standards

Before starting any configuration, your team must have agreed upon development standards. They define the naming convention, frameworks used, coding standards, data storage, etc. Why are they needed? They introduce consistency into your products; they help document work properly and ensure the high quality of projects.

Logins

Do not use *maxadmin* login during configuration and development. Team members should use their own logins (which may belong to *maxadmin* security group) instead.
The purpose of it is to ensure accountability—personal logins help to identify the person creating a particular object.
You may also think about creating a special security group or groups for the developers with a limited access to certain applications, for example: they may not have an access to ***Organizations*** application.
The development logins may be deactivated when the configuration is finished.

Naming convention

This is about how to name new objects: escalation, table, column, action, or report. I suggest using an *X* as a prefix for all the new objects. I have also seen some people use a *C* (for *customer object*), the customer's name or vendor's name (or its shortcut) as prefixes. In my opinion, the best option is to use just an *X* because only a few words begin with it. Do not use the underscore character in the names like *C_FIELD* because it is used by database management systems as a special character. The letter *C* is a very common letter; if you use it, you will not be able to find all your new objects because you will see hundreds of them. The customer's or vendor's names are also not the best solutions because they may be long and use space without bringing any value. Besides, if multiple companies are working for the same customer, you may find objects beginning with: customer... company1..., company2. How can you easily find all the new objects? You can ignore this rule in one case: when you create a new table. The table will be already named X*table*, so you do not need to do the same for the columns. Also, security groups should not be named like this, because usually they bear names of the roles that can be then used in searches. For ordinary users, the name *Driver* is better than the *Xdriver*. Avoid long names, like this one: *clientnamepowergenerationoutage*. They are hard to read, understand and write. Compare it to my proposal: *xpowergenoutage*.

Database objects

- Use the 'same as' functionality for database objects when applicable.
- Be careful when changing the existing objects—avoid changing data types.
- Database tables should be added at the appropriate level: site, system.

System Properties

- All team members should know which properties must be set for a new server and what the default values are.

Security Groups

- You should develop a standard of how to define the groups, which options should be enabled, which ones should remain disabled e.g. always enable the option to run the reports.

Forms

- The form layout should always be consistent with the rest of the system.

- Tables on forms should use the database relationships, not the data sources. This is consistent with the out-of-the-box functionality and is also easier to debug.
- While creating a new Signature Option, use a prefix, e.g. *XHIDECOST*, but also add to the description some information that this is a non-standard option, e.g. *Hide Costs (NEW)*. This will be useful while defining permissions in ***Security Groups*** application. When you look at the list of Signature Options for an application, you will see only descriptions and without a hint, you will not be able to say which option is a standard one and which one has been added.
- In my experience, if you want to change any application, leave the original one intact and create its clone. This may sound like overcomplicating a simple task, but keeping the original application aside allows for easier debugging in the case of some issues. Also, you can check how to re-create original objects that have been removed.
- Store the XML files of the changed forms in the software version control system.

Queries

- When writing a code or queries, always use the *org = :org and site = :site* conditions, even if the current configuration contains only a single organization and site. You never know when the customer extends the scope of the system in the future. In that case, someone should review all the queries.
- Make sure that the keywords are separated with space. Otherwise, the code may generate a lot of errors, because Maximo will not be able to parse the query. This is especially important when the query is multi-line. The new line character may look like a separator, but in fact, the keywords are being interpreted as one word.

Workflows

- Always create a new revision for any workflow change, which gives you the option to go back to the previous working version.
- Start node names with sequential numbers: *7-PO approved?, 8-Send notification to the owner.* You can then easily describe each action and condition as well as the transitions between elements using the convention: *7-8-action Set status to APPR.*

Reports

- Always use *UPPER* function to convert report parameters. Then you will be comparing the same objects.
- Use *org = :org and site = :site* conditions in the queries even if the current configuration contains only single organization and site.
- Follow the below coding standards.
- I suggest including a unique identifier, e.g. a form number (*K-201 Purchase Order with Logo*) or a simple sequential number (*1000—List of Calibration Assets, 1001—PM Forecast*) in the report name to avoid misunderstandings while reporting bugs by users.
- The printout of the report should include a version number.
- Store the report files in the software version control system.

Coding standards

- Follow the best practice of the specific language: either Java, Python or JavaScript.
- Agree upon the content of the script/class header.
- Put comments in the code with the reference to the requirements if applicable.
- Class names should have the prefix '*X*'.
- Always put your classes in the package '*com.custom*'.

- Store the source files in the software version control system.

Translations

If you are implementing Maximo in a multi-language environment, you will need to translate among other things:

- new screen labels (including sections and tables),
- Signature Options,
- database names,
- reports,
- and perhaps the documentation and training materials, too.

In case of new applications, please, do not forget to translate the standard application elements as **Where Clause**, **Save Current Query**...

My recommendation is to never use online translators. Make sure you have a proper budget allocated for professional translation services. Online translators are not a solution.

Style guide for documentation

This may sound trivial but you will be producing numerous documents, so it is worth spending some time preparing document templates, with logos, text styles, etc. Again, this will look more professional from the customer's perspective.

Integrations

Below is a list of potential candidates to integrate with Maximo. I have listed only the generic system classes, not the actual systems. You should map them to the real names. The list is divided into two sections: business integrations that can bring value to the users and technical integrations, which only support Maximo.

Business integrations:

- SCADA systems—Usually one-way integration. SCADA can create a Service Request or Work Order in Maximo when the machine is down, and report the downtime. It can also send information about meter readings and production volume needed to calculate the OEE (Overall Equipment Effectiveness). This applies also to BMS systems in buildings.
- GIS—Uni- or bidirectional integration. In some industries, GIS is a master of asset data, in which case it will send the newly created assets to Maximo. Maximo can complement this data by sending the information about the current status, number of Work Orders or list of the technical parameters. In a simpler environment, Maximo can only send the information about the asset, location or Work Order to be presented on the map.
- ERP—Uni- or bidirectional integration. This one is usually the most complicated interface. The integration can cover sending the general ledger structure, a list of organizations/sites, a list of vendors or a list of items and storeroom balance to Maximo. Maximo can initiate the purchase process by sending a purchase requisition/purchase order to ERP. It can also send issue/return transactions to ERP.
- HR—Uni- or bidirectional integration. HR system can send a list of employees to Maximo (labor records), including lists of crafts and qualifications. Maximo can send back the information about the total working hours for payroll preparation.
- CRM/Billing—Usually unidirectional. It can be found in the companies that are utilities or service providers. CRM/Billing can send the information about external customers and their addresses to Maximo to become the service addresses of the Work Orders. CRM/Billing can also automatically create the Work Order to fix failures.

- Data warehouse—Unidirectional. Maximo can export data to the warehouse for further analysis.
- Other systems—Usually unidirectional. For example: importing currency exchange rates or content of some domains.

Technical integrations:

- Document Management System (DMS)—Bidirectional integration. Maximo has a very simple mechanism for managing attachments. Therefore, if the customer wants to have thousands of files in Maximo, they should have on the spot a document management system that can store a large amount of data.
- Email—Uni- or bidirectional integration for sending notifications, creating service requests from the incoming emails or processing records based on email interactions.
- LDAP—Uni- or bidirectional integration. LDAP sends the list of users and security groups to Maximo. Maximo allows the user to authenticate using LDAP.

Currently, the preferred integration method is the use of Enterprise Service Bus (ESB), which centralizes data exchange and offers additional features like data transformation, validation and monitoring.

As I said, this list contains only samples. You have to ask the customer some questions:

- Which systems should be integrated with Maximo?
- Is the documentation of these systems available?
- Is the target system able to receive the required information? Is there a corresponding database/business object? Are all the fields available? What about the type and length of the fields—do they match?
- What are the available methods of integration?
- How often should the data be exchanged?

- Who will prepare the other system for the integration? It is not only Maximo that needs to be prepared. Who will pay for this?
- Which system will be the master of specific types of data? For example, in utilities, usually GIS is the master of asset information because they plan new pipes or wires on the map, which shows not only the company's infrastructure but also buildings, trees, and rivers. A map of the electrical/gas network offers also simulations of the flow and other advanced functionalities. In this case, Maximo will be only a receiver of the asset information. Try to make the data responsibility very clear, i.e. only one system should be the master of one type of information to avoid scenarios like this: GIS can create assets shared with Maximo, but at the same time, Maximo can create 'temporary assets' that will be sent to GIS.
- Discuss what should happen with the data coming from external systems. Should they be read-only (like the information about companies coming from ERP) or editable (like the Work Orders created by SCADA)? Avoid copying of a lot of information between systems.
- What should happen when the transfer fails? Should there be an entry in a log file? Can you use the standard application, or must a new application be built to review errors? Make sure this is discussed because it may affect your budget and schedule.

Avoid agreeing to integrate with systems that do not exist yet—this will always result in trouble!

Do not forget to compare the business value of the integration with the cost of the actual development. Sometimes, the customer may want to integrate with a system that will send only a few records once a month, but the cost of establishing a connection could be 20 man-days. Do not hesitate to ask the question "Why pay for this effort?" Is it worth it? Maybe it will be cheaper for someone to manually enter this information in Maximo.

Change Control

Implementation projects are always susceptible to changes, especially the long and complex ones. The change can be legally, environmentally or technologically triggered—any of these requires an appropriate reaction of the implementation team. In general, this is a task mainly for Project Manager but the delivery team must be also involved. Each Request For Change must be assessed: what impact it has on the project, if it is feasible, how much effort it will cost. Functional Consultant should also identify possible solutions and make a recommendation. Finally, the changes should be prioritized together with Project Manager.
Here, I want to emphasize here the importance of the assessment phase. You may receive a relatively simple request, such as "please make the field **Supervisor** on the Work Order required". This is 5 minutes work, so the impact on the project may be described as *LOW*. However, there may be an external system generating Work Orders automatically. Mandatory field will then generate errors whenever Work Order will be created. This is quite a trivial example, but it proves how important the right assessment and also testing of the potential solutions are.

Data Migration

Data migration will probably be an iterative process (with the incremental final import right before the production starts). Plan for enough skilled resources and agree upfront on who will be responsible for data cleansing—you or the customer—and how many times the data will be imported. This should be included in the project schedule. Otherwise, someone from your team can get involved in 100% to this task, import data, check for errors and then return it to the customer for further updates. The

agreement should also cover the fact that the customer should use your migration templates, not their spreadsheets.
Please document carefully the migration strategy and scripts. They can be used during the rollout when the customer implements Maximo in the next plant.
While importing data, always include the information about the source system (for example, in the field **SOURCESYSID**). This would allow for reporting data sources but it will be also useful to document migration results.

During the workshops, you should answer these questions:

- Which data will be migrated?
- Which data will NOT be migrated? For example: do not agree to migrate any old transactional records, like Work Orders or Purchase Orders. The effort to convert these records into the format required by Maximo and populate missing information can be a real challenge.
    - In case the historical transactional records are included in the migration, please make sure the required configuration is in place, for example: historical financial periods, exchange rates, but also historical Labor records (the ones which do not work today). Without providing this information, the import will fail or the data quality will suffer.
- Is there a reliable source of data for assets, locations, etc.?
- What is it? The ERP system, a custom system, a spreadsheet?
- What kind of information is there? Does it match the mandatory information in Maximo?

Normally, data migration should always use Maximo Integration Framework (MIF) features. However, when millions of records are being imported, then MIF validation may result in the import time being calculated in days, not hours. In that case, you may decide to bypass MIF and import the data directly into the database. Also, in this case, you need to generate some technical values, like unique IDs, because MIF will not do it. This decision and mechanism should be clearly documented and included in the migration strategy document.

Below is the list of sample steps in the migration process:

- Step 1—Unload data from the old system (the method depends on the platform) to Extract, Transform, Load (ETL) program (in the worst case, ETL will be a spreadsheet). Export the data with the correct code page settings.
- Step 2—Analyze data and list the issues:
    - upper- or lowercase mix, e.g., MOTOR versus Motor versus motor,
    - non-standardized addresses,
    - non-standardized identifiers, e.g. 1000 or 001000,
    - abbreviations vs. full names, e.g. Transformer vs. Trafo,
    - non-standardized languages, e.g. some words in English, some in Spanish,
    - problems with dates (different formats, missing date parts), e.g. 12 Sep; Sep, 12; 12-9-2010; 12-09-2010; 2010-09-12.
- Step 3—Define cleaning strategy:
    - manual work,
    - scripting.
- Step 4—Prepare necessary tools:
    - scripts,
    - macros,
    - programs,
    - ETL configuration.
- Step 5—Execute scripts.
- Step 6—Add required Maximo technical information: IDs, site, org.

- Step 7—Disabling the business logic, which could generate some errors during import. For example: the flag 'Required' for fields, escalations or conditions checking status transitions. For instance, the customer may have a condition checking that *DECOMMISSIONED* status can only be set from *OPERATING* status. When entering historical assets (*DECOMMISSIONED*), which have no previous status, Maximo will throw an error.
- Step 8—Import data.
- Step 9—Check the errors and imported data.
- Step 10—Repeat steps 2-8 until all errors are gone.
- Step 11—Enabling business logic again.

When importing the data, please do not forget about attachments. They should be migrated too; you can copy physical files or just the links to the DMS or network location. Think not only about manuals in PDF format, but also about scanned documents like invoices, warranties or CAD files with equipment details.

I do not need to mention that data migration should always be tested because only a live test will help you discover such unexpected issues as the fields in the database being too short or database triggers being fired (which were added to Maximo database by third-party products), which perform additional data validation.

Training

Please be careful when agreeing to deliver training because one sentence in this section can be in fact a separate project! For example, a customer may request e-learning for end-users. This will require not only standard preparation of the textual content, but also some video and audio materials as well as tests or games to check progress. All of these will cost time and money. Training is usually prepared for two groups (sample content can be found in appendixes): end users and system administrators.

Sometimes, however, the customer may request some additional training for testers, which will be similar to the end user training.
If your project is for multi-national company, probably the training must also be delivered in local languages, which includes preparing the presentation, materials and of course, finding some trainers speaking the local languages.
Usually, training for end-users takes 2-3 days; for administrators, it takes 3-5 days.
You can also face a situation in which a project is planned to take several months but the customer wants the training to be performed at the early stage of implementation. You should then plan for additional training just before go live to refresh the users' memories.
I suggest hiring an experienced trainer to prepare and deliver the end user training. This is part of your public relations. You will be 'selling' the results of the project to the end-users, and they should be happy. If you assign even your best programmer to this task and they do not have the right presenting skills, the whole training effort will fail. But this may work in the case of training for administrators, as they usually have some IT background and speaking their language may be an advantage.

Tests

I repeat my warning from the previous chapter: plan for this step carefully and describe it in detail in the contract. All the tests you will have in the scope—unit, integration, acceptance, performance—require time to prepare the strategy and test cases, not to mention execution and fixing bugs. Some test materials must be prepared only after the configuration is finished, so proper planning is crucial.
Also, you must have bug-tracking software in place (shared with the customer) to report issues.

Go Live

Just one more step and your work will be finished! Go live consists of a few steps—a sample list below:

- final data migration,
- the final checklist:
  - check if the help file is present?;
  - check if auto-numbering is set to the right values? (after the final migration, you may need to set the next numbers manually);
  - check the logs (Maximo, application server, database server);
  - check the loggers—they should not be set to the highest levels because this affects performance;
  - make sure the cron tasks and escalations are enabled (they may be disabled for data import);
  - check the admin mode;
  - check the technical documentation to make sure it contains the latest fixes;
- prepare the documentation needed for the handover to IT operations.

Good luck!

Handovers

A Maximo implementation project for external customers should have at least two handovers:

- Sales Team to Implementation Team,
- Implementation Team to Support Team (if technical support is included in the scope of the contract).

Some also separate the handover of specifications from functional consultants to the technical team.

Figure 4 Handovers

Why should the project include these two handover phases? It's about handing over responsibility to the next team, but also equipping them with all the information they need, e.g. the Support Team should know how the system was configured. They should also be aware of what has not been completed, what problems they may encounter, and how to solve them.

Below are my suggested tasks that should be included in each handover phase.

Sales Team to Implementation Team

- Contract information: scope, timeline, assumptions…
- List of customer contacts,
- License Keys (and installation files, if applicable).

Implementation Team to Support Team

- Documentation,
    - Specifications,
    - Location of scripts/classes, reports,
- License keys,
- Logins and passwords,
- Knowledge Transfer,
    - Configuration,
    - Uncompleted tasks,
    - Existing and potential issues with solutions or workarounds.

This is only a proposal, please discuss internally and consider the actions required by your organization.

Technical Support

Your contract with the customer may embrace not only the implementation process but also the ongoing support. You can play the role of the first-, second- or third-line support. In any case, it must be agreed what minimum information required to process the request is. Too often, the users report a problem, such as, "Maximo does not work"—the support analyst must then call the user and ask a series of questions to understand the issue. To avoid this unnecessary step, users must be instructed to provide the following information (it is best to include a similar list in the contract):

- User ID—without this information nobody can provide any help. The issue may be related only to one user profile because of the lack of access rights.
- When did it happen? Maybe the server was experiencing problems at that time or someone was printing a huge report?
- What did actually happen? The user gets an error message or cannot perform an action?
- Is this issue repetitive or has it happened only once?
- Is this issue related to just one particular record or does it apply to any record?
- What are the steps needed to re-create this issue?
- How urgent is this issue for the user?
- How many people are affected? Just one person, or a group, or all the users? In other words: how much are the business processes affected by this issue?

The last two questions help to identify the priority of the problem using Impact-Urgency-Priority matrix:

		Impact		
		One person	Group	All users
Urgency	Low	1	1	2
	Medium	1	2	3
	High	2	3	3

Figure 5 Impact-Urgency-Priority Matrix

The resulting priority is connected with the SLA agreement defining the response and resolution times.

Lessons Learned

I strongly suggest adding to your project one more (internal) step: a post implementation review (or 'lessons learned', or a postmortem). It is important to include the learning curve in your projects. After you have finished your job, please organize a meeting with the key members of your team and discuss what went well and what went wrong. This is not about blaming anyone, and it is not about complaining. It is about learning from your mistakes and your successes, and making your next projects more successful and less painful.

Below you will find a list of some common issues I have seen in Maximo projects. Some are already addressed in the previous chapters. I have divided the issues in two groups: 'external' and 'internal'.

External

- A fixed-price project: As such, it does not pose a risk, but if the estimates are wrong and you have an open scope (which is another topic on the list), then your project may end up with a loss. The rule is: fixed price = fixed scope with clearly defined assumptions and out-of-scope functions.

- Replacing a legacy system: Sooner or later you will meet a customer who will want to replace their old system with Maximo. It might be a bespoke or in-house developed system with a long history of 15-20 years of use. The users love this software because it was developed to suit their needs, it uses the terminology they understand and has nice colorful icons. This could be a hard time for the supplier, depending on how the customer's management will act on it. From my experience, there are four main scenarios:
    - The management will push the company to use the new system from the very beginning: I have observed the first scenario at the customer who was replacing an old ERP system with Maximo. The management since day 1 was saying that Maximo was their new system and the old terminology and processes were no longer valid, so they all had to follow the new rules. It is the best what you can expect—a bold statement from the managers helps to overcome some natural objections from the users.
    - The management will finally react but it will take a while to make a decision: It was another project. Maximo should have replaced a database program that had been written many years before by the local IT specialist. This person did not want their program to be replaced. Long months, that person was trying to defend their 'child' (this is a typical rhetoric in such situations). Only when the project had a delay, did the developer's manager talk to and convinced them to cooperate with us. Unfortunately, the schedule and budget had already been affected by the unnecessary delay.
    - The management will do nothing, and the users will push you to prepare an 'Old system Version 2.0' in Maximo: This is a real nightmare but it happens very often. Without the project sponsors'

support, the users will push the supplier to re-create the old functions in Maximo. This can cost hundreds of days of effort and generate significant delays, plus, a lot of frustration for the supplier. Instead of the process implementation, you will spend time on discussions, such as, "This field must have the same name as in the old system", "Why must I click 3 times to run a report? In the old system it was only one click", "The screens and reports must look exactly the same as in the legacy program". You may also be required to migrate ALL of the historical data. Except of losing money and time, you will end up with an extremely customized system, which will require additional support during upgrades.

- The users will demand an 'Old system Version 2.0' in Maximo but in the end, they may accept some suggestions from your side: During the workshops, some users may discover that Maximo can offer more functions than the old system or some better options than the one. They will then agree to change or ease some of the requirements. Still, the customer will get a customized system that reflects old processes.
- The impact of the customer's decision to replace the legacy system on your implementation project can be significant. You must be aware of the customer's plans from the very beginning and plan accordingly. I have already emphasized the importance of the initial analysis of the customer's needs. When you discover that the project is about replacing the old system, you must do even more than usually. Check which of the above scenarios is most likely. If this the third one, you had better double check the estimates, increase contingency or maybe even consider not signing the contract. If you do, many of your resources

will be involved in the project, which will get more and more complicated with the each following month. You may need to assign some additional consultants just to get the job done. Frustration will arise on the both sides. The time will pass without any result... Maybe, instead of this project, another (simpler) contract or contracts could have be signed, which would quicker and easier bring money?

- A wrong customer's implementation team: There are at least two variants of this, namely, the team is too small or the wrong people are in it. For example, only the middle and high managers from the headquarters—no end users, no local users, no IT representation.
- The customer's team changes constantly: For example, the first meeting in the work stream is attended by 10 people, to whom the topic is explained and some decisions are made. Several new people come to the next meeting, who know nothing about the topic, so everything must be explained from the very beginning. They may also disagree with the previous decisions causing irritation and delays in the project.
- An open scope or unclear goal of the project: In general, a short list of requirements means problems. The customer will improvise and generate requirements on the fly or multiply single requirements. This process usually grows as the customer learns what Maximo does and they start thinking about how to use it. It applies to the situation when the customer has no clear goal for the project, too.
- A gap between the customer's expectations and the offered solution: Numerous customers do not realize that they buy a product with the out-of-the-box functionality that can be only partially tailored to their needs (it is not a developer's framework). Also, they may not want to

learn how it works and how this ready-to-use option could be used to fulfill the requirements.

- The lack of or wrong communication between the customer and vendor: There should be minimum weekly calls or meetings between both the Project Managers. They should discuss the progress of works (what has been done) and inform about the issues faced; for example, some delays in data preparation on the customer's side or an unexpected bug in the system found by the vendor. This gives a chance to agree on the further steps or resolve the conflicts before they escalate. I know it is Project Manager's job, but I have seen a lot of projects without proper communication, which led to serious tensions between the parties.
- Documentation issues: The customer may not understand the purpose and content of the products and may request the functional specification to be not the description of how Maximo will be tailored to their needs, but a description of all the functions available in the system (each and every field on the screen). They could want the documents to be split into numerous linked files or could ask to produce some additional documentation.
- New requirements or scope changes are submitted to the functional specification or other documents together with the comments: Users may want to quietly smuggle in new requirements. If you do not reply that this is a change to the original scope, they may demand it to be delivered.
- No access to the Internet for your team: It may sound trivial but today, you cannot work without communicating with the rest of the team and accessing the repositories on your own servers.
- The responsibility for issues in the database, application server or standard Maximo functionality: You should not be responsible for bugs in the systems you have no

control of. You can only support your own solution, based on Maximo.

Internal

- Non-existing functionality promised to the customer, usually by the sales department.
- The wrong assumptions: You cannot expect all the work to be done remotely, so plan the on-site presence, especially during the workshops. This issue also covers too optimistic assumptions regarding the technical complexity of the project (e.g. integrations or migration).
- Underestimated workload: I would say this is the continuation of the previous issue. After you read this book, you will discover how complicated a Maximo project is and how much effort it requires. You must include estimates for each team member (including project management) in your calculation.
- A dispersed implementation team: From the perspective of costs, this is a very interesting option, but organizing a remote team improperly, including lack of communication, may be a serious obstacle (no tools to communicate, missing documentation, missing development standards, time difference). This may also cause a problem of unclear responsibilities.
- The lack of internal communication: Missing information about the scope of a project, the responsibilities and work progress can cause one person sitting on a bench, while the other specialists will be working overtime. I have also seen two people working on the same task and someone that was surprised that their work was affected by a change introduced by another team member...
- A too small team: This will soon lead to delays, conflicts in the team, fatigue and poor quality of work.
- The missing skills in the team: You cannot do everything alone, you may need an experienced DBA to do the

tuning or an application server specialist to do the installation.

- Frequent changes in the team: This is not a very unlikely scenario (this covers developers, PMs, consultants, migration specialists…), especially, in larger organizations, where projects have changing priorities. The management will then assign more experienced stuff to a more demanding project.
- An inexperienced PM: As I said before, Maximo is like a small ERP project that requires an experienced PM to deal with demanding, difficult customers. And they must have enough hours booked in the project for project management's tasks.
- Using Maximo as a developer's framework: Some consultants do not want to learn how Maximo works, so instead, they design as new applications functions that are already present in the system.
- Saying 'yes' to all the customer's ideas: You can always meet an aggressive or influential person who can force you to do whatever they think of.
- Contractual issues: The scope of works may be unclear, especially, migration, integration or tests (it may not be clear who does what).
- The missing development standards or a failure to meet them: This may result in an inconsistent appearance of the screens, reports with different layout and other issues.
- No document management: It refers to unauthorized editing of documents.
- The lack of document repository or of skills to manage it: These result in editing the earlier versions, overwriting newer documents, unclear folder structure.

Deliverables

Each of the implementation steps described before requires a specific product or products to be delivered. The list below is only an example. The details of the most important documents can be found in the appendix 'Project Deliverables—sample content'.

Presentations:

- your initial presentation,
- your final presentation.

Workshops and solution design:

- meeting minutes: every meeting must be documented as accurately as possible, the best option is to have someone making notes during the workshops,
- attendance lists,
- functional specification: this is a document that describes the changes in the standard Maximo installation, it is based on the assumption that we have a system with the existing features that are tuned to match the customer's expectations and written in the business language; for example, this screen will be modified, field X will be removed, new text field Y will be added to keep the ID from system Z,
- the integration strategy: for each external system, the mapping of data and integration method should be prepared.

Installation:

- a configuration document: it is a summary of all the addresses, names, and parameters used to install Maximo and its components,
- installation files: usually, they are downloaded using the customer's account but it may be a good idea to download them, burn a disc and hand it over officially,

- a commissioning document to hand over the installed system: the customer must confirm that they take over the responsibility of the installed system because they will receive all the logins and passwords, and can potentially change the configuration, which may cause some issues, so this kind of a hand-over secures your business,
- start/stop scripts.
- high availability scripts,
- backup scripts.

Configuration:

- the technical specification: translating the functional specification into the technical requirements, which is not always demanded; it may be your internal document and it is very useful when your team is geographically dispersed,
- the technical documentation; this describes all the changes made to the out-of-the-box installation of Maximo and is the final document with regards to the configuration/customization,
- the maintenance procedures.
- the end-user manuals.

Data migration:

- the migration strategy,
- migration scripts,
- migration reports: the customer may want to see a report, such as, "There were 1500 records in the source system: 1200 were imported correctly, 200 required manual processing, 100 were not imported because of errors."

Training:

- the training strategy,
- the training materials for end-users: printed documents, presentation files, videos or e-learning materials,

- the training materials for administrators: same as above,
- attendance lists.

Test:

- the test strategy,
- test cases: they should correspond to the business processes described in the functional specification,
- test reports.

Go Live:

- system handover sheet.

I have intentionally skipped the project management documentation because it is pretty standard for all projects.

Also, some industries will require some additional documentation to be prepared. For example, pharmaceutical companies need validation documentation.

The most important thing is to agree upon the structure and content of each product before you start any work. The best way is to present the sample content of the documents before and have the sign off for every chapter, diagram and table. Have an agreed-upon way to describe the changes to the existing screens: how to describe new fields, fields to be removed or no changes. Some people say it is enough to present the table of contents. I do not agree with that—I have seen too many situations when we created and filled out the documents and then the customer said, "This is not what I want. Give me more details, add additional chapters, change the diagram." This will significantly affect your schedule and budget.

Before the approval of the documents, the customer may provide you with some comments or questions. You should agree with the customer about how to report them. I suggest not using the review function in word processors—this is the worst option, especially, if there are many comments. If you reply with your comments and make amendments, then the document becomes unreadable. A good spreadsheet with chapter numbers, page numbers, dates, the name of the reporter and a comment will be the simplest option for both the parties.

No.	Document	Chapter	Page	Orginal Text	Reporting Person	Report Date	Comment	Status	Answer
1	Functional Specification	7	23	new field "Age" will be added	John Doe	23 Nov	This field should be named "Year"	NEW	
2	Migration Strategy	2	5	"Item Master" data will be migrated	Andrew Jones	24 Nov	also photos of the materials must be transferred	NEW	
3									
4									
5									
6									

Figure 6 Sample Comments

You can then add a status column (new, replied, rejected) and your answer. Ask for a consolidated list of comments, as multiple and sometimes contradictory comments on a single sentence of a document should not be allowed.

Implementation Team

Usually, the scale and complexity of Maximo projects make it impossible for them to be performed by only one or two people. You will need an implementation team with clear responsibilities and advanced skills.

Teamwork means to me: assign work to the right people with appropriate skills, to someone who can do their job quickly and at the right level. Senior specialists should not be assigned to such trivial tasks as entering the data. This is counterproductive for the company and demotivating for them. The same applies to the opposite situation: asking junior team members to lead the workshop or preparing advanced system configuration.

For me, the implementation team is in fact two groups:

- a team on your (implementing company's) side.
- a team on the customer's side.

Who should be in each team? I am talking here about roles, not real people, which means one person can play one or more roles. While the customer's team is probably mobilized only for this project, on your side you may have a more permanent organization that can participate in numerous projects.

Who is needed on your side?

- project manager plus project management office: they make sure the project is led according to the chosen PM methodology;
- solution architect/lead consultant who creates the overall concept, manages the implementation from a functional point of view;
- industry consultant who supports the team with some industry experience,
- system (technical) architect who creates the architecture;
- system engineer who installs the software;

- Maximo consultant who designs and implements the solution for specific Maximo areas;
- Java programmer who develops the necessary classes for data validation, integrations, cron tasks;
- mobile programmer who develops and implements the mobile solution;
- Maximo integration framework specialist who designs and implements integration with other systems;
- data migration consultant who designs and loads data from other systems;
- release manager who creates the migration packages to be implemented in any environment;
- report writer who creates the reports;
- technical writer who prepares the documentation;
- tester who tests the software and integrations;
- trainer who trains users and administrators;
- system analyst who provides technical support.

Once the implementation is finished, you may also have a technical support team on the spot that will take the responsibility for supporting the solution.
If you want to read more about the required skills, see the appendix for the team roles.

The size of the team (the list of the roles and the number of people per role) depends on the scale of the project and the skills of your people. Some will be needed for only a short time, like system engineer or report writer, while the Maximo consultants will work longer.

The customer's team should consist of:

- project manager,
- management representative, to approve the design decisions,
- experts from the maintenance department,

- future Maximo administrators, because they should have at least some basic orientation in the system,
- end users' representative: for multiple sites, there should be people from different locations because they usually have different opinions; for the same reason, you will also need people for different roles in the future system; try to avoid having the decisions about how the system will work being made by people who will never use it.

This is the minimum staff. Of course, there may be people engaged from different areas (maintenance, production, storeroom) in the team. You can also invite people from IT, finance, HR and administrators of other systems to participate in a specific workshop.

Tools

Even the perfect team will not be productive without proper tools. Below is a list of the most common programs or systems you will need during a Maximo project.

- A document repository for all the project files: often back up your files!
- A project management tool to prepare the plan of the project and monitor its execution.
- Task management software: you will have hundreds of tasks to be done during the implementation and this kind of software will help you assign tasks and monitor their execution (see, the bug tracking program).
- A requirement management system to document the requirements and make sure all of them have been addressed properly.
- A text editor: you will write a lot of documents, so make sure all your team members have the required writing skills; try some new on-line solutions that allow parallel editing of the same document, which can greatly speed up preparing documents.
- A team communication tool: a text/audio/video chat.
- A spreadsheet: it is a must-have for all data transformations, calculations or even contact lists.
- Presentation software to prepare the initial and final presentations, and training.
- A program for taking screenshots to prepare the documentation and training materials.
- Screencast software for recording screen content to prepare the training materials.
- Computer-based training software (e-learning software).
- A system for software version control for Java/Jython code, reports, XML files.
- A process drawing tool to prepare process diagrams and describe the steps.
- A screen mock-up tool to prepare the layout of screens.

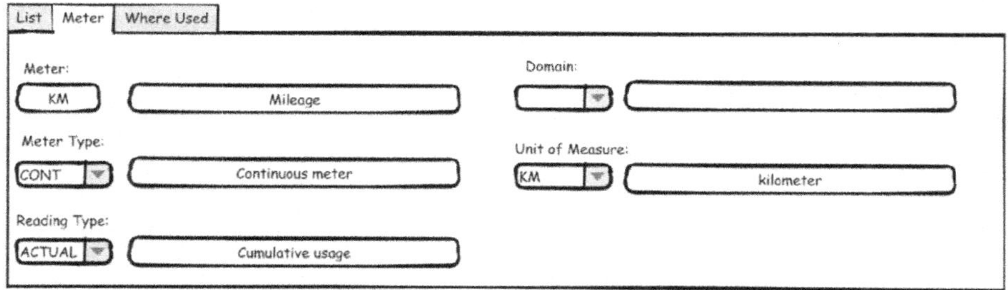

Figure 7 A Sample Mock-up Screen

- Software to prepare test cases: a lot of teams use spreadsheets for this but there are alternatives like on-line systems.
- Automatic testing tools.
- TDToolkit to manage Maximo translations.
- Maximo Help Customization Toolkit to edit standard help files and attach, for example, user instructions.
- ETL tools: you can consider MXLoader (https://bportaluri.com/mxloader) to load data.
- A fake SMTP program to test notifications without spamming.
- A programmers' editor/framework: let the team choose the one they prefer.
- Report writing tools: this will depend on the system.
- A bug tracking program: this will be required during the support phase but some teams also use it for task management.
- Database tools to run queries, view table content, export query. NOTE: This tool should be only operated by users who are experienced in SQL and even then, handled with caution while updating the records! I always suggest updating the records solely through Maximo UI, not in the database. One *update table* command can destroy many days of configuration.
- Log viewers.

Before the contract gets signed

Let us go back in time now to the moment when the customer was only your prospect. Your account manager has approached them, identified the opportunity and decided to present Maximo.
To avoid project problems related to misunderstanding by the customer of what Maximo can and cannot do, I recommend involving Maximo consultants in the presales phase and let them lead the system presentation.

Usually, the presentation starts with an introduction of your company—leave it to your account manager. You will focus entirely on the Maximo presentation.
To prepare a successful event, please follow the three following steps:

Research—Prepare—Rehearse

Research—I have already discussed that in the prerequisites for the implementation. Try to find as much information about the customer and their problems as possible, and prepare the presentation accordingly.

Prepare—This is all about the content: slides and live demo. You can have one or more presentation templates (for different industries), which can be tailored to specific needs based on the results of your research. Design your slides carefully, make them clean, avoid excessive text on slides, do not use all the colors of the rainbow, and use only a few fonts. The slides should look professional and neat, not like a stack of random ideas.

Below you will find some topics you can include in your presentation—these are the points I consider most important:

- History of Maximo—to confirm that this is a mature software;

- Enterprise grade software—emphasize that Maximo is multiplatform software, scalable, based on modern technology, supporting complex organizations and processes, secure, and ensuring data reliability and consistency;
- IBM as the owner— one of the largest IT companies in the world guarantees continuous development and support;
- Functionality highlights, e.g.
  - configurable downtime reporting,
  - Work Centers,
  - Nested, Conditional and Dynamic Job Plans,
  - assets/locations/work—can be shown on a map without integration with GIS system,
  - SLAs,
  - Work Orders—can be assigned first to the group and then to individuals,
  - classifications with attributes,
  - ad-hoc reporting,
  - Service Requests application,
  - ...;
- Flexible configuration:
  - graphical workflow designer,
  - Database Formulas,
  - multi-language support—not only labels but also data (domain values, descriptions) can be translated,
  - Maximo Integration Framework—EAM systems never exist as 'islands'; Maximo offers multiple integration methods: WebService, REST API—this enables integration with any system,
  - database configuration—it is possible to extend the length of the standard fields, add new fields or tables,

    - customizable layouts of the screens: fields, tables, tabs can be added; it is possible to display fields from other applications through dot notation,
    - advanced configuration—extending standard Java classes,
    - Migration Manager—to deploy changes on servers, among others, the application layout can be transferred between them;
- Preview site—available for customers to play with the system;
- Licensing—a free license for requestors;
- Free database license—in the package;
- Partner eco-system—there are hundreds of companies around the globe that implement Maximo, which is important because it ensures serviceability of Maximo; you can use my "IBM Maximo Asset Management (Partner) World Map" (an actual version can be found at: https://robert-zientara.blogspot.com/2019/12/ibm-maximo-asset-management-partner.html).

Prepare the backup slides, as there might be some topics you have not planned to present but the customer will ask for, so it is good to have them ready-made.

An important part of your presentation will be the live demo of Maximo. This will work best when you prepare some scenarios, like ordering materials for a work order, or reporting a failure by the users and then processing the work order. Each scenario should not be too complicated, avoid going into deep details, focus on the flow and the main steps. Make sure you have different users defined in the system to perform the actions in the process, each with its own role = security group. The groups should have their own Start Centers with Favorites, result sets, and/or Inbox portlets. This will allow you to show the records coming and going to/from the "To Do" list.

If you want to demonstrate a mobile application, show not only its features but also the built-in functions, like speech-to-text for making notes without typing, attaching photos, using GPS to record the location of work, etc.
If you have a proper budget, buy an infrared camera or an endoscope, which can be attached to a mobile device. Show how easy it is to attach photos from these instruments.
Remember to emphasize that mobile apps are tailored for the use in tough environments; for example, they have simplified interfaces and sometimes, also color schemes optimized to be visible on a sunny day.

Make sure that your technology will work if you are going to present the system online—ask the customer to confirm that there will be a wireless or cable Internet connection in the room. As a backup, bring your phone or modem with you.
Test if are able to connect your mobile device to the notebook to share the screen since sometimes, it requires a cable connection, or a specific software to be installed.
If you have one, then use the presenter tool—a remote to control the slides and a laser pointer to show something on the screen (do you have fresh batteries inside?).
I am a person who likes drawing on a flipchart—if you want to do the same, check if there will be a whiteboard or flipchart available. Also, take a spare marker with you.
Pack your notebook, charger, mobile device charger, and all the required cables.

Rehearse—do not trust yourself and the technology. To avoid forgetting something during the presentation or seeing an error on the screen in front of the customer, have a dry run of your presentation. Switch the roles to show the flow of the process, explain what you are doing and what will be the result, draw the steps on the flipchart parallelly to help the audience to follow what you are doing. If possible, you can also use two beamers: one to present the process diagram and another to show your steps.

First, do all of those alone, then ask your colleague(s) to be your audience. This will help you to polish your presentation but also to make sure that you will fit in the time slot planned for your show.

Right before the presentation—mute your speakers, and close all the communicators and your email client to avoid notifications being displayed on the screen.

Once the presentation is over, be patient. Even the best presentation may not convince the customer or they will need more time to take their final decision. In my experience, the sales cycle for Maximo projects may take from 3 months up to even 2 years.

Summary of Part I

In the first part of the book, I have described my vision of a Maximo implementation project. You should understand now what the steps of the implementation are, who should be in your team, what products you are about to deliver, and what kind of tools you can use to make it faster, easier and of better quality.

A lot of times have I said, "You should not do this; you should avoid that." I perfectly understand that business is not black and white, and frequently, you just cannot say 'no'. My intention was to make you aware of all the risks you may face. Once you know your enemy, you can arm yourself accordingly.

Part II—Maximo Applications

The second part of this book is focused strictly on Maximo applications and the functions they offer. You will find here some technical information, but everything was written from the point of view of a functional consultant: what can help, what can be done better...
I am going to explain how the out-of-the-box features work and how applications cooperate together. You can find here some use cases from real projects which will give you some fuel to think, experiment and design your own solutions.
This part is organized by the modules and applications in Maximo.

Module Administration

Application Organizations

One or more sites?

Organization and site configuration is a basic step in Maximo implementation and must be carefully planned because there are several limitations in the system:

- you cannot delete the site or organization, you can only deactivate them (but you should remember that in some places Maximo can still show inactive sites);
- site identifiers must be unique across all the organizations.

NOTE: to add a new site the user must have the flag **Can Access Inactive Sites** in the User's record checked.

The question that must be answered during the design phase is: one or more sites? There are no ready-made answers. Instead, you have to take several factors into account:

- Is it just one legal entity or a group of companies?
- Is there just one location or multiple plants/offices?
- Is it a national or international company?
- How is the ownership of the assets defined? Is there just one owner or many companies?
- What currencies are in use? One organization can have only two currencies defined.
- Is the chart of accounts the same in all companies?
- How often are the machines moved between the production plants? The history of the maintenance work is kept in the site where it was performed. In the case of frequent changes, it may be better to have just one site.
- Integration may also influence the setup; for example, an ERP system can have multiple instances.

Here are a few examples to give you a better understanding of this issue:

- one production company with one plant equals one organization, one site;
- one production company with three plants equals one organization, three sites;
- one international facility management company equals multiple organizations (countries), multiple sites (shopping centers, buildings or campuses);
- a utility company covering the whole country area with the internal structure, divided into three regions equals one organization, one site. Why is 'only one site' the solution? Theoretically, you could create three sites, but there are always some issues with the infrastructure at the border between regions, like towers or poles. If you separate the sites, the regions could see only their own infrastructures, but in real life, sometimes the closest technician (even from another region) can come and fix a failure. Separate sites make this almost impossible (but please read the next bullet for a solution). Another argument against multiple sites is ownership. A lot of times have I heard that the region's structure is invariable. Then after two years, the borders of the regions changed. Of course, you can move the assets between sites in Maximo, but the history remains within the original site, which may be unacceptable. On the other hand, I have an example in which a utility company used two sites. The company had a very specific geographical setup, operating in two remote areas of the country. There is no chance that the infrastructure from one region will be moved to the other region.
- a production company had two facilities on both sides of the road. Both of them were defined as separate sites, because they were producing different items and had their own machines and technology. However, they

were also sharing some equipment like special trucks, which were owned by one site, but repaired by the second one. The setup was extended to include third site for shared equipment. Thanks to Maximo security groups, users can have access to multiple sites. Site A can create new asset and work order for it, Site B can process it, including issuing material from their own storerooms.

- a railways company has three regions (which own the trains) and five workshops where the work is being done—this can be reflected as one organization, three sites, and five Repair Facilities (they can belong to different sites). Trains are moving and the work is performed at the closest Repair Facility (not necessarily the default one).

Even if you decide to go with one site only, when creating saved queries and reports, you should always use the relationship: *orgid = :orgid and siteid = :siteid.*

Company and Item Sets

Company and Item Sets are defined in ***Sets*** application, but because they are part of the organization and sites discussion, I include them here.

Sets are defined to group the companies (for example, vendors) and items (a catalog of materials). In Maximo, you can define as many sets as needed but each organization can have only one Company and one Item Set. Multiple organizations can use the same Company or Item Set, which means they will all see the same companies or items list (this can introduce standardization of material lists).

Sets are especially important for larger organizations; for example, one with the following structure:

- Organization *USA*
    - Site *US-East*

  - Site *US-West*
- Organization *Europe*
  - Site *United Kingdom*
  - Site *France*

The question is how to define the material catalogs for this customer? A potential answer will be two Item Sets:

- Metric
- Imperial

Organization *USA* will use *Imperial* set, *Europe* will use *Metric* Item Sets.

We can also group the vendors (companies). All the American companies can go into set *US* and the European vendors into set *EU*. As a result: organization *USA* will use company set *US* while *Europe* will use *EU*.

However, if you look from the perspective of the *United Kingdom* and *France* sites, the above setup may not be optimal, because they may have totally different vendors in each country and one company set will mean they will share the same data.

This could suggest changing the organization setup as follows:

- Organization: *USA*, Item Set *Imperial*, Company Set *US*
  - Site *US-East*
  - Site *US-West*
- Organization *United Kingdom*, Item Set *Metric*, Company Set *UK*
  - Site *Bristol*
  - Site *Manchester*
- Organization *France*, Item Set: *Metric*, Company Set *FR*
  - Site *Bordeaux*
  - Site *Marseille*

Application Conditional Expression Manager

This is one of the most powerful features in Maximo as the queries defined here can be used in restrictions or to control conditional UI. And importantly, the conditions defined here may be re-used, so you can avoid writing the same conditions multiple times.

Unfortunately, this feature has also a 'dark side'—too many conditions used in one application may affect the system performance, so you have to balance functionality versus system responsiveness.

Known Issues and Initial Changes

By default, the expression manager shows in **Reference Count** field the information about the number of times the expression was used, which is not very helpful during debugging because you do not know where exactly it is used. I suggest investing some time into modifying this application and creating an XML template to be used in your projects. You should add the tables which will list the usage of the condition in the following objects (search for condition ID in the tables below):

- domains (tables: **CROSSOVERDOMAIN** and **MAXDOMVALCOND**),
- security restrictions (table: **SECURITYRESTRICT**),
- signature options (table: **APPLICATIONAUTH**),
- conditional UI (table: **CTRLCONDITION, CTRLGROUP**).

NOTE: in Crossover Domains, the condition can be referenced to Source and/or Destination—please check both.

Hide sensitive data with restrictions

A classic example of using conditional expressions is hiding sensitive information. In my example, it will be an hourly cost. You need an expression like the one below to show the hourly rates only for *TECHN* group members:

> *exists (select 1 from groupuser where userid = :&USERNAME& and groupname = 'TECHN')*

Now, in ***Security Groups*** application, in **Global Data Restrictions** action, on **Attribute Restrictions** tab, you should define the above condition and **Type** = *HIDDEN* for all the columns below (this will hide the hourly rates in all places in Maximo).

- LABTRANS.PAYRATE
- LABTRANS.LINECOST
- WPLABOR.DISPLAYRATE
- WPLABOR.LINCEOST
- LABORCRAFTRATE.DISPLAYRATE

Application Classifications

Classifications should be used as much as possible because a lot of internal mechanisms in Maximo are based on them, such as SLAs. Classifications also make data analysis easier because you can group information. The technical attributes are on the electronic nameplate of the device. They allow, among other things, for a quick search for devices with the specific technical parameters. An important feature of the attributes is that they can be re-used with multiple classifications. For example: width, height and power can be applied to a vehicle, transformer or pump.

Classifications and attributes have the options which can automatically generate record descriptions. This ensures data standardization and minimizes manual errors. It has some drawbacks, too; for example, all the numeric values contain decimal places, which is not always an expected result. To enable this mechanism for classifications, the checkboxes **Generate Description** and **Use Classification** must be marked. In the case of the attributes, **Use in Description Generation** must be checked. For example: an asset that is assigned to *Cars/Passenger Car* classification and has attributes *Engine Type=DIESEL, Number of Passengers=5.0* can automatically generate a following description: *Cars, Passenger Car, DIESEL, 5.0.* Attributes have an additional parameter *Description Prefix.*

A prefix equal to *Seats* will generate a following description: *Cars, Passenger Car, DIESEL, Seats 5.0.* The separator of the elements in a description is defined in ***Organizations*** application, option **System Settings**.

You should use the above option instead of assigning a domain to **Description** field with the predefined values, which is intended to introduce standardization, but in my opinion is not as flexible as classifications.

Additionally, in SRs and WOs, classifications can be used as 'wizards' or forms that can improve and speed up collecting information that is required to diagnose the issue. Classifications can also be used to assign a proper group of specialists to the task.
You should use the feature that allows the classification to be shared by different objects in the system; for example, SR and WO, Item and Asset.

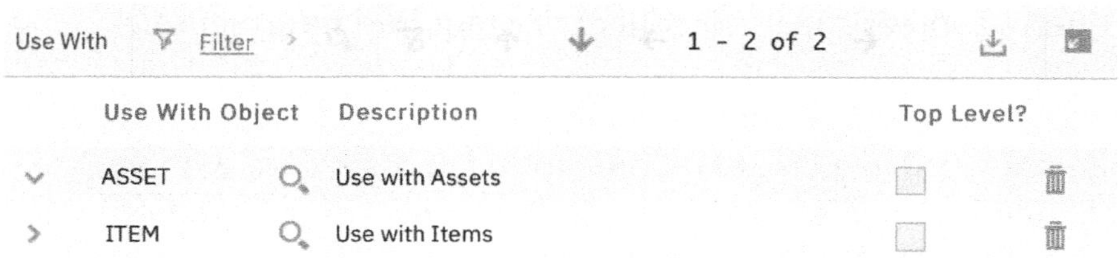

Use With Filter 1 - 2 of 2

Use With Object	Description	Top Level?
ASSET	Use with Assets	☐
ITEM	Use with Items	☐

Figure 8 A Classification Associated with ITEM and ASSET Objects

This feature allows you to create WO from SR or a rotating asset, which will inherit the classification and attributes from the other object.
NOTE: While applying an item to asset, which has classification assigned to *ITEM* only, this classification will still be applied to asset causing the *ASSET* classification and their attributes to be removed and replaced with the new ones.

Please be careful while designing classifications because once they are defined, you cannot change the IDs (only the descriptions).

Try not to re-invent the classification which may already exist in the industry or country. For example, IBM partially uses *UNSPSC* classification in the demo database. If you decide to use one of the above classifications, do not copy the whole set but use only the applicable parts of it. And while designing the hierarchy, make sure there are not too many levels of details (2-3 levels work best for the users).

I have already mentioned that the preparation of the classifications should be a task for the client. As a part of this activity, a list of the technical attributes and a list of the classifications should be prepared, and finally, the attributes should be assigned to each classification. This activity has an additional benefit for the customer because the data will be clearer and more thoughtful. You may support this task by offering spreadsheets to collect the required information.

Some customers prefer to maintain all the technical attributes at item level. They create records for each asset type with very detailed specifications. The rotating assets will only inherit this classification (and the technical details) from the item record. This setup speeds up the asset creation and improves the data quality. To complement this configuration, you should prevent changing the data in ***Assets*** application. On **Specifications** tab remove **New Row** button and **Mark Row for Delete** icon, and make the content of **Specifications** table read-only.

Creating Hierarchy of Classifications

In numerous cases, classifications will be organized in tree structures, e.g.

- VEHICLE
    - CAR
    - TRUCK
    - TRAILER

The method to create this hierarchy is top-to-bottom. That means:

- create the top-level classification,
- then click **New Row** button in **Children** section and create the lower level classification,
- if you need to build another level of hierarchy, then click the menu by the children record and choose **Move To** option; in the children record, click **New Row** button in **Children** section and add grandchildren records.

Figure 9 Children Classifications

Sometimes, when the hierarchy is already in use, someone can decide to modify it and introduce a new top-level classification:

- <u>FLEET</u>
    - VEHICLE
        - CAR
        - TRUCK
        - TRAILER

To change the tree in Maximo you have to define new classification *FLEET* first (remember to assign it to the same objects as *VEHICLE*) and then navigate to *VEHICLE* record. Next, click the menu by **Parent Classification** field and choose **Select Parent Classification** option.

Figure 10 Parent Classification Field Menu

Find and select *FLEET* classification, save the record. Maximo will then update all the objects associated with your classifications to reflect the new hierarchy, namely, the current classification.

VEHICLE \ CAR

will be transformed into

FLEET \ VEHICLE \ CAR

To copy the attributes from the parent classification to the children, please select the **Apply Down Hierarchy** checkbox

Known Issues and Initial Changes

To start with, a typical problem you might encounter while working with classifications is when you cannot see the required classification in **Classify** window; for example, in ***Assets*** application. Then this classification has probably no entry for *ASSET* object in **Use With** table.

Internally, Maximo does not use the visible classification ID (like *MOTOR*) but the numeric class structure ID, e.g. 1243. The simplest way to find it is, for example, to filter the assets by any classification in **Advanced Search** window and then check **Where clause** dialog. There will be a numeric identifier of the classification:

> *(siteid = 'BEDFORD') and (exists (select 1 from maximo.classancestor where ((ancestor = '**1013**')) and (classstructureid = asset.classstructureid)))*

Sometimes, you will need this information to create a query in Maximo or for report writing but this ID is not visible on the form. You can add a read-only field with the attribute **CLASSSTRUCTURE.CLASSSTRUCTUREID**. Then you will be able to check this value at any time.

However, a recommended method to find objects having the classification MOTOR is to use the following query with a readable ID:

> *classstructureid = (select classstructureid from classstructure where classificationid = 'MOTOR')*

This is especially important when you migrate classifications between DEV, TEST and PROD servers. The same classification may have different internal IDs on each of the servers!

Quite often, classification is no longer needed, and you do not want it to be visible. However, in ***Classifications*** application there is no status field, which could deactivate the record. The solution is to add a new logical **Inactive** field to the classification record and create a global data restriction for object **CLASSSTRUCTURE** and an application where it should be hidden, e.g. *ASSET*. Use the condition: *:xinactive = 0* and set **Restriction Type** to *QUALIFIED*.

There are many other use cases that regard classifications. For instance, the customer may need to hide classification *MOTOR* for all the users who belong to Person Group *MECHANIC*. Again, the global data restriction for object **CLASSSTRUCTURE**, **Type** *QUALIFIED* would help. You would need to define the following condition:

> *:classificationid != 'MOTOR' and exists (select 1 from persongroupteam where resppartygroup = :&usernane& and persongroup = 'MECHANIC')*

The customer may have more than just one classification for motors, for example:

- MOTOR
  - AC MOTOR
  - DC MOTOR

But still, the requirement to hide ALL the motors for all *MECHANIC* Person Group members is valid. In that case, the above query must be modified to find *MOTOR* classification and all of its children.

> *:classificationid not in (select classificationid from classancestor where ancestor = (select classstructureid from classstructure where classificationid = 'MOTOR')) and exists (select 1 from persongroupteam where resppartygroup = :&username& and persongroup = 'MECHANIC')*

If the classification has a large number of attributes, please do not forget to increase the number of rows in a respective table that contains parameters in ***Assets*** or ***Locations*** application. There is nothing worse for the user than to see a table of 10 rows that occupies one-third of the screen and to have to click through the list of 50+ attributes!

Classifications attributes have only two data types:

- alphanumeric including table attribute,
- numeric.

Each type is presented in **Specifications** table as a separate column. This is one of the biggest problems for users because they have to learn to look for information in different places, which may not be user-friendly.

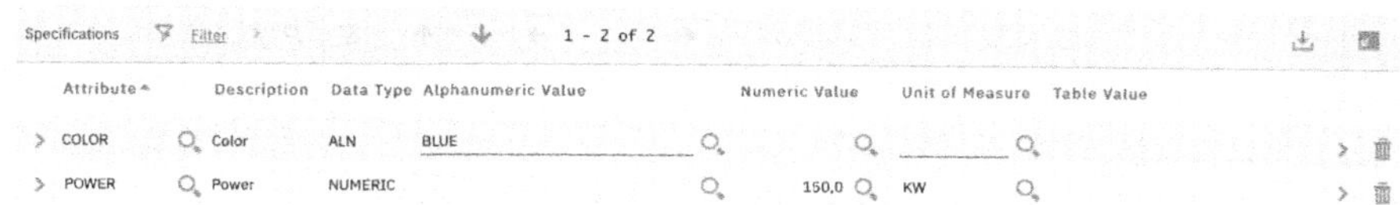

Figure 11 A Classic Specification Table

There is a trick which allows replacing these three columns with only one. All you need to do is edit **Specifications** table in ***Application Designer*** application, delete the columns: **Alphanumeric Value**, **Numeric Value** and **Table Value**. Then add a new column, you can call it just **Value**, and enter *{CLASSSPECVALUE}* as the attribute name. Now, the table is much more readable and the attributes have even lookups where appropriate. I recommend updating all the applications with specifications, among others: ***Assets***, ***Locations***, ***Item Master***.

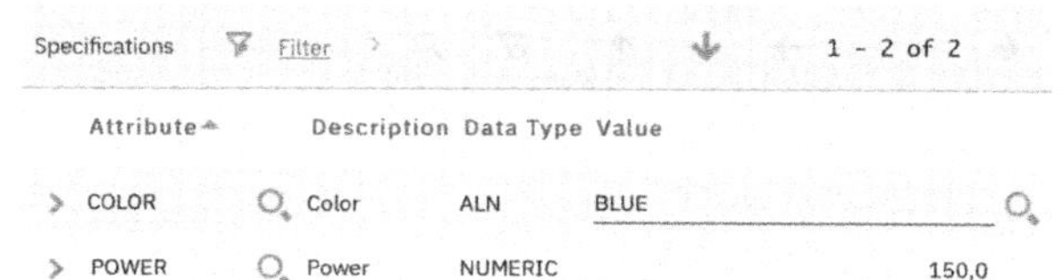

Figure 12 A Modified Specifications Table

There is no date type for attributes, which some customers consider a limitation. However, it may be bypassed because you can define these dates (like the production date or warranty expiry date) not as attributes but as fields at the asset/location level.

NOTE: As of Maximo version 7.6.1.2, this is no longer true. In this version, IBM introduced a new data type: *DATE*.

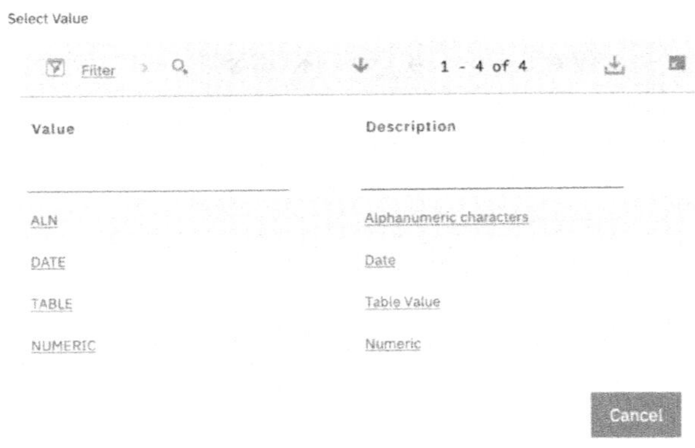

Figure 13 A New Data Type

In the **Use with Object Detail** window of the attribute, it is possible to define the default value, which will be then replicated to the objects with this classification.

By default, when a new attribute is added to the classification, it is automatically added to all the objects that have the same classification, for example:

Before change

Classification: CAR, Car
Attribute: POWER, Power in hp
Attribute: SEATS, Number of seats

Asset 1
Classification: CAR
Attribute: POWER: 100
Attribute: SEATS: 4

Asset 2
Classification: CAR
Attribute: POWER: 120
Attribute: SEATS: 5

Classification change:

Classification: CAR, Car
Attribute: POWER, Power in hp
Attribute: SEATS, Number of seats
New attribute: COLOR, Color

Asset 1
Classification: CAR
Attribute: POWER: 100
Attribute: SEATS: 4
Attribute: COLOR: <empty>

Asset 2
Classification: CAR
Attribute: POWER: 120
Attribute: SEATS: 5
Attribute: COLOR: <empty>

NOTE: Adding new attributes to the classification associated to thousands of records may have a significant impact on the performance, because Maximo will try to add the new attribute to all of them after saving. This can affect the response time of the server or result in a timeout. In that case, you may consider adding the new attribute without updating the existing records, e.g. the assets, and later importing them from the file. To achieve this, add a new attribute and before saving the classification, uncheck **Use In Specifications** flag in **Use with Object Detail** window.

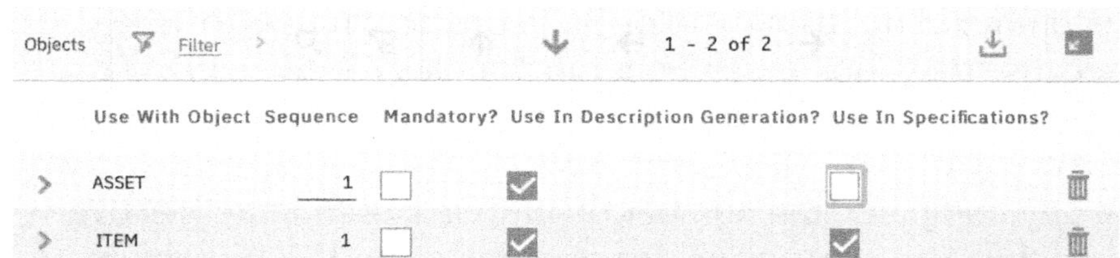

Figure 14 The Attribute for ASSET Object Disabled

Then, after the classification is saved, check this flag again.

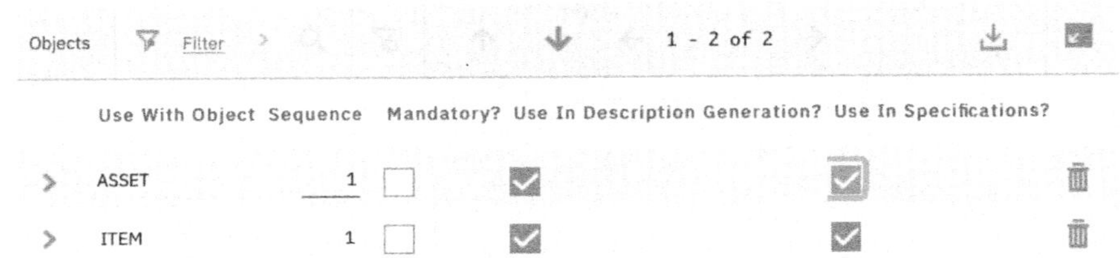

Figure 15 The Attribute for ASSET Object Enabled Again

The final step will be to perform a mass update of the existing records with new attribute values using import files (after business hours).

The number of records presented in **Classify** window (drilldown) is defined globally in **CONTROL-REGISTRY.XML** file and for the specific application in **LIBRARY.XML** file (in both cases the parameter is called *maxchildren*). You may want to change the default values to match the size of your classification tree.

There is an option to add a picture to the classification; however, users must be granted an access to **Add/Modify Image** option in ***Classifications*** application first. The purpose of it is to display a graphical map of related assets on **Topology** tab in **Assets** application. You can only add *GIF* or *JPG* pictures. NOTE: ***Classifications*** application shows pictures as squares, while **Topology** view presents the same pictures as rectangles, which is a little inconsistent. I suggest trying different aspect ratios to achieve the best results in **Topology** view. And I recommend not using photos but icons or symbols instead, because they look much better in **Topology** view. UPDATE: topology viewer was deprecated starting from version 7.6.0.7.

In any company, the number of attributes used increases over time, but also some attributes stop being used. The problem then arises of how to find the attributes that are no longer used. To make this task easier, you should add a new tab to the application with a table **Unused Attributes**. Use the following relationship between **CLASSSTRUCTURE** and **ASSETATTRIBUTE** objects:

assetattrid not in (select distinct assetattrid from classspec)

The resulting table will help the data administrator remove the obsolete records.

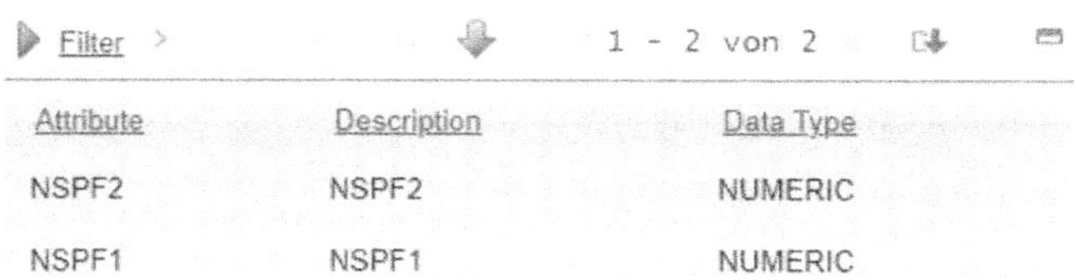

Attribute	Description	Data Type
NSPF2	NSPF2	NUMERIC
NSPF1	NSPF1	NUMERIC

Figure 16 Unused Attributes

Saved Queries

This below query will find all the classifications with pictures.

exists (select 1 from imglib where refobjectid = classstructureuid and refobject = 'CLASSSTRUCTURE')

If you want to find the classifications with *XYZ* attribute, use the following query.

exists (select 1 from classspec where assetattrid = 'XYZ' and classspec.classstructureid = classstructure.classstructureid)

Application Bulletin Board

In multiple projects, this application is greatly underestimated, but I still think it can improve communication between different groups.

Usually, you will limit the access to creating new messages; otherwise, someone may generate a lot of spam. The candidates to create messages are:

- system administrator,
- business data administrator,
- department managers.

Bulletin Board can be used to inform users about the upcoming events:

- planned machine downtime,
- an outage,
- planned changes in Maximo start centers (so the users can refresh it),
- planned changes in Maximo dictionaries; for example, a new value for a Work Order type,
- some new asset attributes that must be manually populated in existing records.

Bulletin Board requires *BBCron* cron task to be enabled, so make sure it is active.

Known Issues and Initial Changes

On the messages list, there is only **Post Date** column. I usually add **Expiration Date** column there to know when the message expires.

I also suggest moving the fields: **Post Date**, **Expiration Date**, **Posted By**, and **Status** to the left side of the screen on **Bulletin Board** tab. The standard layout requires horizontal scrolling.

In order to automatically remove the expired messages you have to enable system property *mxe.crontask.deleteBB* and configure escalation *ESCBLTNEXP* to run once a day.

Sub-module Reporting

Maximo is a transactional system, and it generates a lot of data that should be somehow consumed, which is they should be reviewed, and some decisions should be made. Therefore, it is important to ask the customer at the beginning of the project what kind of information they will need and for whom—internal needs or external authorities. Why is this information needed? What actions could be initiated based on this input?
You should then ask who the recipient of such information is (who will need and read this report?). Compare the effort to create a report with the value of the data presented in it. It may be easier to run a saved query and export the data to a spreadsheet. Sometimes, the reports are prepared week-by-week or month-by-month because everybody have done so before, but in fact, nobody even reads them. The implementation of Maximo should be an opportunity to change that, perhaps by removing this report or replacing it with something more useful. Information needs may sometimes influence your design because some additional attributes will be needed, or an additional effort should be planned to prepare the reports.

Reporting in Maximo is not only about BIRT/Cognos reports, because the required information can be also presented on start centers in the form of tables and predefined queries that are complemented by KPIs. There are a few methods of presenting the KPI values:

- a gauge on a Start Center,
- a list of KPIs on a Start Center (with a trend indicator, goal, current value and difference),
- a gauge in the KPI record,
- a list of historical values in the KPI record,
- a graph in the KPI record.

The information should not always be printed. In most cases, the on-screen report (perhaps sent by e-mail) should be enough.

Please present all these options, preferably during the initial presentation.

Application KPI Manager

Maximo KPI is an SQL statement where you can use any calculation function and method available in the RDBMS, e.g.

> *SUM, COUNT, AVG* or *(select count(*) from workorder where worktype = 'CM') / (select count(*) from workorder where worktype = 'PM') * 100 from sysibm.sysdummy1.*

KPIs are usually presented on the Start Centers but there is also an application for end-users, ***KPI Viewer***, where all the public KPIs can be viewed.
NOTE: KPI's Long Description will be shown in this application as an explanation for the users.

If you plan to define many identical KPIs, for example, for organizations, sites or person groups, and you prefer not to duplicate KPIs, it is recommended to use ***KPI Templates*** application. You will define templates with the usage of one or more variables which will be used to generate the KPIs for each combination of variable values. For example, the variable *${vassettype}* in this query will be replaced with *PRODUCTION, FLEET* etc. to generate KPIs for each Asset Type:

> *select count(assetnum) from asset where assettype = ${vassettype} and status = 'OPERATING'*

Known Issues and Initial Changes

In Maximo 7.6, the graph in the KPI record has the form of a square/triangle, generated for each point in the data series, which makes it unreadable if you have numerous data points.

In some earlier versions of Maximo 7.5, the graph could draw only a flat line and display *NaN* for the X axis labels (check for a fix or install a newer version of Maximo).

You should give to the users enough permission to see the KPIs. But if you give them a read-only access to the KPI, they will not be able to change the default KPI timeframe (fields **From** and **To** on **Historical Trends** tab).

KPIs are calculated by the cron task *KPICronTask*. Version 7.6 has solved the issue that all KPIs must have shared the same frequency. Now, there is a pre-defined instance of the above cron task called *KPINONREALTIME*. It is a default instance for all KPIs, but you can create additional instances with their own schedules: once a day, once a week etc.

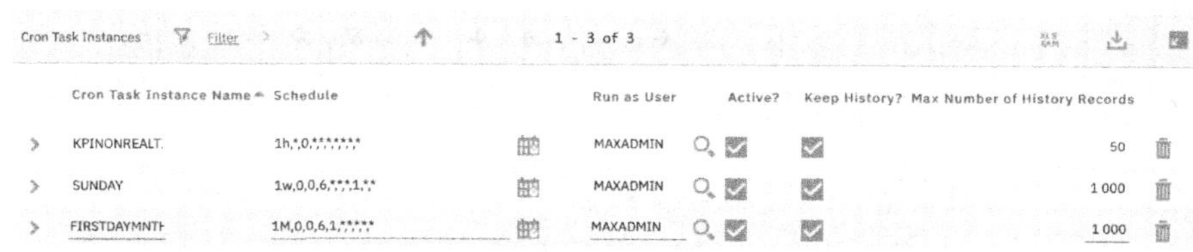

Cron Task Instances
Filter
1 - 3 of 3
Cron Task Instance Name
Schedule
Run as User
Active?
Keep History?
Max Number of History Records
KPINONREALT.
1h,*,0,*,*,*,*,*,*,*
MAXADMIN
50
SUNDAY
1w,0,0,6,*,*,*,1,*,*
MAXADMIN
1 000
FIRSTDAYMNTH
1M,0,0,6,1,*,*,*,*,*
MAXADMIN
1 000

Figure 17 Sample KPICronTask Instances

You can then link one or more KPIs with the new instances. This can be done with the **Add Schedule/Remove Schedule** or **Schedule KPI** actions—for multiple or just one KPI respectively.

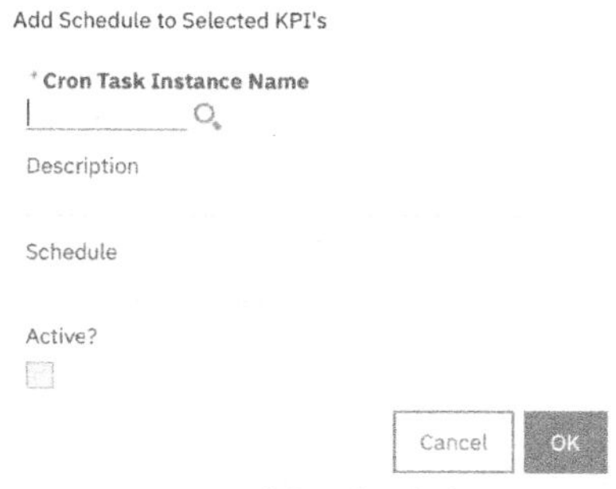

Figure 18 Add Schedule Action

A KPI has an important attribute: **Target** to compare the current readings 'to'. You can use industry benchmarks to set this value.

KPIs can gather historical values but you may decide to remove them automatically, for example, after *180* days. Cron task *KPIHISTORY* can be configured to delete the old values.

You can authorize only selected groups to access the KPI on **Security** tab.

KPI Examples

I always create two types of KPIs:

- business KPIs,
- system administration KPIs.

Here is a list of sample business KPIs:

- Corrective Work Orders to preventive maintenance Work Orders ratio (%): This KPI should be based on the **Work Type**. The best companies should have this indicator at less than 30%.
    - o *DB2 select (select count(*) from workorder where worktype = 'CM') / (select count(*) from workorder where worktype = 'PM') * 100 from sysibm.sysdummy1*
- The percent of the PM Work Orders completed on time:
    - o *select count(*) from workorder where pmnum is not null and actfinish <= targcompdate*
- The number of the Work Orders past due:
    - o *select count(*) from workorder where actfinish > targcompdate*
- The percent of the Work Orders that have actual values (material cost, labor time) above estimates.
- The number of the Work Orders created today (you can do the same for the Service Requests). This is very useful for observing trends on a graph.

- *DB2 select count(*) from workorder where date(reportdate) = date((select current timestamp from sysibm.sysdummy1))*

- The number of the Work Orders created today by the preventive maintenance mechanism
  - *DB2 select count(*) from workorder where pmnum is not null and date(reportdate) = date((select current timestamp from sysibm.sysdummy1))*
- How to measure the performance of the users? One method will be to check how many Work Orders were modified today.
  - *DB2 select count(*) from workorder where date((select current timestamp from sysibm.sysdummy1)) = date(changedate)*
- Backlog monitoring: How many Work Orders are still open?
  - *select count(*) from workorder where status not in ('COMP', 'CLOSED')*
- How good is the planning process? The percentage of the Work Orders completed within the planned dates.
- SLA compliance: The percent of the Work Orders completed within the target dates.
- The mean time between failures (MTBF): This should be calculated for the main machines. Below is a sample SQL to calculate MTBF for a specific asset defined as a difference between report dates.
  - *DB2 select (select sum(numrec) from (select days(lag(reportdate, 1) over (order by reportdate desc)) - days(reportdate) as numrec from workorder where worktype = 'CM' and assetnum = '1000' order by reportdate desc)) / (select count(*) - 1 from workorder where worktype = 'CM' and assetnum = '1000') from sysibm.sysdummy1*

- The mean time to repair (MTTR): Again, this should be calculated for the main machines. This should be the time spent off-line. You have to define this period with the customer. Usually, this will be the time between the date when the issue was reported and *RESOLVED* status.
- The KPIs related to Maximo data quality, e.g.
    - The percent of person records without email addresses.
    - However, "The number of the failure Work Orders without failure codes" is a bad example of such a KPI. This should never happen because you can make the failure code fields required at a certain stage. What I understand by data quality KPI is to report the situation when there is no influence on the data entry. In my example, person records might come from an external system and you cannot make the email address required. Instead, the KPI will show you which data requires attention.

You can modify these examples to limit the scope (e.g. adding sites or dates) or change the KPI object, for example, to monitor Service Requests. You can also add the clause: *woclass = 'WORKORDER' or woclass = 'ACTIVITY'*

The second type of KPIs is designed for system administrators, allowing them to monitor Maximo from Maximo. Here are a few examples:

- the number of the users currently logged-in: There is an out-of-the-box KPI for that, but I suggest creating new ones—one per license type (see, License Types). The one below can be used for the license compliance checks.
    - *select count (*) from maxsession where issystem != 1 and exists (select 1 from maxuser where maxuser.userid = maxsession.userid and type = 'AUTH')*

- Database size: This KPI can be related to another one, for example, the number of the Work Orders registered per day, to determine if there is a correlation between the two values.
    - *DB2 select sum(data_object_p_size) / 1024 as obj_sz_mb from sysibmadm.admintabinfo where tabschema = 'MAXIMO'*
- Used DB Space:
    - *DB2 select float(tbsp_page_top)/float(tbsp_usable_pages) * 100 as usedspace from table(mon_get_tablespace('', -2)) where tbsp_name = 'MAXDATA'*
- The number of database locks:
    - *DB2 select count(*) from table(mon_get_locks(null, -2))*
- The number of database connections:
    - *DB2 select count(*) from table(mon_get_connection(cast(null as bigint), -2))*
- The number of deadlocks:
    - *DB2 select sum(deadlocks) from table(mon_get_connection(cast(null as bigint), -2))*
- The number of failed logins today—can be a sign of a security incident (Requires Login Tracking to be enabled):
    - *DB2 select count(*) from logintracking where attemptresult = 'FAILED' and date(attemptdate) = (select current date from sysibm.sysdummy1)*

Status	KPI	Actual	Target	Variance
↓	Number of Database Connections	15	10	5
↓	Database Processor Load	13932	1000	12932
—	Number of Deadlocks	0	0	0
↓	Number of Locks	9	20	-11
—	Database Size in MB	3626	2000	1626
↑	TCP/IP Transmission in KB	373	100	273
↓	Number of Failed Logins Today	0	0	0

Figure 19 A Sample Start Center with System KPIs

NOTE: Executing some of these queries may require some additional database privileges for *maxadmin* user.

Application Report Administration

Adding New Reports

While designing a new report, the Report Writer always decides what is the application, from which it will be run, e.g. ***Work Order Tracking*** application. However, it is possible to add the same report to other applications, too. For example: you have prepared a custom report with the graph showing the number of normal and overtime hours. This report can be attached to ***Labor Reporting*** and ***Work Order Tracking*** applications. Users can run the report without changing the application.

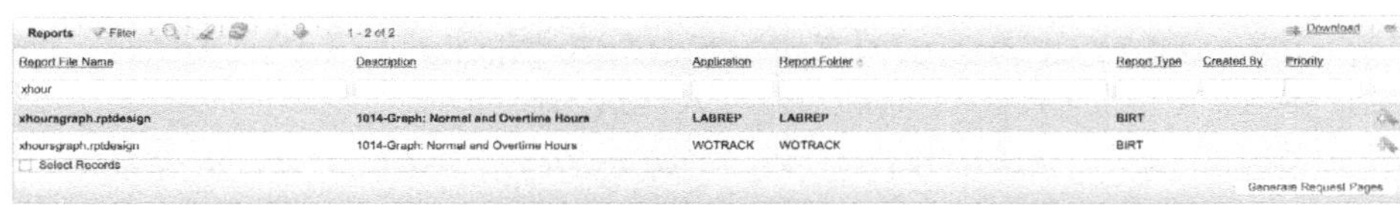

Figure 20 Report Attached to More Than One Application

Reports and Security

Report Security tab is very useful because you can authorize only selected groups to access the report.
Reports can not only be printed or previewed on the screen but users can also schedule the reports to be sent out via email. This is a potential backdoor that allows sensitive information to be shared with non-authorized personnel.
NOTE: There is no validation of email addresses in this dialog, the user can enter any external address.
To verify the list of recipients of the scheduled reports, you can open **Run Reports** dialog in any application and go to **Scheduling Status** tab. It will list all the scheduled reports in all the applications, so you can quickly check if the addresses are correct. The same list will also be displayed after choosing the

action **View Scheduled Reports** in *Report Administration* application.
Emailing reports can be used to print the documents automatically. Some printers have unique email addresses assigned to them. Instead of specifying a person as the recipient, the user can provide the email address of a printer.

And only as a reminder: make sure that the users who can access the reports have the appropriate Maximo license.

Report Performance

Running reports can affect the performance of the system. A poorly defined report or a report that processes a lot of information can slow down the system, because the database will be busy preparing the necessary information.
You can control these issues to some extent. The easiest way is to set the limit of records that can be processed by the report (check **Limit Records** flag and enter **Max Record Limit**), but this is good only for the main section of the report. What about a situation when the report displays only one main record but has a lot of sub-reports and each will process thousands of records? Starting with version 7.6, there is an additional setting that can limit the number of records processed by a report. This option is set at a Security Group level (not the report). You can access it from **Set Security Group Limits** action on **List** tab in *Report Administration* application. Enter the value for **Report Server Limits** as well as for **Ad Hoc Preview Records Limit** and **Scheduled Reports Limit**.

When designing the reports, you should consider some questions:

- Verify the frequency of scheduled reports. Try to minimize the number of calls during working hours, cron tasks, escalations or backups.
- Double check the SQL statements used in the reports. Always test them in the database tool first and then check

the execution plan. If required, ask the DBA to optimize them. The result of this analysis may affect the database setup: it may be necessary to add one or more indexes.

OEE Reports

The OEE is one of the most important indicators for the maintenance industry. Maximo comes with ready-to-use data structures to calculate the OEE as well as with the reports. These data structures are important because the OEE is calculated based on the information about:

- equipment availability,
- production volume,
- quality factors.

The latter two do not exist in Maximo. Therefore, you should provide integration with the production systems to download this information periodically into **KPIOEE** table. Remember that the OEE should be calculated only for the main machines, e.g. production lines, and not for the components.

Report Parameters

Please do not forget to define **Display Sequence** and **Required** flag for the parameters. This will ensure consistency; especially, when you are using the same parameters in multiple reports, such as, *Start Date* and *End Date*. They should have the same wording and be presented in the same order in all the reports. Parameters can have the **Lookup Name** defined, too. There is a huge list of system lookups that could be used, e.g.

- asset,
- contract,
- craft,
- datelookup—calendar control,
- failurecode,
- item,
- jobplan,
- labor,

- location,
- site,
- storeroom,
- valuelist—values from a domain,
- yornlookuplist—Yes/No values.

Sometimes, it is worth setting the **Default Value** for a parameter to avoid entering the obvious values.

Report Usage

The *REPORTUSAGECLEANUP* cron task collects information about the reports used in the last *30* days (you may adjust this value). This information is saved in the **REPORTUSAGLOG** table and can be viewed in the standard report called *Report Usage*. Analyzing data from this report provides information about what reports are actually used, how often, and who uses them.

You can also use the information from the **REPORTUSAGLOG** table to create an escalation with a security notification that some users have executed a certain report.

Known Issues and Initial Changes

After installing Maximo, always remember to open *Report Administration* application. On **List** tab, click **Generate Request Pages** button in the bottom right corner. This will create request pages for all the out-of-the-box reports in the system. During the configuration, you will need to generate a request page for each new report that is added to the system. This action should also be repeated if you are changing the numbers or types of the parameters of the report.

NOTE: in a multi-language environment, you have to generate request pages for each language installed in the system separately.

Out-of-the-box reports may have some issues with printing the descriptions which are multi-language enabled. Some reports refer to the original **DESCRIPTION** column, which may be empty in the local language. The localized content will be stored in the language table: **L_...** You will then need to modify the report queries to display the correct value:

select description from L_item where langcode='XX'

If you plan to use the automatic cost rollup, do not forget to schedule the report in ***Assets*** application: *Maintenance Cost Rollup Update* to run every day or every week.

There may be a need to create a report with barcodes. The easiest way to do this is to use a barcode font, which automatically encodes the strings or numbers.
NOTE: This font should be installed on the report server to prepare the printouts. Free fonts are available on the market but they may not be sufficient because they do not support all the codes and their qualities may not be acceptable. But if you decide to use paid fonts, you should include this price in your or the customer's budgets. Always try to print and scan the codes using the target-scanning device until you will get repeatable results. Some industries will require the use of special labels that are resistant to external conditions, which may cause some problems during barcode reading.

Saved Queries

The query below will help you find all the reports with the parameters:

exists (select 1 from reportlookup where reportlookup.reportname = report.reportname)

Sub-Module Resources

Application Crafts

This is, in fact, a simple dictionary of the occupations of the workers, but it is widely used in the planning process. Therefore, it must be defined in the system. It can be entered manually or, if possible, populated through the integration from the HR system, in which such information should be available.

Please be aware that some mobile solutions may also require the craft to be assigned to the worker for them to use the application.

I always ask my customers to prepare this list as part of their homework (see, chapter Homework), but you can suggest using either country specific classifications, like *Standard Occupational Classification System*, or an international classification, like *International Standard Classification of Occupations*. This is to avoid reinventing the wheel but also it may be required for reporting purposes.

Premium Pay Codes

You may work for a customer who charges different rates for the time working under normal conditions, overtime and/or extreme conditions, such as, at heights or underground. This information can be defined in *Crafts* application, action **Manage Premium Pay Codes**. The codes can be defined as a multiplier of the standard rate (e.g. *1.5*), increment or hourly factor, which should fulfill requirements of any customer.

Application Qualifications

A qualification is a formal confirmation of the skills.
You can define here:

- medical certificates,
- safety training,
- drivers' licenses,
- IDs and passports,
- and even badges issued for the workers.

Known Issues and Initial Changes

Before defining any qualification, domain **QUALTYPE** must be first populated.

Saved Queries

This query will find all the qualifications that are not used:

status = 'ACTIVE' and not exists (select 1 from laborqual where status = 'ACTIVE' and laborqual.qualificationid = qualification.qualificationid)

Application People

Known Issues and Initial Changes

The email address of a person must be unique mainly because of the incoming email processing mechanism. Also, one person's record can only be related to one user's record. Normally, this is not an issue, but I have found a couple of companies (or rather a group of companies) with non-standard employment terms. One person can be an employee of several different companies but can have only one email address (in Maximo, such a group of companies will be reflected as different organizations). This requirement cannot be implemented in Maximo, so you should discuss other options, such as, creating separate users for the same person (with different logins and email addresses) for each company where they are employed. Please remember that not only email addresses must be unique but also phone numbers cannot be duplicated.

Maximo has a couple of technical logins (and, of course, corresponding person records): *maxadmin, mxintadm, maxreg* (and you may create some additional ones). The problem is that users can see them on the lists while choosing person records. To improve user experience, I suggest creating a data restriction with the below query based on **System Account** field from *Users* application. Any user marked as system user will not be displayed on the person list.

not exists (select 1 from maxuser where maxuser.personid = person.personid and status = 'ACTIVE' and sysuser = 1)

Person data can have one more application: you can use it as a phone and address book. All you need to do is to create a clone of *People* application with first name, surname, department, email and phone information. Then grant the read access to this application to everyone. A phone book can be added to **Favorite Application** portlet on a Start Center.

People can be assigned to one or more Person Groups, but you cannot determine it in *People* application as you do in *Users* application, which lists all the Security Groups the user belongs to. I suggest adding a new tab, **Person Groups**, in *People* and putting a table there with all the groups this person was assigned to. To do that, you have to define a new relationship in **PERSON** table to find the related records in **PERSONGROUP** table:

persongroup in (select persongroup from persongroupteam where resppartygroup = :personid)

Anonymization

People application has a lot of information about people: names, phone numbers, email addresses, contact information. In some countries, this may be considered sensitive information, which is protected by personal data law. It may be required by this law to anonymize the information when no longer required in *People* application, but also in *Service Requests*, *Work Order Tracking*, *Purchase Requisitions* applications and anywhere where personal data is visible, for example, in the **Work Log** and **Communication Log**. Anonymization means replacing the name, surname and other information with static text, like *XXXXXX*. This would require creating a new escalation with the actions to replace these fields.

Alternatively, you can define the Global Attribute Restrictions of the type *HIDDEN* for **WORKORDER** object to hide fields that contain personal information, like **Reported By**. This restriction can have the following condition:

DB2 *days((select current timestamp from sysibm.sysdummy1)) – days(reportdate) >= 180*

This will hide the information for 6 months after the **Report Date**.

NOTE: Personal data protection may influence your setup of the person and user identifiers. In numerous systems, it looks like *johndoe* or *jdoe* for *John Doe*, which still can be considered personal information if you replace the surname: *John Doe* with *XXXXX*. In such cases, the solution will be to use system-generated ID's for the person and user records.

Do not forget about possible sensitive information in the qualifications section of the person—it needs to be handled with, too.

NOTE: In the newer Maximo versions, there is **Maximo People Data Management Utility**, which can help you scramble or delete personal information. Please refer to the official documentation of this utility for more information.

Saved Queries

Very often you can face a situation when someone will complain, "I am not receiving any emails from the system." The root cause could be a missing email address of this person. The query below verifies that everybody has an email address assigned. You can also use it on the system administrators' Start Center in a result set portlet.

status = 'ACTIVE' and *not exists (select emailaddress from email, person where person.personid = owner and email.isprimary = 1 and email.personid = person.personid)*

The people in more than one Person Group:

status = 'ACTIVE' and exists (select 1 from persongroupteam where resppartygroup = personid group by resppartygroup having count(*) > 1)

Dialog Profile

Profile is not an application in *ADMINISTRATION* module but a dialog in the main system menu. However, it is closely related to the content of *People* application, so it should be modified accordingly. For example, if the customer decides not to use the procurement cards, you may need to remove these fields from **Personal Information** window to avoid confusion. Some users think they should enter private card details there and complain that this is against privacy rules.

In the case when Maximo has no integration with the system which provides information about people, you can use this dialog to keep at least users information up to date. You should prepare a procedure which obliges the users to update their personal information initially (after the first logging in) and whenever their phone or address information changes.

Application Labor

I suggest keeping Person ID, Labor ID and User ID the same, even if Maximo allows them to be different. Some applications and mobile solutions expect them to be the same, and it is also much easier to maintain the identifiers if you know they are identical.
NOTE: make sure that the attributes **MAXUSER.USERID** and **LABOR.LABORCODE** have the same length as **PERSON.PERSONID**. Otherwise, you may get an error that the field is too short.

Labor can have its own inventory (storeroom). You can create it using the action **Create Labor Inventory Location**.

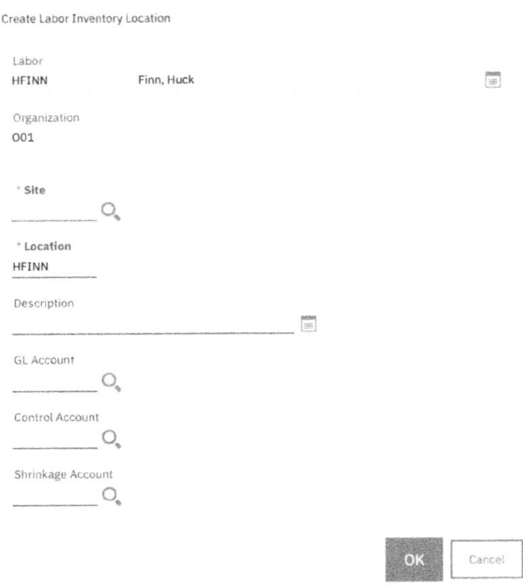

Figure 21 Create Labor Inventory Location

This can be used, for example, to monitor the location of tools or safety equipment, which can be returned to the main storeroom after the worker leaves the company.

Known Issues and Initial Changes

The first step I make in the new Maximo environment is to reorder the fields on **Qualifications** tab. I put the dates and status fields close to each other.

Figure 22 A Proposed Layout

You can also add a person lookup to **Validated By** field if the customer wants to keep the name of the HR specialist who has verified the certificate.

An escalation can be defined so that it will automatically change the status of the qualification to *EXPIRED* after it reaches

its expiry date. It can also send a warning to the boss of the employee (or HR specialist) before the expiry date to remind that the re-certification is required.
NOTE: You have to change the definition of **LABORQUAL** object in the ***Database Configuration*** and make it the main object; otherwise, it will not be available in the roles and communication templates.
Also, you will need to define *EXPIRED* status (internal value *INACTIVE*) in **QUALSTAT** domain.

Saved Queries

Here are some queries that can help you check the labor information.

Labor without qualifications:

> *status = 'ACTIVE' and not exists (select 1 from laborqual where laborqual.laborcode = labor.laborcode)*

Labor with expired qualifications:

> *DB2 status = 'ACTIVE' and exists (select 1 from laborqual where laborqual.laborcode = labor.laborcode and status = 'ACTIVE' and enddate is not null and enddate <= (select current date from sysibm.sysdummy1))*

Labor with craft but without qualifications:

> *status = 'ACTIVE' and exists (select 1 from laborcraftrate where laborcraftrate.laborcode = labor.laborcode) and not exists (select 1 from laborqual where status = 'ACTIVE' and laborqual.laborcode = labor.laborcode)*

Application Person Groups

This is a simple application that allows for grouping people for different purposes:

- to send notifications from the workflow or escalations,
- to be used in ***Bulletin Board*** to send out messages,
- to assign work.

The groups can contain people:

- from the same locations (city, site or building),
- with similar skills (mechanics, drivers),
- from the same departments,
- of the same sexes (to send more personalized messages).

You can combine a group with the information about the organization and site (fields: **Use for Organization** and **Use for Site**). For example, you could have a group *ELEC*, containing the electricians from all the locations. The work order will be assigned to this *ELEC* group, but then you can filter the group members by WO's site, so only the relevant people can be assigned.

Known Issues and Initial Changes

Please modify the out-of-the-box application and move the field **Sequence** below **Person** followed by **Group Default**. This will make entering the data much easier.

Figure 23 The New Layout of Person Groups Application

Module Assets

Application Meters

Meter is a definition of how to collect the metering data. Once associated with an asset or location, it stores the readings for them. Meter can be used by multiple assets/locations and one asset/location can have more than one meter.

Meter is not equal to a physical metering device and cannot be used to manage it. For this purpose you need to create an asset. The purpose of meters is to control the meter-based Preventive Maintenance and Condition Monitoring, but also to collect the consumption of energy or fuel.
Maximo has the following meter types:

- continuous meter that usually presents the mileage of the device, e.g. the number of the hours worked. New reading must be greater than or equal to the previous one. NOTE: If you forget to enter one value, you can still do that, but the reading date must be lower than the latest entry. Maximo automatically calculates the daily average. This value is used to determine the next Preventive Maintenance date. You can enter the meter reading as *ACTUAL* value (what the meter says, e.g. *78423 mi*) or *DELTA* value (how much the meter has changed since the last reading, e.g. *169 mi*). This is defined for the meter as **Reading Type,** but you can always overwrite this setting while entering the value for the asset/location. Both the values will update the actual value.
- gauge meters that present the current condition of the device, e.g. temperature. The readings are not dependent on the previous values and can repeat: *73, 68, 77, 73...*
- characteristic value, which is the reading that can be only one of the predefined text values, e.g. the number of

broken fibers in the line: *<5, 5-10, >10* or colors: *Red, Yellow, Green.*

Copying the Meter Readings

Assets are usually organized in vertical structures:

- An engine is a part of a truck and they both have the same mileage meters.

It is expected that both the engine and the truck will have the separate histories of meter readings because the engine can be moved between vehicles. At the same time, the meter reading from the truck can be copied over to the engine's meter to avoid a double-entry. Maximo allows for copying meter readings between parent asset and children, but also the reading from the location can be copied over to the assets in this location. In both cases the delta values are copied to the meters with the same names.

This mechanism can be enabled/disabled by choosing an appropriate value in **Accept Rolldown From** field on **Meters** tab in ***Assets*** application:

- From parent asset (*ASSET*),
- From location (*LOCATION*),
- Do not copy the readings from other objects (*NONE*).

NOTE: The meter reading will not be rolled down to the child assets when the reading date is earlier than the date of creating an asset hierarchy.

A meter readings rolldown does not work for Locations because they can belong to different systems. This has an important consequence for the 1:1 setup (1 Location—1 Asset—described later). You can define the structure of locations and assign meters to them. The asset meters can be defined to get the readings from the associated location. But, because the location will not inherit the readings from their parents, this setup will not distribute the readings down the asset hierarchy as expected.

Fuel Consumption Registration

In order to collect the information about fuel consumption, the meter with the same name, e.g. *DIESEL*, must be assigned to the non-rotating item (fuel) and the asset (truck).
Each issue transaction of the item (fuel) for the asset that has meter *DIESEL* will increase the asset's meter reading and add the same number of gallons/liters. This can be combined with the mileage meter and give fuel economy in l/100 km or mpg.

Known Issues and Initial Changes

On **Where Used** tab there are sub-tabs with the tables that present assets, locations, PMs, items and measurement points associated with the current meter. However, all the tables are static, you cannot open the related record. You will need to add the following information for each of the tables:

- Lookup,
- Go To Applications,
- Menu Type.

You will also need to change the **Input Mode** of the table from *Read Only* to an empty value; otherwise, your configuration will not work.

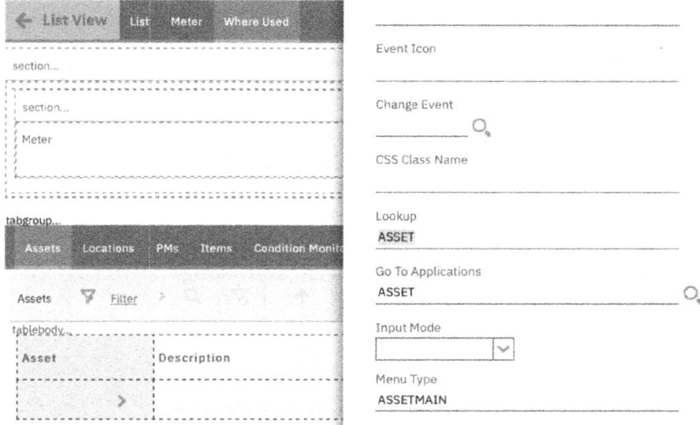

Figure 24 A Sample Modification of the Asset Table on Where Used Tab

Application Meter Groups

To facilitate the management of multiple meters you can put them in groups. Instead of assigning *8* or *12* meters separately to an asset or location, it is enough to enter **Meter Group** information. And groups offer an additional benefit of adding a new meter to all the associated assets/locations automatically. In case there are *50* assets already, each with *8* meters, and you want to add an additional meter, this may be a time-consuming action. Fortunately, *Meter Groups* application has a checkbox **Apply New Meters Where Groups Is Used**. When selected, it adds the new meter in a group to all the associated objects. NOTE: this checkbox does not support deleting meters from objects.

Application Collections

This application belongs to *IT INFRASTRUCTURE* module, but I have mentioned it here, because it is closely related to assets and locations.

I could describe this application as 'underused'. What it does is another form of grouping (categorizing) assets and locations. One asset/location can be part of one or more collections giving more reporting options. You can add the objects to the collection:

- in *Collections* application, or
- in *Assets* or *Locations* application, action: **Manage Asset Collections/Manage Location Collections**.

Categorizing is not everything collections can offer. The collections can restrict an access to the selected assets/location for users. You can define it in *Security Groups* application, tab **Data Restrictions**, sub-tab **Collection Restrictions**. This feature can be very helpful if you want to give the operators the option to report issues with any production machine located in a specific building.

Application Relationships

It is also part of *IT INFRASTRUCTURE* module but can be used for Assets. The relationship defines the rules that determine how the assets relate to each other. There are two type of relationships:

- UNIDIRECTIONAL, e.g. USES,
- BIDIRECTIONAL, e.g. CONNECTS.

Be creative, instead of naming the relationship *BEGINS* or *TERMINATES*, you can use symbols: |--> and -->|.

You can also define the rules for a relationship to define which assets (belonging to which classification) should be the source and target of this relationship. The rules can be really complex, you can include conditions, like *attribute >= 50*, the conditions can be connected by operators *OR/AND*.

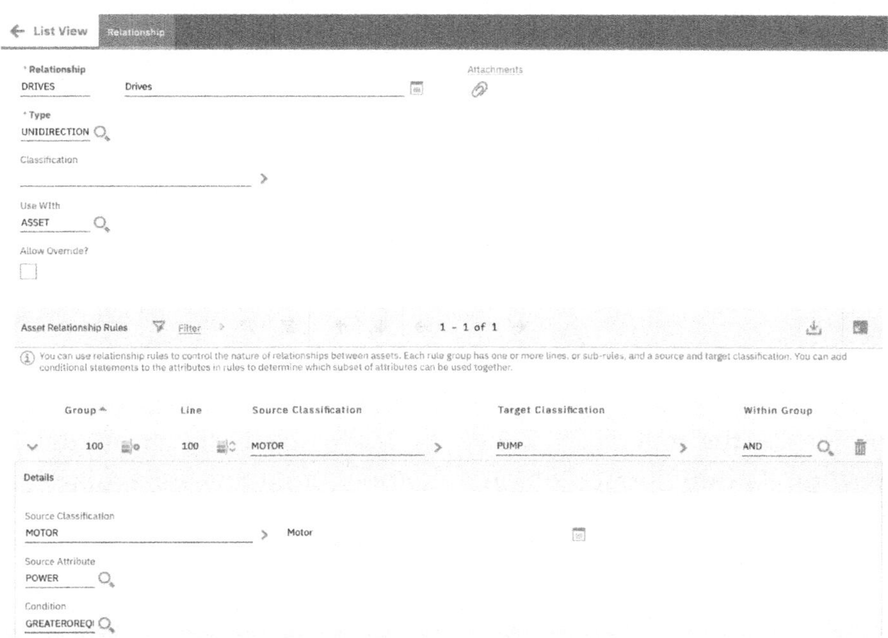

Figure 25 Relationship's Rules

Relationships can be used to define relations which are not simple machine-component connections but define also logical dependencies between the assets.

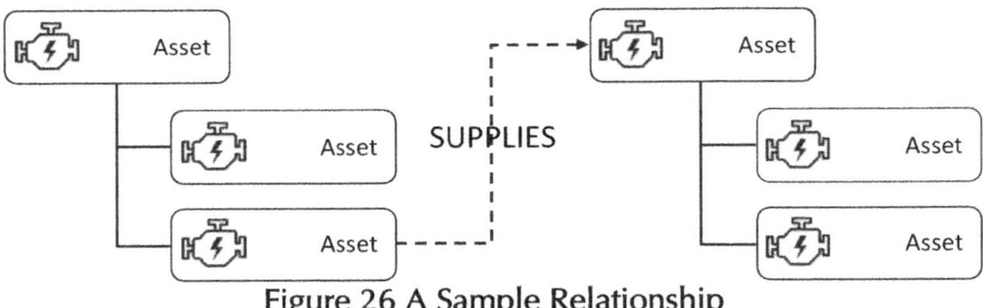

Figure 26 A Sample Relationship

Known Issues and Initial Changes

If you decide to use the relationships, it is worth changing the layout of the tab **Relationships** in ***Assets*** application and grouping the source and target fields:

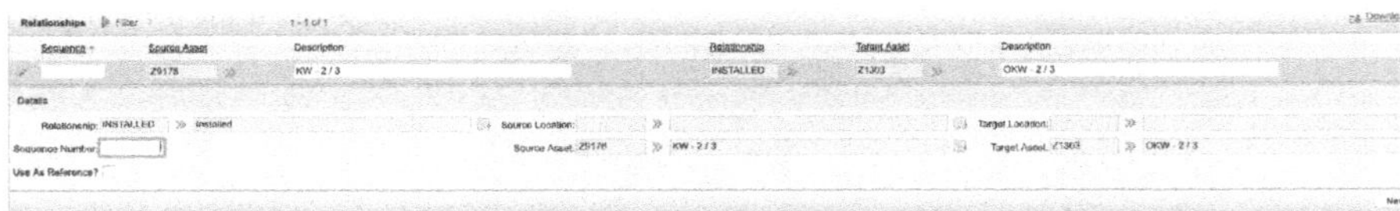
Figure 27 A Proposed Layout for Asset's Relationships Table

You can also add the Asset description columns to the table, by default only IDs are shown (use *SOURCEASSET* and *TARGETASSET* database relationships to get the descriptions).

Application Locations

One of the fundamental architectural decisions in Maximo projects is the reflection of the physical assets in the computer system. As I mentioned before, a variety of means are available: locations, assets, classifications, collections, relationships…

However, the most important feature that Maximo offers are locations and the method of connecting them together which is called 'systems'.

A location can be a physical place (building, room, zone, etc.) where the assets are installed. One or more assets may have a relation to this physical location. It can be subject to maintenance (painting, meter readings, inspections).

But we can also have the so called functional locations in the system (you should use **Classification** field to categorize locations). A functional location plays the role of the logical element of the infrastructure. For example, when you look at the Piping and Instrumentation Diagram/Drawing, the structure of the elements in the depicted production process will always be the same: there will be a tank and a pump needed. The diagram does not say who the manufacturer of the pump should be and which serial number it has. From the diagram the requirements for the elements may be calculated: the flor rate and pressure for the pump, the volume for the tank, etc.

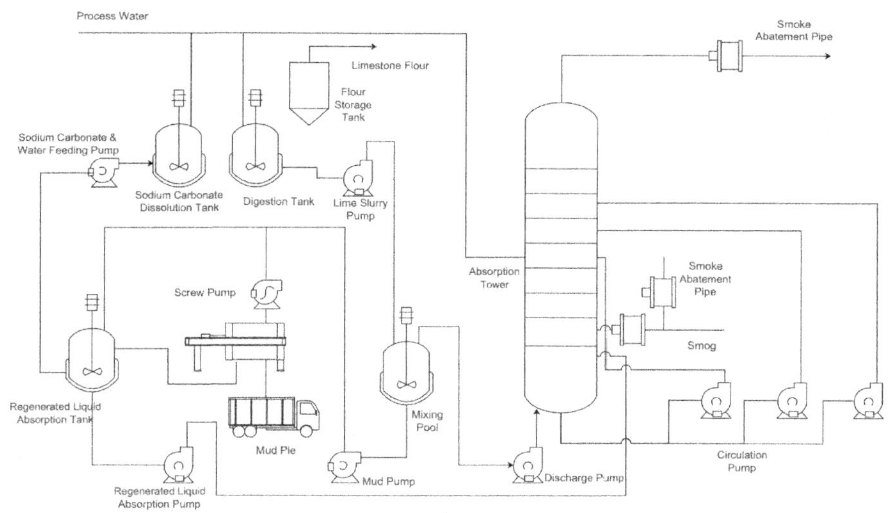

Figure 28 A Sample Piping & Instrumentation Diagram
EdrawSoft, Producing PID Template, accessed 13 June 2020, retrieved from https://www.edrawsoft.com/template-producing-pid.php

Similarly, for the Energy Transmission System Operator, the location can be a substation, a bay and a transformer. In a grid structure, there will always be a place for these substation, bay and transformer (until a major re-design of the grid happens).

A functional location may have no assets at all or just one asset, which will be considered as the physical representation of this logical element: it will have the manufacturer information, serial number, installation date, purchase price, etc.

Figure 29 Functional Location—Asset Relation

In other words, during the lifecycle of the plant or the substation, the structure of the elements will not change. What can happen is that the devices installed as a 'tank', 'pump' or 'transformer' can be replaced with another device from a different manufacturer and with a different serial number.

If the functional location has the technical specification defined: power, volume, etc., we can use this as a guideline to check if the asset to be installed has the same technical attributes. All you need to do is to define the classification for *LOCATIONS* and *ASSET* objects and assign the technical attributes to it.

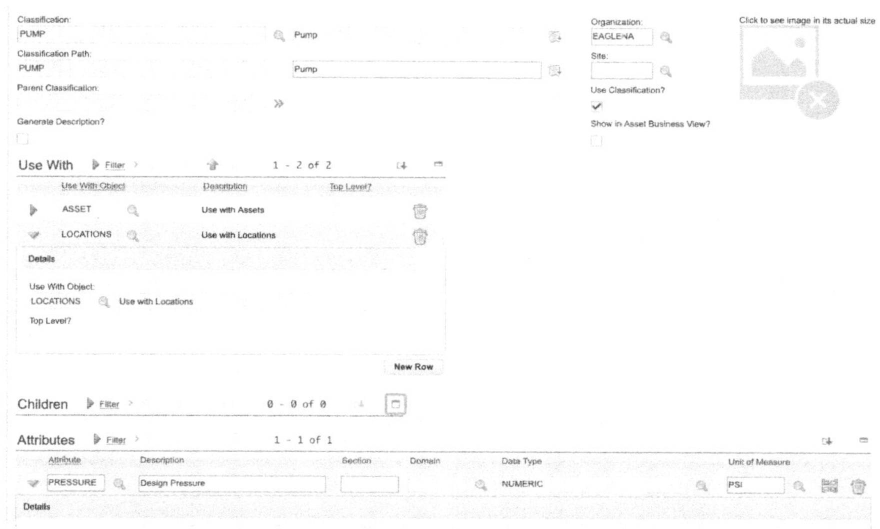

Figure 30 The Classification for Locations and Assets

Then you can build some logic to compare the specification of the asset and location and take an appropriate action, e.g. throw an error when the attribute values do not match.

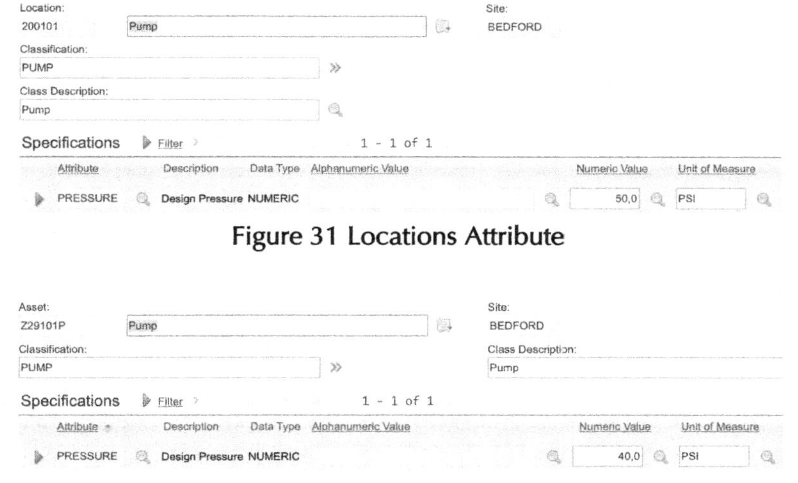

Figure 31 Locations Attribute

Figure 32 Assets Attribute

A *1:1* relation with the assets has another effect. You will define the Preventive Maintenance measures not for the asset but for the functional location. The benefit of this setup is that the PM record will always be the same, regardless of the asset installed there.

For example, we have the functional location: *Tank* with the associated asset record.

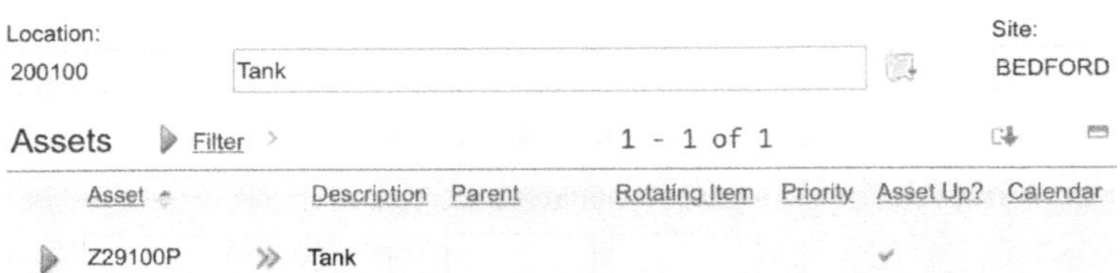

Figure 33 A Functional Location with an Asset

We will define the Preventive Maintenance for the Location:

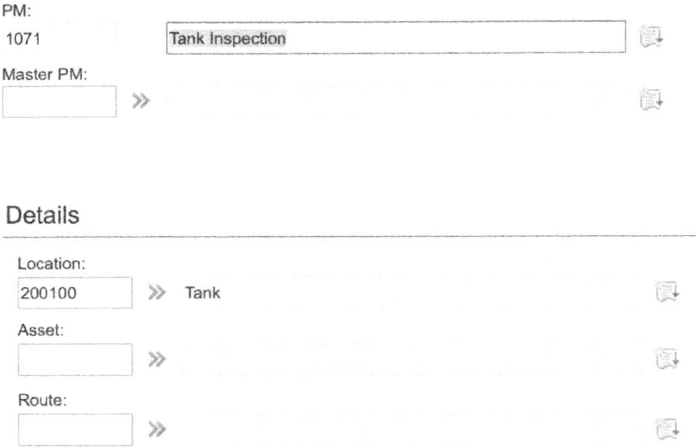

Figure 34 The Preventive Maintenance for the Location

However, because a *1:1* relation between Location and Asset exists, when WO is generated, it will also have the asset information!

Work Order:
1392 Tank inspection
Location:
200100 Tank
Asset:
Z29100P Tank

Figure 35 A Work Order with the Location and Asset Information

The Work Order will collect the costs of the maintenance on the asset level. The costs will go with the asset when it will be replaced, but the history of work will keep the fact that the maintenance was done for this functional location.
And you can switch between these two views: Locations and Assets when using **Open Drilldown** action in ***Assets*** or ***Locations*** applications.

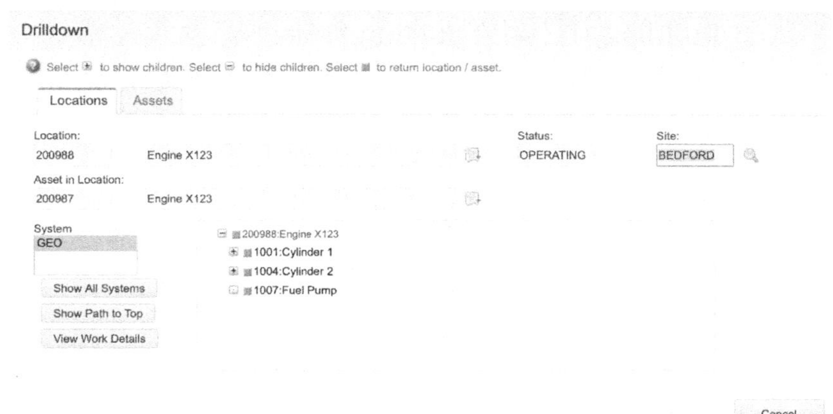

Figure 36 Drilldown with the Locations and Assets Tabs

That allows you to see not only the machine—component structure, but also to find the physical and functional locations in different layouts. The relations between the locations which are equal to the different layers on Engineering Drawings can be defined in Maximo using systems. There are two types of the systems:

- hierarchical,
- network.

One location can belong to multiple network systems but only to one hierarchical system.

Hierarchical systems are usually used to represent geographical structures, such as, this one:

- Site
    - Building 101—Office
        - Floor 1
            - Room 1-1
            - Room 1-2
            - ...
        - Floor 2
            - Room 2-1
            - Room 2-2
            - ...
    - Building 102—Production floor
        - Floor 1
            - Zone A
            - Zone B
        - Floor 2
            - Room 10
            - Room 11
            - ...

In a hierarchical system, one location can have only one parent element but many children.

A network system is built around a different principle: one location can have multiple parents and can belong to multiple network systems; these can be electrical, air condition, water supply...

Please observe the picture of a high voltage network:

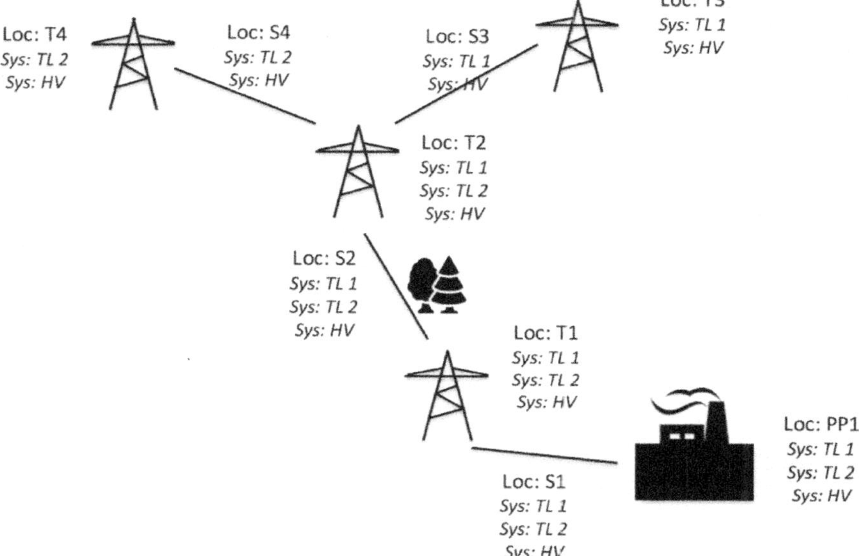

Figure 37 A Sample Energy Network

In this example, we have the following functional locations:

- towers 1-4 (T1-T4),
- spans 1-4 (S1-S4),
- power plant (PP1).

Towers and spans belong to systems:

- TL 1—transmission line 1,
- TL 2—transmission line 2,
- HV—high voltage.

If you expand this diagram and include substations, you can add medium voltage to the system, too. You can also add Common Information Model (CIM) nodes as locations.

All the locations will be part of *HV* system. Locations *T1, S1, T2, S2, T3,* and *S3* will additionally belong to part of *TL 1* system, while *T1, S1, T2, S2, T4,* and *S4* will belong to *TL 2* system. This picture shows the locations of the parents of *S1* in *TL 1* system.

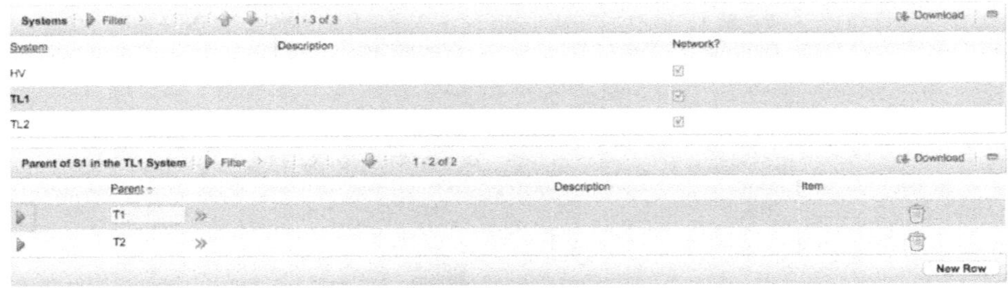

Figure 38 Sample Systems

The tower locations will contain the assets (the towers and corresponding equipment), while the span locations will be empty.

This structure enables to easily find all the locations in a high voltage system and/or belonging to the transmission lines *1* or *2*. The Work Orders in this setup can be created not only against the towers but also against the span locations to trim or cut the trees. In the case of an inspection Work Order for transmission line 1, you can quickly identify all the locations in system *TL 1* and enter them in the table: **Multiple Assets, Locations and CIs** in the Work Order record.

Design the system structures carefully because adding new elements is not easy and what is more, changing the hierarchy requires additional steps (action **View/Modify Parents**).

NOTE: You can change a system from a hierarchical one to a network type but not vice versa.

Location Types

Locations are divided into types. The purpose of having multiple types of locations is to have better information about the location of assets. Make sure that you are using more location types than only *OPERATING*. You have the following types to choose from:

- *OPERATING*—a place where the asset is used as intended; you can call it the production environment,
- *STOREROOM*—this type is hidden; in fact, all the storerooms in ***INVENTORY*** module are the locations of this type, but there is a condition in application ***Locations*** that prevents them from being seen there,
- *HOLDING*—this is a temporary location, used for receiving rotating items. NOTE: The location of this type is automatically created for each site. That also means you cannot create another location with that name because it already exists.
- *VENDOR*—usually, you can create such a location for each external workshop; moving an asset there indicates that asset is off-site,
- *REPAIR*—similar to the previous one but this one is for on-site workshops,
- *COURIER*—used to indicate that an asset is in transit between locations,
- *LABOR*—this can be used in a similar way to *COURIER* location (when the worker is transferring the assets to another location) or it can be used to the record tools or personal protective equipment issued to this person; the tools can be later returned to the storeroom,
- *SALVAGE*—locations used to indicate that the assets have reached their end-of-life; they may be named, e.g. *Sold*, *Scrapped* or *Destroyed*.

Known Issues and Initial Changes

Both ***Assets*** and ***Locations*** applications have a field called **Priority**. **ASSET.PRIORITY** is a persistent field but **LOCATIONS.LOCPRIORITY** is not persistent. You will find the persistent value for Location's Priority in another database table: **LOCOPER.LOCPRIORITY**.

The *HOLDING* location must have the **GL Account** field populated in order to receive the rotating assets.

Saved Queries

Here are a few helpful queries for Locations.
Locations with meters—this one is good, for example, for checking the energy consumption:

> *type = 'OPERATING' and exists (select 1 from locationmeter where locationmeter.location = locations.location and locationmeter.siteid = locations.siteid)*

Locations with missing meter readings—this is a variation of the above query that allows for finding locations for which readings were not entered during the last 30 days (change the number as required):

> *DB2 type = 'OPERATING' and exists (select 1 from locationmeter where locationmeter.location = locations.location and locationmeter.siteid = locations.siteid and ((days((select current timestamp from sysibm.sysdummy1)) - days(lastreadingdate) > 30) or lastreadingdate is null))*

Locations with safety information:

> *exists (select 1 from safetylexicon where safetylexicon.location = locations.location and safetylexicon.siteid = locations.siteid)*

Locations with attachments:

> *exists (select 1 from doclinks where ownertable = 'LOCATIONS' and ownerid = locationsid)*

Locations with classifications:

> *classstructureid is not null*

Locations with classifications and attributes:

classstructureid is not null and exists (select 1 from locationspec where locationspec.location = locations.location and locationspec.siteid = locations.siteid)

Application Assets

When you start discussing Maximo and asset management, the customer may ask a question, "What is actually an asset?". The below points should help you identify the assets:

- In case of a failure, it will be fixed, not replaced.
- It has a unique identifier.
- It has meters.
- It has attributes.
- It has a warranty or service contract.
- It is controlled by external bodies.
- The producer obliges the user to maintain the machine.
- It must be presented on a map (GIS) or plan (CAD).
- It is owned by someone else (leased or owned).
- It is very important for the infrastructure.
- It is very expensive.
- The history of work and costs must be recorded.
- It has a special value because of the safety or access procedures.
- It must be registered because of the regulatory compliance (industry regulations, safety, environmental).

A machine will be an asset if one or more of these characteristics apply.
Once you identify the assets, you have to define the breadth and depth of the asset database. By breadth I mean the scope of data:

- production assets,
- fleet,
- IT assets,
- building equipment.

All the elements may fit the asset definition but they will be not necessarily stored in Maximo database because of the different responsibilities or at least, they will not be entered in the first batch (the customer may start with production assets because they are most important, then include the installations in buildings, then the fleet, etc.).

The depth of the database is the number of its component levels, i.e. the technical hierarchy of the assets. Usually, the customers ask, "Should we enter everything that is part of the machine down to the smallest screw?". The answer is 'no' because according to the above characteristics, a screw is not an asset. However, the number of levels depends on the industry, the reporting needs and the already gathered information.

Some industries have a good understanding of the hierarchies, and they will tell you how many levels they need; a typical example is energy transmission and distribution.

Reporting needs define:

- at which level the Work Order will be reported—usually at the lowest level of the assets to keep the history of events at the most granular level,
- at which level a failure code should be reported,
- at which level the costs will be collected.

Finally, as part of the data migration, you will ask if the customer already has the information about the machines and their components. In many cases, they already have it in a legacy system or at least in a spreadsheet, but the level of detail may vary from *0* to *2-3*. In such cases I suggest to use an *n-1* approach. Create the assets for the main machines (level *n*) and their main components (level *n-1*). If the customer has more information, they can enter it, but *n-1* is a starting point. Any further details will be entered later. One solution to keep the

database growing is to enter a new component every time it is broken.
NOTE: Maximo does not keep (in a simple form) the history of asset structure, i.e. it is not possible to answer the question what the hierarchy of the assets was on March 27. Maximo keeps only the current picture of the assets and their relations.

The asset statuses should reflect the standard asset life cycle:

- planning,
- acquisition,
- operation and maintenance,
- renew/upgrade,
- decommission.

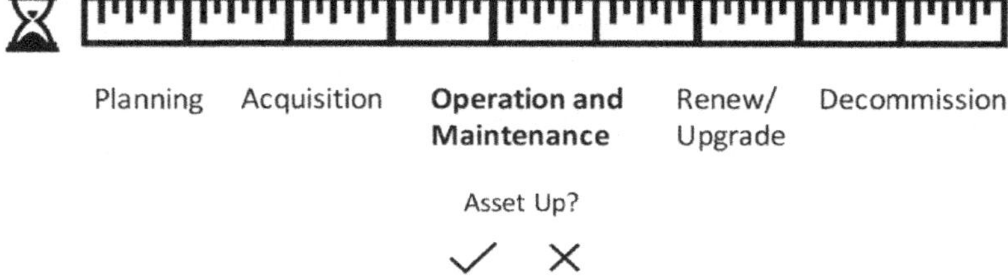

Figure 39 The Asset Lifecycle

As you can see there is no place for status *FAILURE* or *REPAIR*, which is used in some implementations. The fact that an asset is temporarily out of service does not mean we are leaving *Operation and Maintenance* phase. Instead of changing the status, **Asset Up** flag should be used with a correct downtime code.
Each step in the life cycle requires specific actions.

- Acquisition:

- Enter the details of the asset in Maximo:
  - asset number,
  - location,
  - rotating item (if applicable),
  - GL account,
  - failure codes,
  - classification and technical parameters,
  - criticality (asset priority),
  - hazards and precautions,
  - attachments (manuals, scanned invoice, warranty document, inspection documents),
  - spare parts,
  - define the meters,
  - components (hierarchy of assets).
- Create the maintenance plan:
  - Job Plans,
  - Preventive Maintenance records.
- Prepare the machine:
  - create the Work Orders for unpacking, cleaning, regulations, tests, etc.
- Change the status to *OPERATING*.

- Operation and maintenance:
  - register any failures,
  - enter the meter readings,
  - enter the movements between locations and sites,
  - report any downtimes.
- Decommission:
  - move to *SCRAPPED* location,
  - change the status to *DECOMMISSIONED*,
  - deactivate Preventive Maintenance records and Job Plans (if applicable),
  - deactivate safety plans,
  - optionally, remove the spare parts.

During *Operation and Maintenance* phase, you should not use a status like *Failure*, which indicates the machine is down.

Failure is only a temporary state, not a step in the life cycle and downtime reporting should be used for that purpose which will update **Asset Up** flag.

Known Issues and Initial Changes

When the asset is decommissioned, you may want to create an escalation which will inactivate the PMs, Job Plans and other objects associated with this record.

Assets application has its own status field but does not keep the history of changes. If you need it, then an e-Audit for **Status** field should be enabled and a new tab with the history of changes should be added (see, History Tab chapter). The same comment applies to Users/Custodians functionality: Maximo does not track the history of the ownership, so again, the e-Audit must be enabled for this.
NOTE: New relationship to **A_ASSET** table should be added *assetnum = :assetnum and siteid = :siteid.*
NOTE: from version 7.5.0.9 Maximo has a dialog to view the status changes. This article describes how to enable it: https://www.ibm.com/support/pages/view-asset-status-history-not-available-assets-application.

The action **Create Work Order** is very useful in the application because it allows users to create a work order directly from the asset record (the same action is available in ***Locations*** application). This action should be presented during the users training, since it helps to increase the percentage of failures reported. However, at least one element is missing on this dialog—**Work Type** field. Users may want to choose a work type from the list because they can report either a failure or only an inspection. You should edit the dialog in the application and add this field, as presented below:

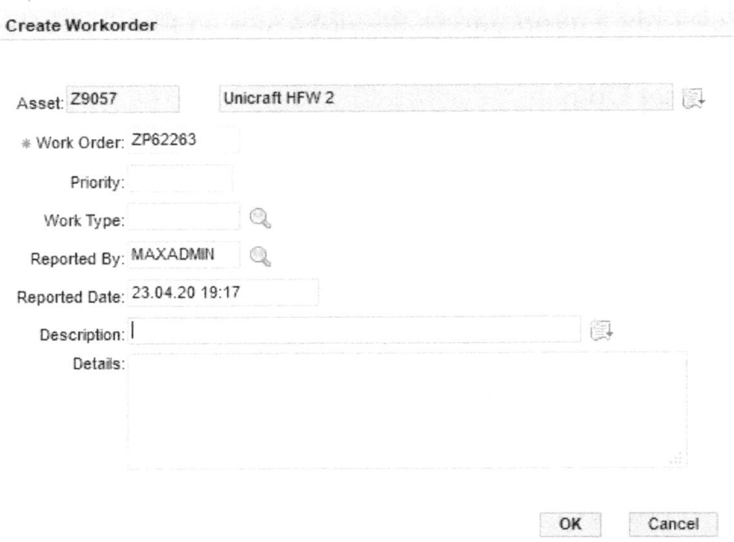

Figure 40 Create Workorder Dialog with Work Type Field

You can add the same field in other places, e.g. in action **View Work Details** and on **Work** tab.

View Work Details action can be further improved. This dialog has the checkboxes **Include Children, Include Ancestors**; however, the tables below have no Asset and Location columns, which means you may see the list of the Work Orders, but you will not know to which object they refer to.
The reason this information is missing is that the dialog uses **WORKVIEW** object, which does NOT contain Asset and Location information. You will need to use the relationships: **TICKET** and **WORKORDER** to retrieve the **ASSETNUM** and **LOCATION** from the tables e.g. **WORKORDER.ASSETNUM**.

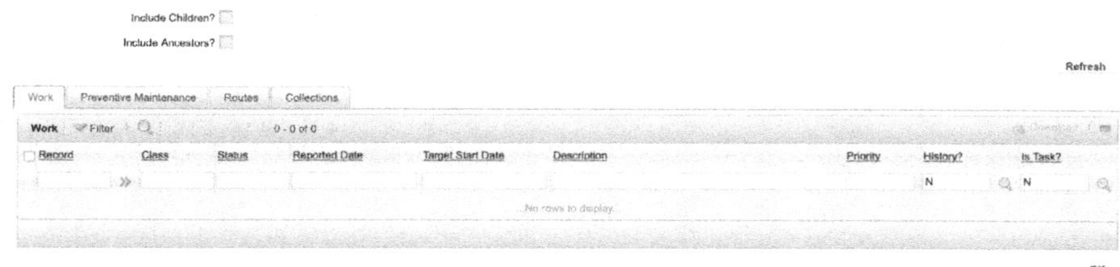

Figure 41 View Work Details Dialog

In the standard lookup that shows the asset list there is another important column missing: serial number. If there are tens of the same devices, the user will not be able to find the right one based on the very name and Maximo ID. You should add **Serial Number** field to that dialog.

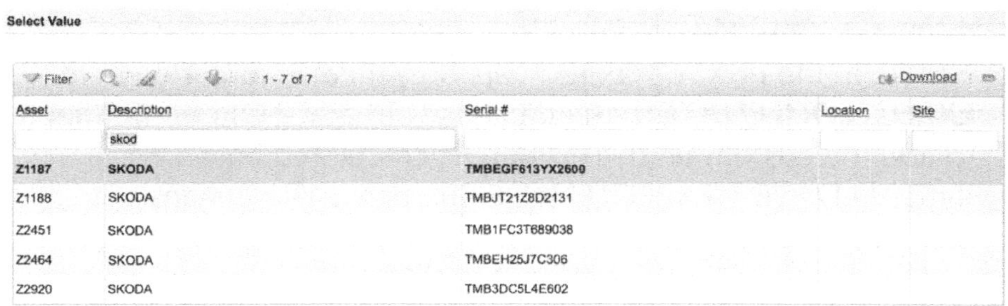

Figure 42 A New Serial Number Column

Move/Modify Assets dialog allows you to change the rotating asset condition, too. However, **Condition Code** field has no lookup by default, you can only enter the value manually (if you remember the condition names well). To fix this you will need to edit **LIBRARY.XML** file and add a lookup *conditioncode* to the above field.

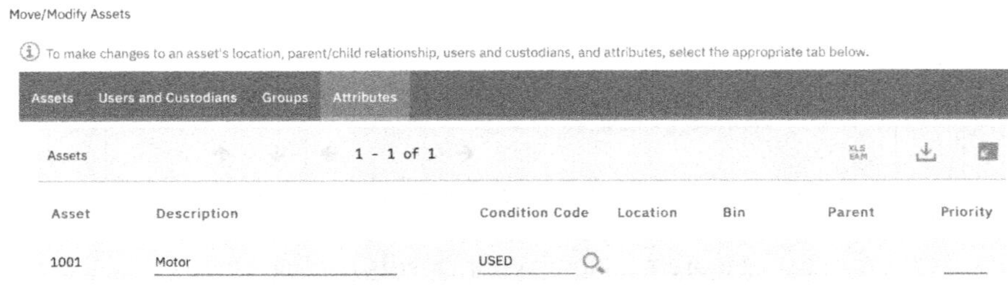

Figure 43 A Fixed Condition Code Field

Sometimes, the customer defines the rules for replacing the assets after a certain period of time (or it may result from some regulations). To support this functionality, you can add a new date field **End Date** to Assets application and create an escalation which will in advance inform the asset custodian that this asset should be decommissioned.
NOTE: In the newer Maximo versions, there is a hidden field **EXPECTEDLIFEDATE** in the database already—you do not need to add the custom field. This date is calculated based on **INSTALLDATE** + **EXPECTEDLIFE** (in years). That means you have to put all the three fields together on the screen. You can also add a new custom field **XEXPECTEDLIFE** (in years) to *Item Master* application. This will define the lifespan for all the rotating assets of the same type, for example, the same car model (ensure there is a mechanism, e.g. a crossover domain, to copy this information to the assets **EXPECTEDLIFE** field).

Any changes to the asset's attributes are saved in the history and can be reviewed in **View Asset Specification History** window.

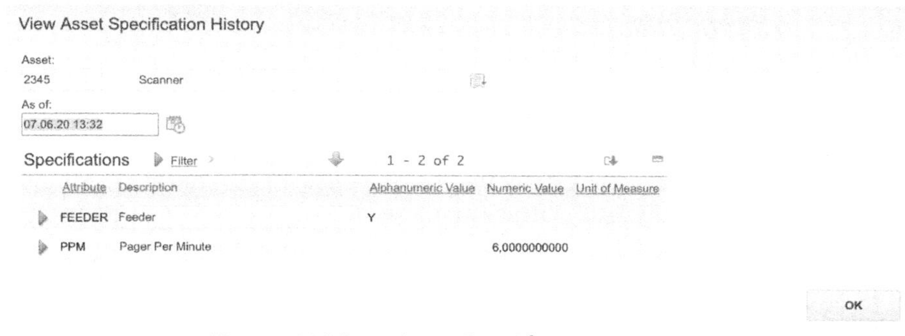

Figure 44 View Asset Specification History

This dialog always shows the list of the asset's attributes "as of date", which means you cannot see the history of changes, but only a 'picture' of the asset state. To bypass this limitation, you can either change this dialog, add a new tab to the application, or build a custom report.

It is worth preparing a visual indicator of the asset age. Use Conditional UI to make, for example, **Asset Number** field red when the asset age (difference between the today's date and **Installation Date**) is greater than *20* years, make it yellow when it is between *10* and *20* years, etc. You can use a similar query to create the conditional expressions, such as:

> *DB2 installdate is not null and (year((select current timestamp from sysibm.sysdummy1)) - year(installdate) > 10) and (year((select current timestamp from sysibm.sysdummy1)) - year(installdate) <= 20)*

There are different methods for maintaining assets. Basically, there is a run-to-failure approach and different preventive maintenance models. To help customers implement this basic division, I suggest adding to the asset record a new logical field **To Be Maintained.** When checked, it will suggest that this asset should have a corresponding Preventive Maintenance record (at least one). Then you can use the query below to quickly find all the assets without mandatory PMs.

xtobemaintained = 1 and not exists (select 1 from pm where pm.assetnum = asset.assetnum and pm.siteid = asset.siteid and pm.status = 'ACTIVE')

As you know, Maximo has a well-developed functionality of Warranty Contracts but some customers are overwhelmed by the complexity of this application (lots of information to be entered, status changes are required). But at the same time, everybody is interested in monitoring warranties. The asset table has a hidden field **WARRANTYEXPDATE**, which can be used for the same purpose but in a simplified form. You can put this field on the screen and create an escalation to inform the asset custodian in advance about an expiring warranty.
NOTE: when the above field contains a future date, it generates a reminder in ***Work Order Tracking*** application that the asset is still under warranty, but it does not select **Warranties Exists** checkbox.

A simple trick can help asset managers check when the asset was broken the last time. Just create a new relationship from **ASSET** to **WORKORDER** table, which will show the last Work Order of the type *Failure*, and then add **REPORTDATE** field to the asset details and asset list.

assetnum = :assetnum and siteid = :siteid and reportdate = (select max(reportdate) from workorder where assetnum = :assetnum and siteid = :siteid) and worktype = 'CM'

If the customer uses the meters' functionality, you will need to add the following new columns in **Manage Meter Reading History** dialog (*METHIST*):

- **Reading Date**,
- **Reading Type** (it will show: *ACTUAL*, *DELTA* or *RESET*—for Reset/Replace action),
- the work order number (you can also add the description if needed) from which the reading comes.

To display Work Order information prepare a new relationship from *METERREADING* object to *WOMETER* object with **Where Clause**: meterreadingid = :meterreadingid. You can do the same in ***Locations*** application and then the source object will be: *LOCMETERREADING.*

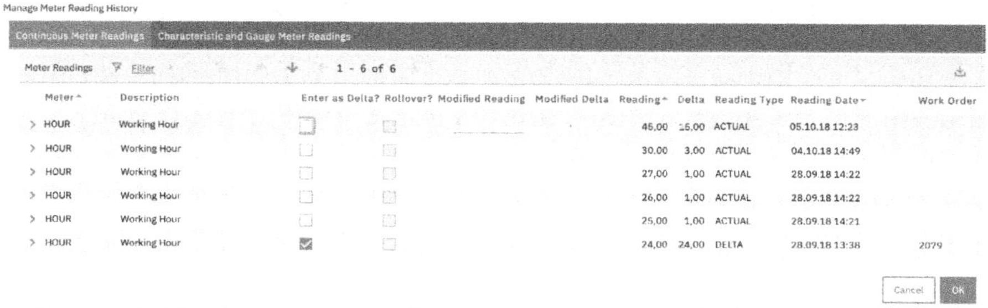

Manage Meter Reading History

Continuous Meter Readings | Characteristic and Gauge Meter Readings

Meter Readings Filter 1 - 6 of 6

Meter	Description	Enter as Delta?	Rollover?	Modified Reading	Modified Delta	Reading	Delta	Reading Type	Reading Date	Work Order
HOUR	Working Hour	☐	☐			46,00	16,00	ACTUAL	05.10.18 12:23	
HOUR	Working Hour	☐	☐			30.00	3.00	ACTUAL	04.10.18 14:49	
HOUR	Working Hour	☐	☐			27,00	1,00	ACTUAL	28.09.18 14:22	
HOUR	Working Hour	☐	☐			26,00	1,00	ACTUAL	28.09.18 14:22	
HOUR	Working Hour	☐	☐			25,00	1,00	ACTUAL	28.09.18 14:21	
HOUR	Working Hour	☑	☐			24,00	24,00	DELTA	28.09.18 13:38	2079

Cancel OK

Figure 45 Manage Meter Reading History Dialog with the New Columns

Some customers tend not to create Work Orders for simpler works, like changing light bulbs, but at the same time, they issue light bulbs directly for this asset. However, the costs section in the asset details shows only the costs related to the Work Orders. In such a case, the customer will be confused because there will be a difference between the Work Order costs and direct costs. You can fix this by adding a new calculated summary field (below: **Material Cost**) for direct costs. NOTE: You will need to write an Automation Script or Java class to do this calculation.

Costs

Material Cost:	8 569,17
Total Cost:	9 625,75
YTD Cost:	9 625,75
* Budgeted:	0,00
Inventory:	0,00

Figure 46 A New Calculated Material Cost Field

Rotating or non-rotating

Rotating assets are interchangeable, like motors or pumps in a storeroom, or they can be tools in a tool storeroom. They move in and out of storerooms and can be tracked as inventory, so you can always say how many motors you have. They can also exist in courier and/or labor locations. You can apply Item Assembly Structure to rotating assets to build asset hierarchies. The relation between a rotating asset and a rotating item ensures that all the assets share the same classification and attributes (inherited from the item). A rotating asset must be received in *Receiving* application.

Non-rotating assets are not located in storerooms.
NOTE: If you plan to use the meters functionality with IAS, define the meters of *DELTA* type. Also, make sure that **Accept Rolldown From** field is not equal to *NONE*.

Move/Modify Assets

Once the asset record is saved, fields like **Parent** and **Location** become read-only, preventing ad-hoc, undocumented changes. Instead, Maximo is forcing users to use the **Move/Modify Assets** or its variance: **Swap Assets** action.

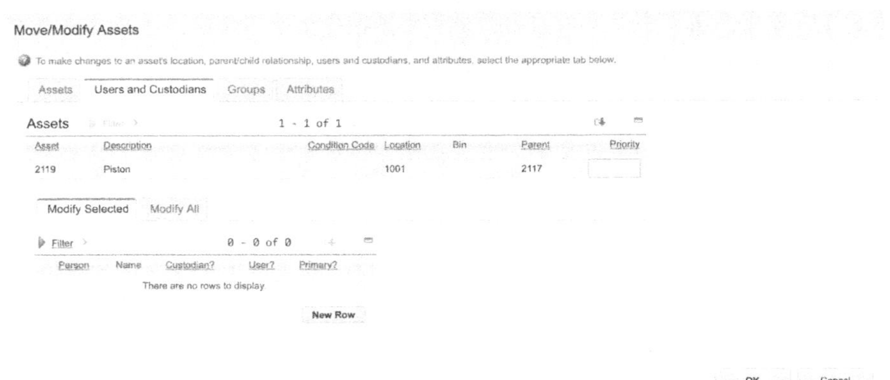

Figure 47 Move/Modify Assets Dialog

You can move the asset to a new location, change its parent record, change the site, but also modify the custodians/users and even attributes.
The changes made to the asset record, can be later checked using **View Asset Move History** action. Please observe that the above actions will work not only with a single asset but with multiple ones too, allowing mass-move of objects.

In *Work Order Tracking* application there is a similar action called **Move/Swap/Modify**.

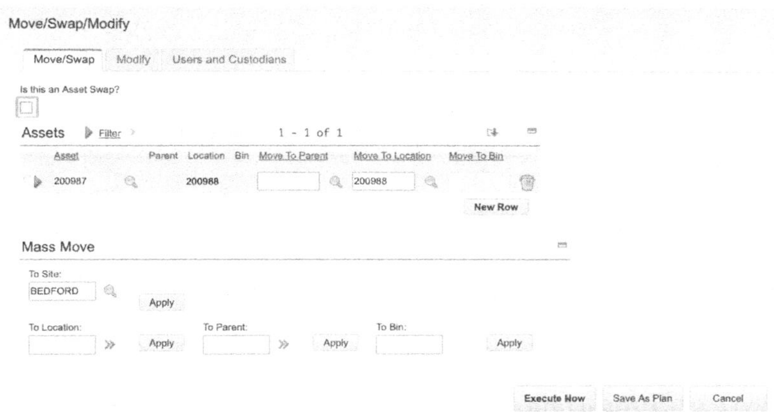

Figure 48 Move/Swap/Modify Dialog

It is designed not only to perform the changes in the asset record immediately but more importantly to schedule them. The changes will be then automatically applied when the WO status changes to *COMP*.

Ownership of assets

Assets application offers a very useful but rarely used feature: the action **Associate Users and Custodians**.

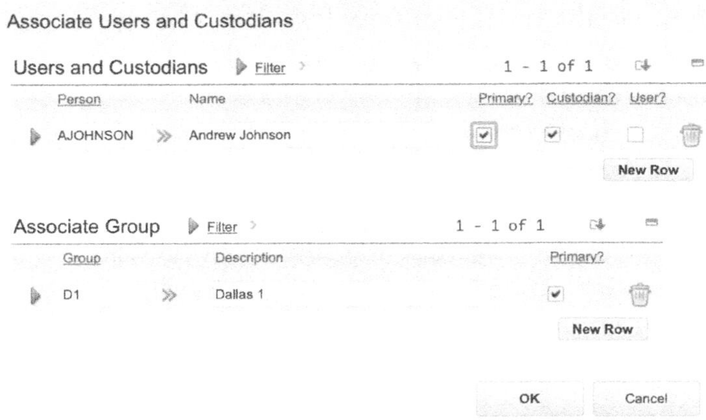

Figure 49 Associate Users and Custodians Dialog

That action defines the ownership of the equipment: users and custodians, but also associated groups. Usually, the custodian is the one who is responsible for the asset from the financial or maintenance points of view, while users can be, for example, the operators from the production department. Why define custodian and user? This may complement your workflow and notifications. For example, in case of a failure, Maximo can send a message to the users informing them about the event. The Work Order to fix this machine can be approved by its custodian.

NOTE: Contrary to the asset move history, it is not possible to register the custodian's and user's changes. If you want to monitor these changes, you must define an e-Audit for this information.

Downtime Codes

As I mentioned at the beginning of this chapter, any temporary break should not be reported as a status change but with the usage of **Report Downtime** action. This action is available in ***Assets*** and ***Work Order Tracking*** applications. To report a downtime, you will first need to define values for **DOWNCODE** domain. Below you may find sample codes:

- ADJUST—Adjust Machine,

- CLEAN—Clean,
- LUNCH—Lunch Break,
- REPAIR—Repair,
- STANDBY—Machine in standby mode, e.g. in a power plant one steam generator may be running while the other is in the standby mode,
- TRAINING—Training,
- WMAT—Waiting for Material.

Additionally, you may define that specific work order types will require entering downtime codes (you can do this in ***Organizations*** application by setting **Downtime Prompt** for specific work types).
Downtimes can be reported manually, at the moment of the event or later (in this case the operator will enter the start and end date of the downtime). It is recommended that the downtimes are imported from SCADA systems because the integration ensures that the dates are entered accurately.

The information about a downtime is saved in **ASSETSTATUS** table but in a specific format: each line is equal to one status change.

ASSETNUM	CHANGEDATE	DOWNTIME CODE	WONUM	ISRUNNING
2056	March 19	REPAIR	1209	0
2056	March 21	REPAIR	1209	1

The whole downtime period is two lines: one for *DOWN (0)* status, the other one for *UP (1)*.

To present the above information in a more user-friendly format:

ASSETNUM	STARTDATE	ENDDATE
2056	March 19	March 21

you may use the following SQL:

select e.assetnum, max(s.changedate) as startdate, e.changedate as enddate from assetstatus e left join assetstatus s on s.assetnum = e.assetnum and s.changedate < e.changedate and s.isrunning = 0 where e.isrunning = 1 and e.assetnum = '2056' group by e.assetnum, e.changedate

Downtime codes can be used to calculate the MTBF/MTTR indicators (earlier, in KPI Examples chapter, I present an alternative way to calculate this indicator for the machine). They can be also used in Predictive Maintenance as an input for calculations.
NOTE: A downtime, unlike meter readings, is not rolled down to child Assets.

Unique Serial Numbers

Only asset numbers are checked for uniqueness but some customers ask also to prevent serial numbers from being duplicated. This is a risky decision I could say. In the case of enterprise assets, it is very likely that the serial numbers will be repeated (I have even seen serial numbers as *1, 2, 3*). So, even if technically this is possible in Maximo, I suggest not preventing entering duplicated numbers or using conditional UI instead. For example, you could make the text in the field **Serial Number** red if this number already exists.

Map Tab

Not every customer needs or can afford to buy a GIS system to display the assets and/or locations on the map. In numerous cases, the standard Maximo function will be helpful. If the customer wants to use it, you have to enable the maps in ***Map Manager*** application. You will also need to order/buy an API Key from the chosen map provider to make them active.
If your customer does not need the maps because it is a relatively small plant, you can delete or hide this tab not to distract the users.

Depreciation

Depreciation Schedule was already introduced in Maximo some time ago to calculate the actual value of tangible assets (field **Current Value**). There are two depreciation methods available:

- Straight Line,
- Double Declining Balance.

You can define depreciation schedules, which are time- or meter-based. The calculations are done by the cron task *DepreciationFinTransCronTask*, which must be enabled and configured.

As it sounds, depreciation is more a financial term than maintenance. Not every customer may need it. Depreciation schedules were included in Maximo to keep all the information about the assets in one place, but in fact, the depreciation is in most cases calculated in a financial system (Fixed Assets module). This will require building an interface between the ERP system and Maximo. You need to check if Fixed Asset number can be linked to an asset record in Maximo (a new attribute may be added to ***Assets*** application to build this relation). You should also design how the information about the current value of assets will be transferred between the financial system and Maximo.

Saved Queries

The assets with safety information:

> *exists (select 1 from safetylexicon where safetylexicon.assetnum = asset.assetnum and safetylexicon.siteid = asset.siteid)*

The assets with meters:

> *exists (select 1 from assetmeter where assetmeter.assetnum = asset.assetnum and assetmeter.siteid = asset.siteid)*

The assets with attachments:

exists (select 1 from doclinks where ownertable = 'ASSET' and ownerid = assetuid)

The assets with relationships—the query consists of two parts because an asset can be a source or target of the relationship:

exists (select 1 from assetlocrelation where sourceassetnu m = assetnum) or exists (select 1 from assetlocrelation where targetassetnum = assetnum)

The assets with classifications:

classstructureid is not null

The assets with classifications and attributes:

classstructureid is not null and exists (select 1 from assetspec where assetspec.assetnum = asset.assetnum and assetspec.siteid = asset.siteid)

Application Asset Templates

You can use the templates defined here to both create and update the existing records. However, the main function of the application is to create new records. Of course, the user can create new assets with the usage of Purchase Orders. This is the preferred method because thus, you can find the origin of the asset. Not every company uses a purchasing module in Maximo, though. Sometimes, it is also easier to create a lot of asset records without POs. For example, utility companies may create hundreds of energy or water meters for their customers. The built-in feature can generate asset records with all the required information:

- asset numbers (generated automatically, even with a prefix and/or suffix),
- name,
- spare part list,
- meters,

- Preventive Maintenance schedule (based on a Master PM),
- depreciation schedule,
- other details, like a classification and attributes.

The action **Generate New Assets** can even copy the skeleton of the serial number to the new assets, where you can complete the full number. Yet, this will work only for the sequential serial numbers, e.g. GHQ7090, GHQ7091, GHQ7092, and so on. You can also enter here **PM Start Date** and **Depreciation Start Date** assuming all the new assets begin their cycles together.

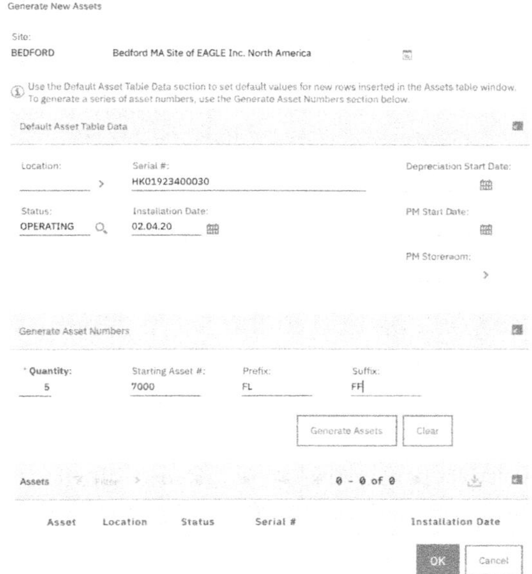

Figure 50 Generate New Asset

NOTE: you cannot generate rotating assets from the Asset Template yet.

As mentioned before, ***Asset Templates*** application can also update the existing assets and change some attributes—the action **Apply to Existing Assets** serves that purpose.

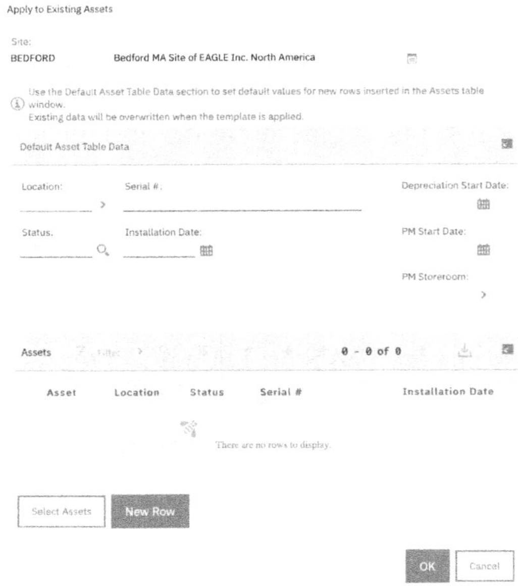

Figure 51 Apply To Existing Assets

Surprisingly, in the update window you can select any asset, not only those created by the given Asset Template. This gives you an opportunity to standardize the information and increase data quality, because you can add to the assets the missing information about Vendor, replace the description with some new text, or add a classification and attributes.

NOTE: you can also apply the Asset Template to the assets created by another template—this will replace the information about the associated template.

Please be careful while choosing the assets because the data will be overwritten without any further warning.

Application Failure Codes

Maintenance should not be about fighting fires—it is about learning from the past. If something happens, it should be fixed, but afterwards, it must be analyzed to take some corrective actions that may prevent the same event from happening again.

The basic mechanism supporting data analysis in Maximo is Failure Codes. A failure code is a reason for which an asset has failed. The catalog of codes represents the most common failures in infrastructure. Failure codes can be industry-specific; for example, in the automotive world, *VMRS* (*Vehicle Maintenance Reporting Standards*) may be used. When designing a catalog, make sure the lists are not too long (10-20 positions) and include *OTHER* position for all the issues not listed before.

Sample Failure Codes:

- Class
  - Boiler
  - Conveyor
  - Pump
  - Valve
- Problem
  - Corrosion
  - Fatigue
  - Leaking
  - Short Circuit
  - Vibration
- Cause
  - Human Error
  - Working Conditions
  - Wrong Material
- Remedy
  - Adjust
  - Clean
  - Repair
  - Replace

You can force entering failure report in a completed or closed Work Order by selecting **Failure Prompt** checkbox in ***Organizations*** application for specific work types.

The analysis of Work Orders with Failure Codes may result in changing the list of tasks in a Job Plan or modifying PM frequency.

Application Condition Monitoring

In this application, you will define the Measure Points for the assets or locations to collect the readings from non-continuous meters (*CHARACTERISTIC* or *GAUGE*).
Each measure point is a checkpoint for the object condition with the option to automatically generate a Work Order when the current reading reaches the threshold. This gives us a tool to depict inspections in Maximo.

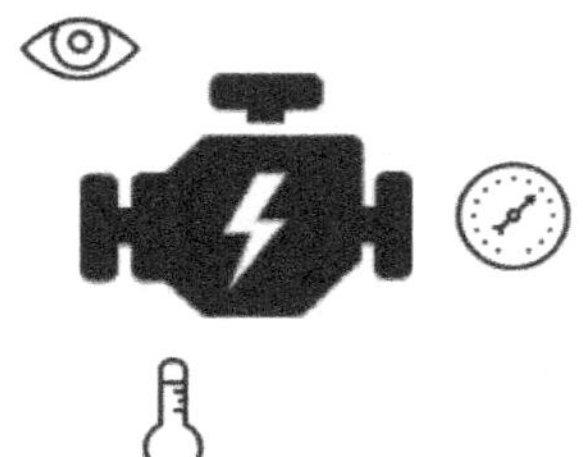

Figure 52 The Inspection: Visual Inspection, Temperature and Pressure Measurement

Inspections do not cost much and can be repeated relatively often, as they require only a worker to come to the device, check the condition visually and measure something. In the above example, this will be temperature and pressure, but it could be a drone inspection, vibration analysis, thermography or any other type of Non-Destructive Testing. The inspections may discover early symptoms of a failure, which gives an opportunity to perform some further diagnostics or schedule the repair work. We can automate inspections using Maximo. The first step is to define a Job Plan with a corresponding Meter *CHARACTERISTIC* or *GAUGE*).

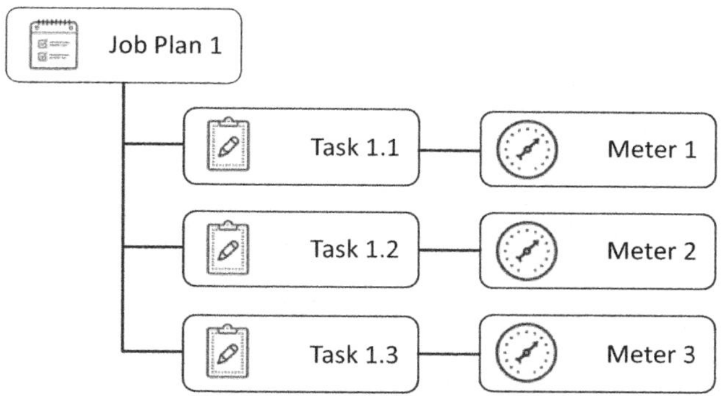

Figure 53 A Job Plan with Meters

In our example, it will be:

- Visual Inspection, Characteristic Meter: Visual Condition with values: *Perfect, Good, Poor, Bad,*
- Measure Temperature, Gauge Meter: Temperature,
- Measure Pressure, Gauge Meter: Pressure.

Each of these meters must be assigned to the object of which the asset or location we want to inspect.

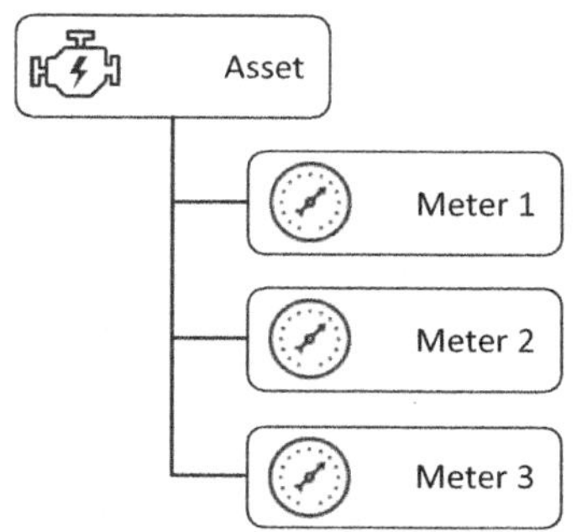

Figure 54 An Asset with Meters

NOTE: If multiple meters are to be assigned to objects, you can group them in **Meter Groups** application.

Additionally, for each combination of a meter and an object, a Measurement Point must be entered:

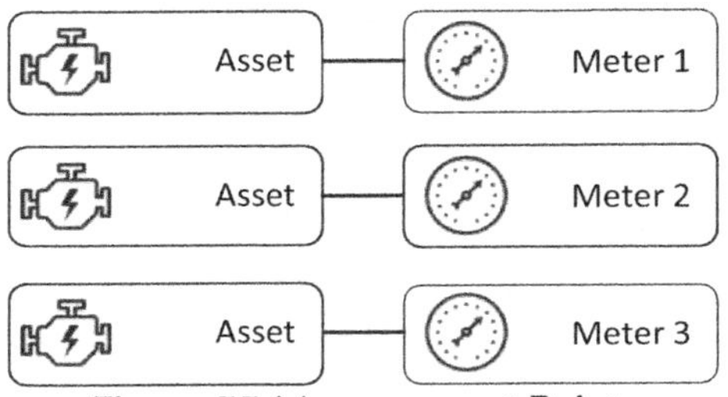

Figure 55 Measurement Points

Once we have the Job Plan and meters ready, we can define the PM for the object. The PM will then create an inspection Work Order:

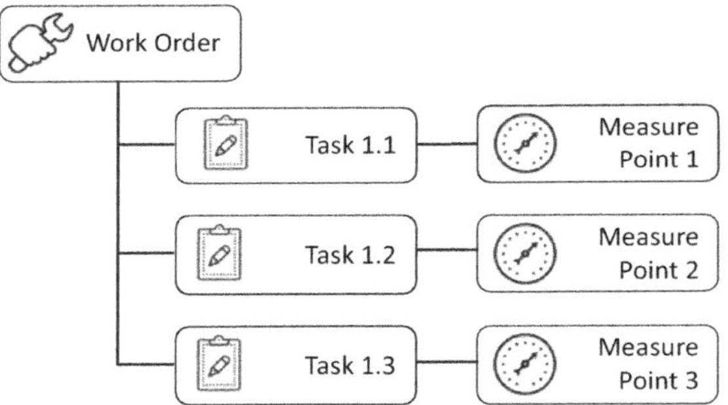

Figure 56 An Inspection Work Order

The worker will go to the object and for each of the tasks they will enter the corresponding meter value—observation or measure which can create a new Work Order if the threshold value is reached.
The thresholds are defined in *Condition Monitoring* applications for each Measurement Point.
For *GAUGE* meters this will be the lower and upper threshold; see, the example:

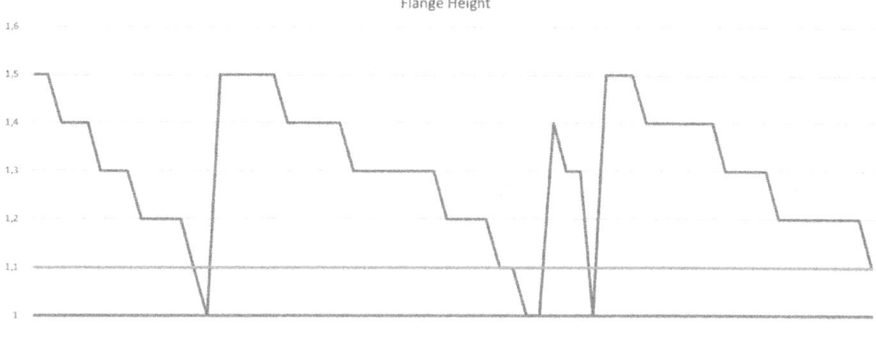

Figure 57 A Flange Height Example with Thresholds

Because the flange height of a train wheel will always decrease, there is no upper threshold, we have only lower warning at *1,1* and lower action at *1,0* (if you do not need either point, use dummy values like *99999*, because these fields are mandatory and cannot be left empty). That means, when the current reading exceeds the action level, a Work Order will be automatically generated, based either on the Job Plan or PM chosen for this measurement point, to replace the flange for the wheel.
NOTE: *MeasurePointWoGen* cron task must be enabled first!

Defining the right thresholds is the key. It must be based either on experience or the vendor's suggestions.
NOTE: The same meter for different objects may have different thresholds!

The second type of meters, *CHARACTERISTIC*, has a list of possible values, we can define our measurement point to generate the Work Order when the reading is equal to a certain value, for example: *Poor*.

Here are some examples of *CHARACTERISTIC* meters:

- general appearance: *Excellent/Good/Fair/Repair Required/Replacement Required*,

- the electrical cord condition: *Good/Average/Bad,*
- thickness: *1-5mm, 6-9mm, above 10mm,*
- rust: *Yes/No,*
- secured to floor: *Yes/No/N/A.*

Readings for a Measurement Point can come also from other sources:

- a manual input in the application,
- integration.

A manual input is rather unlikely, as customers usually plan the integration with SCADA system, which can report different conditions, like temperature, vibration, pressure, etc. However, you should then evaluate the available options. Numerous SCADA systems can analyze the data internally (comparing the current reading with the thresholds) and trigger an alarm. Then it will be easier to accept such an alarm through integration and create a Work Order in Maximo.

WOs are not generated

Condition Monitoring must be configured to generate Work Orders but it is possible that one day there will be no new WOs, even though the threshold has been exceeded. Here are some possible reasons:

- *MeasurePointWoGen* cron task is not active,
- WO generation is not active for the site (**Organizations** application, **PM Options**),
- admin mode is on,
- Asset/Location is not active.

Known Issues and Initial Changes

Originally, the records in this application are presented in a textual form, which is not especially helpful. If you want to make it more readable, you can add a graph on the screen that will show the readings of *GAUGE* meter combined with lower and upper limits.

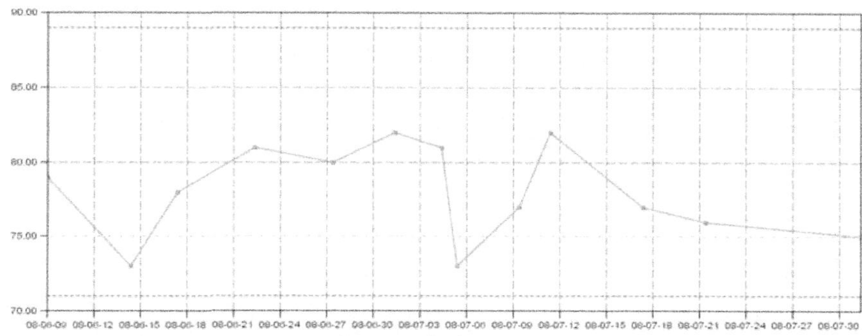

Figure 58 A Sample Graph for a Measurement Point

There is no **Work Type** field on the screen, so the Work Orders created by the Condition Monitoring mechanism do not have this information. You can fix it by adding a new field and creating a crossover domain that will copy its content to the Work Order. Usually, such Work Order will have the type: *INSPECTION* (but you can define also a new Work Type for this type of action).

There is no function regarding warning limits. You will need to create your own escalation, which can send an email that the reading has exceeded the threshold for the warning or an action, which could, for example, increase the priority of this asset.

In the table **History** (with the list of the generated Work Orders), you cannot open the related record. You may need to add 'Go To' functionality to Work Order column.

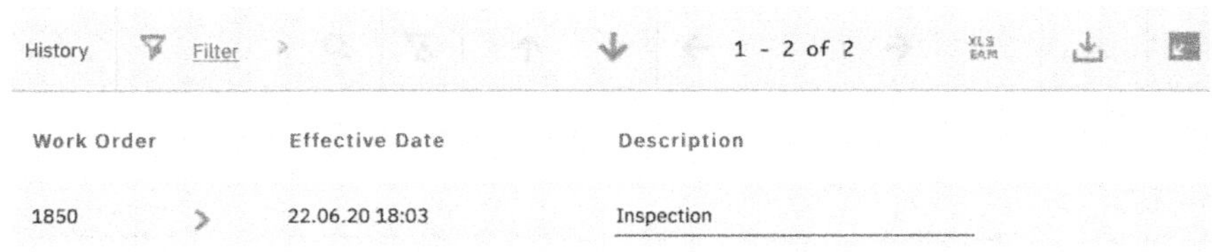

Figure 59 History Table with 'Go To' Work Order Tracking

NOTE: While generating a Work Order, Maximo creates a record in the **WORKORDER** and **POINTWO** database tables. The table **History** shows the records from the latter source. This may be confusing because you can delete a Work Order but the entry in **POINTWO** will be kept.

Module Contracts

Formal agreements with the vendors can be defined in this module. As a formal document, a contract defines the rights and obligations of each party and is valid for a period of time. In Maximo, the contract is not only a representation of a signed paper document but there can also be created payment schedules for generating invoices, or Purchase Orders based on contract conditions. However, contract applications may be not always used in Maximo. This is because a lot of companies manage vendors and contracts in other systems, and it is not necessary (or too costly) to integrate with these systems. Please discuss the business requirements first.

Maximo offers the following contract types:

- Master Contracts,
- Purchase Contracts,
- Lease/Rental Contracts,
- Labor Rate Contracts,
- Warranty Contracts.

Master Contracts—they define frame agreements with a vendor. Then, new contracts (of all the below types) can be generated from this contract, and they will inherit all the terms and conditions.

Purchase Contracts—are used to purchase of materials and services at the agreed prices and in the agreed quantities. A Purchase Order must be created for each purchase. There are three Purchase Contract types available:

- Purchase—quantity and price are defined,
- Price—only price is defined,
- Blanket (Volume)—defines maximum amount of all the purchases.

Lease/Rental Contracts—very often companies do not buy expensive equipment but they rent it as this may be financially more advantageous. The items listed in the contract lines must be rotating items with the corresponding rotating assets. This contract type has a payment schedule feature to generate invoices. There are two contract types available:

- a rental contract—it can be terminated and at the end, the asset must be always returned,
- a lease contract—it is a method of hire-purchase of an asset (finance lease) because it has an option at the end of the contract to purchase the equipment (buy-out option). The action **End Lease** allows to either purchase or return the assets.

Labor Rate Contracts—contracting external labor, very useful when there is a lack of specialists with certain skills. The contract defines hourly rates per craft and skill. The action **Create Invoice** in ***Labor Reporting*** application can create invoices for all the approved external hours.

Warranty Contracts—define the warranty and maintenance terms and conditions for assets and/or locations. Two contract types are available:

- Warranty—usually related to the purchase of an asset. The duration can be defined as a time period and/or usage (meter based), e.g. *1* year or *15000* miles. The contract must contain a list of assets/locations associated with it. You can add objects only to the approved contracts. If the warranty for an asset/location is still active, the user will see a warning in ***Work Order Tracking*** application and the checkbox **Warranties Exists?** will be selected,
- Service—maintenance services offered by an external company for assets and/or locations. This contract type also offers a payment schedule to generate invoices. The invoice must reference the Work Orders for the affected assets/locations.

Warranty Contracts are theoretically very useful but in my experience, not often used, because the configuration of the contracts is really labor-intensive. In addition, there are complex vendor agreements for the equipment and its components, e.g.

- Boiler 2 years
    - Pump 1 year
    - Motor 15000 hours

Sometimes, the customers decide to implement a simpler solution in the form of a warranty expiry date (see, the chapter **Application Assets** for details).

Before approving them, contracts must be authorized for the use in specific sites (action **Authorize Sites**).

A very useful feature is the action **Apply Price Adjustment**, which can change the prices. For example, once a year an inflation factor of *2,5%* may be applied to all the contract lines.

All the contracts are revision controlled, meaning the current, approved version of a contract can be applied to the Purchase Order while a new version of the contract can be discussed and approved later.

Module Financial

Application Chart of Accounts

Usually, the chart of accounts should be the same as in the ERP system, but if you do not exchange data with ERP, you can introduce a different accounts schema in Maximo only for internal reporting or even use a dummy GL account when it is not needed. In the latter case, you should turn off the GL account validation (**Validation Options/Deactivate GL Validation**).

NOTE: Please define financial periods; otherwise, transactions cannot be saved.

Application Financial Control

This is in fact only a framework, not a real application. You can use it, for example, to manage projects, but it requires customization and usually integration with an ERP system. The idea is to import from the ERP system-approved budgets for projects, which will be read only in Maximo. Each Work Order will be then assigned to this budget position. The costs associated with the WO will 'consume' the budget, so the customer can quickly check the actual consumption and the remaining financial resources. Normally, the budget has start and end dates, so it will be natural to introduce a mechanism in ***Work Order Tracking*** application that will prevent assigning a Work Order to a budget that has already reached its end date.

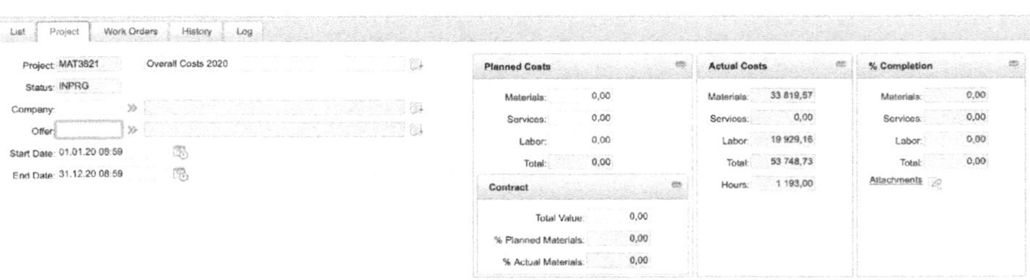

Figure 60 A Customized Financial Control Application

All the tools are already in the system: you have *Financial Control* application. In **WORKORDER** table, there are the columns **FCPROJECTID** and **FCTASKID**, but you have to design the concept and implement it.

* Work Order: ZP62295
* Work Type:
Parent WO:
Location:
Asset:
Asset Up?
Project:
Position:
Classification:

Figure 61 Project Fields on the Work Order

The GL accounts segments can help you to monitor the spending, too, but there is no budget part. *Financial Control* application offers more options: you can give permission to specific groups of users to open it and analyze the budget.

Known Issues and Initial Changes

The status field in this application is named (non-standard) **FCSTATUS**.

Application Budget Monitoring

Budget Monitoring application is relatively new, introduced in one of the minor releases of 7.6 version, and is really powerful because it is highly configurable. By default, you define the budget for assets, location and GL components, but you can introduce also new, so-called focal points. Budget positions include all the standard cost elements: materials, labor cost and labor hours, tools and services. Maximo will automatically calculate budget consumption, based on the information from material and purchase transactions.

Especially interesting is the option to collect the cost for locations, because by default, Maximo does that only for assets.

Budget Monitoring makes it possible to know, too, what the costs for the physical or functional locations were. Create a new budget, enter the year, then add a new Focal Point: *LOCATIONS*. You can enter a condition here, e.g. *location like 'CAMP1-%'*. Run the action **Generate Budget Lines** and approve the budget.

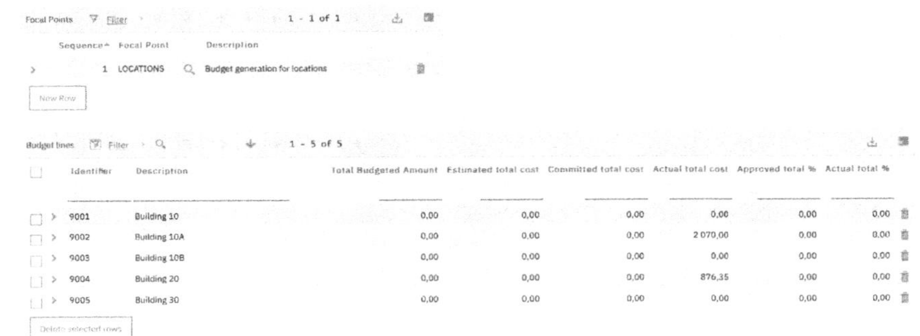

Figure 62 Budget Monitoring for Locations

Next, you can generate some Work Orders for the locations with costs. The calculations are done by the cron task *BUDGETUPD*, which must be enabled and configured.

Known Issues and Initial Changes

You must configure calculation rules first. Run the action **Manage Rules**, click on **Auto-Configuration** button.

Module Integration

This module requires a separate book, so I will limit my comments to only a few points.
Before starting any integration, make sure the integration user *mxintadm* has a default insert site defined; otherwise, the data will not be imported.

I mention it repeatedly in this book: do not reinvent what is already available in the system. Maximo comes with multiple ready-to-use object structures, like *MXMETERDATA* for importing meter readings—just use them!

When importing data, you may have different requirements—some customers may expect that the imported data will be read-only in Maximo. You can easily achieve this by creating a Conditional UI based on the special information already included in Maximo's data model. There are columns in many tables—**SOURCESYSID, SENDERSYSID, EXTERNALREFID, OWNERSYSID**—that should contain the name of the source system and ID of the record in the source system. They are combined with some internal switches that control the data. Please use this default mechanism to control the Conditional UI. It is also a good practice to include similar fields in your new custom objects.

In ***Object Structures*** application you can configure a very useful feature: export and import from the application. For example, you can add them to ***Assets*** application (options: **Add/Modify Application Export Support** and **Add/Modify Application Import Support**). After you enable it in the object structure, you have to grant appropriate access in ***Security Groups*** application to a selected group or groups. This would allow the authorized users to export and/or import data from the application. The purpose of this could be data cleansing in a spreadsheet or importing large amounts of data.

Please do not forget about REST API—this is a very powerful tool for quick and easy integration with the external world, including Internet of Things (IoT). One of the potential applications is connecting Maximo to Zapier (zapier.com) or IFTTT (ifttt.com)—web applications integration platforms. This enables the integration with tens of web applications without programming allowing, among others, for:

- creating a Work Order based on a case registered in the helpdesk or CRM system,
- creating a Work Order for snow removal based on weather forecast,
- using external applications as a mobile solution for Maximo,
- creating a new company record based on CRM information,
- sending meter readings to Maximo via text messages,
- entering a new meter reading based on the external temperature.

NOTE: because the REST API calls require a login and password, you should create special Maximo users for this purpose with limited access rights.

Module Inventory

Application Item Master

In general, the material is something that will be regularly ordered and kept in a storeroom. Usually, these are:

- rotating items,
- spare parts and consumables,
- devices that will be replaced, not fixed, in the case of a failure, such as small pumps,
- work wear and personal protective equipment.

Item Assembly Structure

This feature implements the Bill of Material concept in Maximo. What is Bill of Material (BOM)? Most of the definitions describe BOM as a structured list of components which make up a technical object. In Maximo you will create hierarchical structure of items: the rotating and non-rotating ones. Each child has a **Quantity** field to describe how many elements of this type are needed.

Item Assembly Structure (IAS) can be applied to Assets and Locations.

NOTE: Location must be associated with a hierarchical system first.

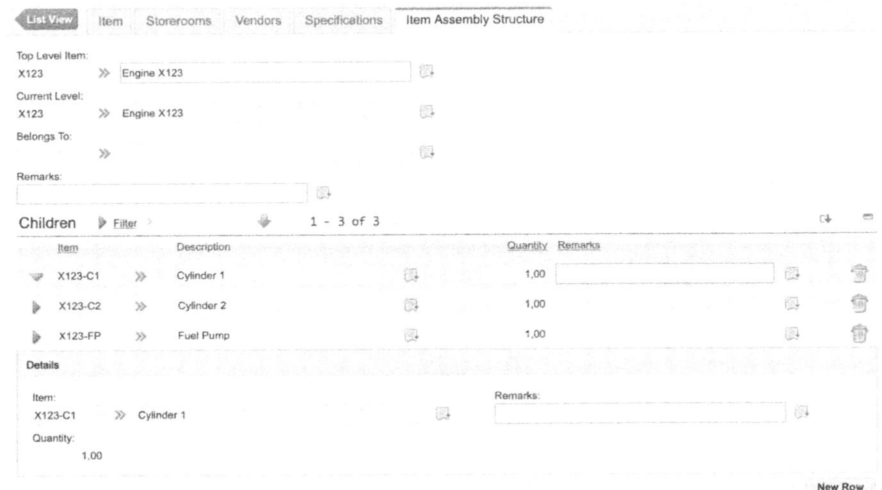

Figure 63 The Item Assembly Structure

When applied to an Asset record, the mixture of rotating and non-rotating components will populate **Spare Parts** tab in ***Assets*** application. The rotating items of IAS will become **Subassemblies** (assets) of the Asset, the non-rotating items will be **Spare Parts**:

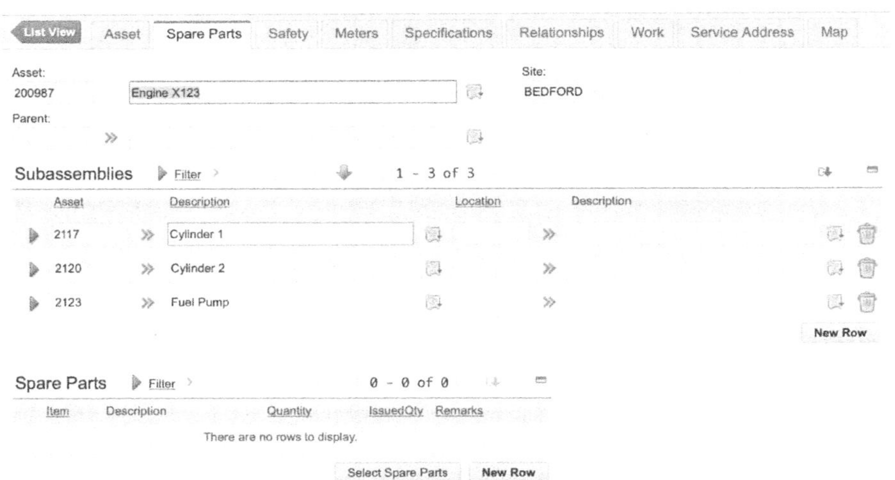

Figure 64 Spare Parts Tab

You define the IAS on the **Item Assembly Structure** tab in *Item Master* application.
NOTE: All the elements must be entered as active Items first.

You will then add the new subassemblies in **Children** table. If you need to create a multi-level structure, you should continue working here: navigate to the children record using **Move To XXX** menu and add its children. Repeat for all the children and grandchildren.

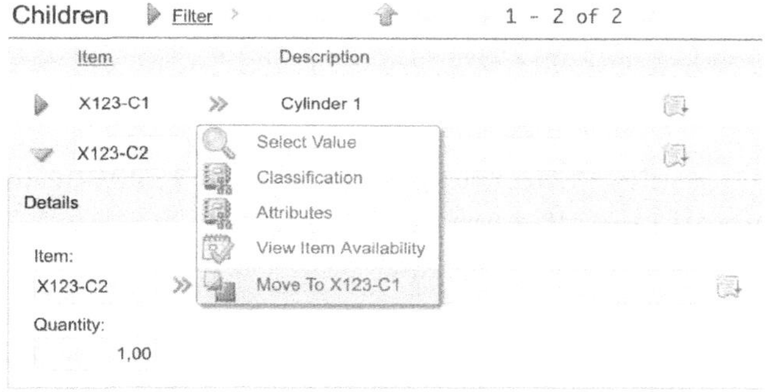

Figure 65 Move To Item Menu

Once the structure is finished, you can apply it to the asset/location record using the action **Apply Item Assembly Structure** in the *Assets/Locations* application. Use **Autonumber All** button to generate IDs for all the children records. This will generate new assets/locations and put them in the structure:

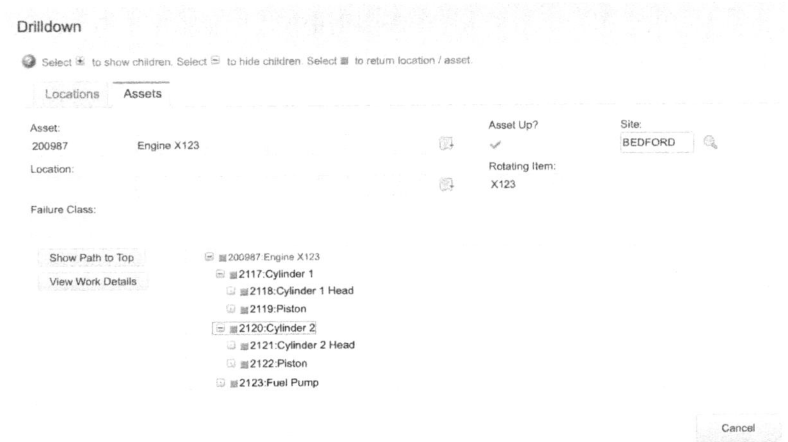

Figure 66 The Hierarchy of Assets from IAS

NOTE: The asset/location record must have **Rotating Item** information equal to the top element of IAS.

Some may expect that when a new spare part is added to the IAS, it automatically appears in all the asset records associated with this structure. Unfortunately, this does not happen. To refresh the list of spare parts, the user must execute the action **Apply Item Assembly Structure** for each asset again.

Lotted Items

A lot (number) is used to identify a particular batch of material from a manufacturer which was quality tested. This can be used to trace back the origin of the item in the case of any issues. Lots (usually) have expiration dates. Many of the chemical materials are produced in batches and must be marked as 'Lotted'. There is a field **Lot Type** in ***Item Master*** application with the default value *NOLOT* but you can change it to *LOT*. NOTE: You can change the Item **Lot Type** from *LOT* to *NOLOT* or vice-versa only before the positive balance is added to the storeroom.

While ordering and receiving such items you will need to enter the **Lot** information. Please observe that there is an unusual lookup which contains all the previously entered values, but you can still add your own text. You can also define the expiration date for this item. In order to do that, you can either enter the date directly into **Expiration Date** (INVBALANCES.USEBY) field or specify **Shelf Life (Days)**. This number will be added to the transaction date and calculate **Expiration Date.**

To monitor the items, which near or exceed their expiration date, you can add a Result Set to the Start Center with the list of such materials or create an escalation.

NOTE: To define the escalation, you have to change first the definition of the **INVBALANCES** object in the ***Database Configuration*** and make it the main object.

Kits

Do not forget about the kits functionality, which is a powerful means to improve the planned maintenance. A kit is a group of individually separate but related consumables that are issued together to perform well-defined tasks. This task can be a preventive Work Order, but you can also prepare kits for new employees with the necessary supplies.

The technician gets all the items needed to do the work instead of making multiple trips to the storeroom and looking for the necessary parts.

Kits are usually built by the internal storeroom staff based on the maintenance planner's guidelines. Parts may be packaged into containers or boxes. The prepared kits should be stored in the staging area (probably, having a separate bin number) for easy retrieval.

To create a kit in Maximo, add a new item and mark it as a **Kit**; **Order Unit** and **Issue Unit** will be *EACH*. The components of a kit are other items which you will add on **Item Assembly Structure** tab (one item can be part of multiple kits).

NOTE: You cannot use rotating items, lotted items or condition enabled items as components of a kit.

Once you defined your kit, add it to the storeroom; **Issue Cost Type** will be *STANDARD*. Finally, you have to enter **Unit Cost** value.
So far, we have only a template of a kit, with *0* balance. Now the storeroom manager must prepare physical kits and confirm they were prepared. This will be done in ***Inventory*** application. The user must find the kit and the storeroom, and run the action **Assemble Kit**.

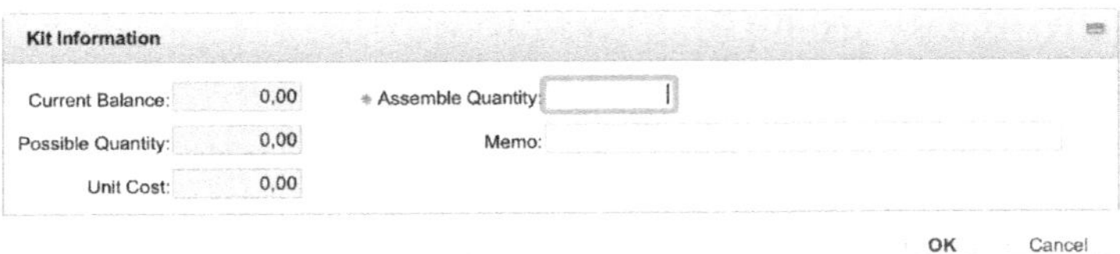

Figure 67 Assemble Kit Action

The field **Possible Quantity** shows how many kits can be built based on the availability of components. **Assemble Quantity** is the confirmation of how many Kits were actually built. Clicking **OK** will increase the current balance of kits and decrease the balances for all the kit components.
NOTE: Each kit should be clearly labeled, so the user should have an option to print and attach kit labels.
You can also disassemble a kit using the action **Disassemble Kit** in ***Inventory*** application; however, this action should be an exception rather than a rule, because it means the kits were incorrectly planned.
NOTE: as a kit is just another item in Maximo, you can use it as a component for other kits.

Known Issues and Initial Changes

If you cannot use an item in other applications and you receive some errors saying the item is not active, this could happen because the checkbox **Roll New Status to Organizations and Inventory** was not set while activating the item in **Change Status** dialog.

It is easy to fix: simply, change the status of this item back to *Pending* and then once again to *Active*, but in each case the checkbox **Roll New Status to Organizations and Inventory** must be selected.

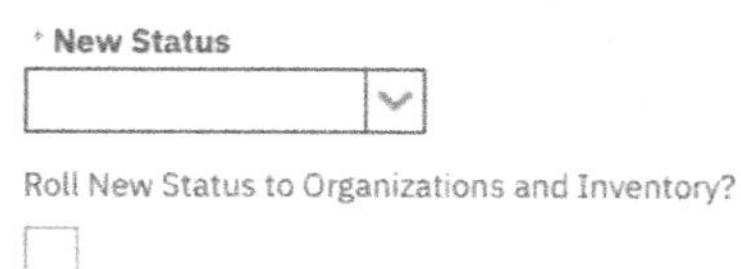

Figure 68 Roll New Status to Organizations and Inventory Checkbox

Because the **Order Unit** and **Issue Unit** fields are required in purchasing applications, I suggest making these required fields in ***Item Master*** application, because normally they are optional, and it is easy to skip one value in there.

Some customers want to change **Rotating** flag for an item (on or off). This can be done only for the items that have a zero balance in all the storerooms.

How to find an item which was defined as a spare part for an asset? You may of course go to ***Assets*** application and check **Spare Parts** tab, but you can also use the power of **Advanced Search** dialog in ***Item Master*** application. Edit **searchmore** dialog and add a new textbox with the field **SPAREPART.ASSETNUM.** You will also need to edit the database relationship **ITEM.SPAREPART**, because there is an error. It contains the following query:

itemnum = :itemnum and siteid = :siteid and itemsetid = :itemsetid

but Item records do not contain the Site ID! Please change the relationship to:

itemnum = :itemnum and itemsetid = :itemsetid

NOTE: You can also consider adding a new tab to ***Item Master*** application called: **Where Used**. You can add a table with the above relationship: **ITEM.SPAREPART** to display all the assets, for which this item was marked as a spare part.

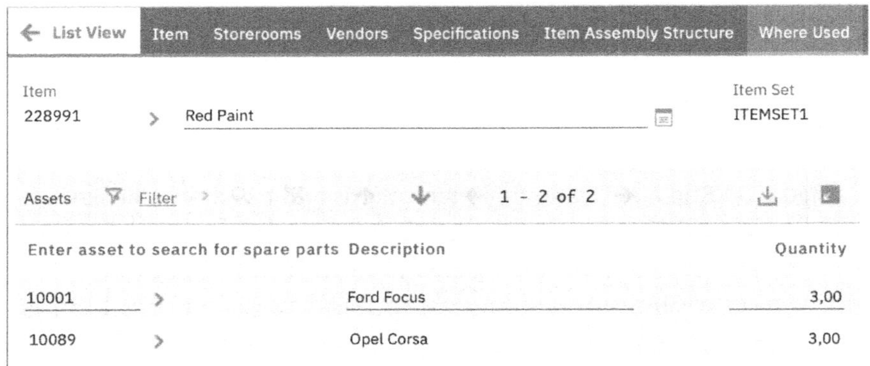

Figure 69 A Sample Where Used Tab

NOTE: To automatically add items to assets upon (the first) issue, check the box **Add as Spare Part** on the Item record. **Issued Quantity** field on **Spare Parts** tab in ***Assets*** application will be then updated with the amount of the item that was issued. The other field: **Quantity** on the above tab is only manually updated and represents the quantity of the item needed to be performed a maintenance of.

One item can be purchased from different vendors and each company may have its own catalog number for that. Customers often want to search by this vendor number. To do that you will need to edit **searchmore** dialog again and add a new textbox with the field: **INVVENDOR.CATALOGCODE**.
NOTE: **Catalog #** field on **Vendors** tab becomes read only immediately after a new vendor is saved.

Saved Queries

The items with classifications:

classstructureid is not null

The items with classifications and attributes:

classstructureid is not null and exists (select 1 from itemspec where itemspec.itemnum = item.itemnum and itemspec.itemsetid = item.itemsetid)

Application Service Items

These are standard services which are purchased because of the lack of skills, tools or people. Here are examples of such services:

- cleaning,
- lawn mowing and gardening services,
- calibration,
- repairing tools,
- thermography or vibration analysis,
- training for workers,
- professional membership,
- subscription services,
- transportation services.

They can be used as **Line Type**: *Standard Service* on Work Orders, Purchase Requisitions, Requests for Quotations, Purchase Orders and contracts.

Application Inventory

Consignment Storeroom

Instead of buying spare parts, companies decide for "pay on use" model. They sign a contract with a vendor which declares to keep a stock of the predefined materials in one or more company's location (consignment storeroom). For the end-users, it is just another storeroom, they can issue or return items; it is also possible to transfer parts from this storeroom to another. The difference is that when an issue / transfer happens, an invoice will be generated in Maximo for the consumed parts—company pays only for the actual use, does not need to invest and 'freeze' money in stock.

To refill the consignment storeroom, a PO will be generated and then a standard receiving process will follow. However, the PO for the consignment items is not linked to an obligation to pay, it is rather a request to replenish the storeroom.

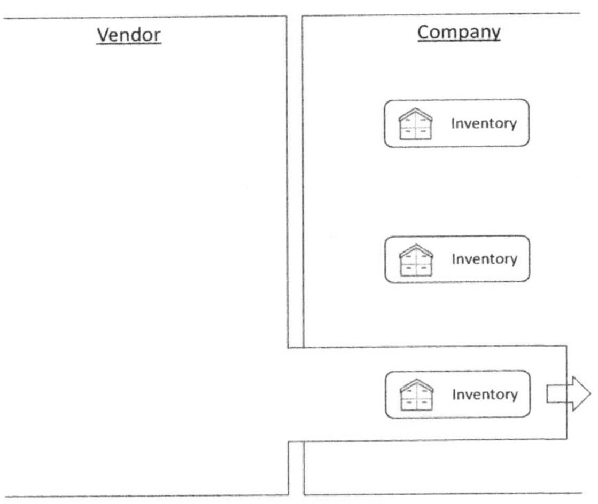

Figure 70 The Consignment Storeroom

To define items as the consignment ones, you must run the action **View/Edit Consignment Details** and select the checkbox **Consignment**. Next, the vendor of the consignment items and the method of issuing an invoice must be selected:

- consumption—generate the invoice after each issue/transfer transaction,
- frequency, e.g. 1 month,
- manual.

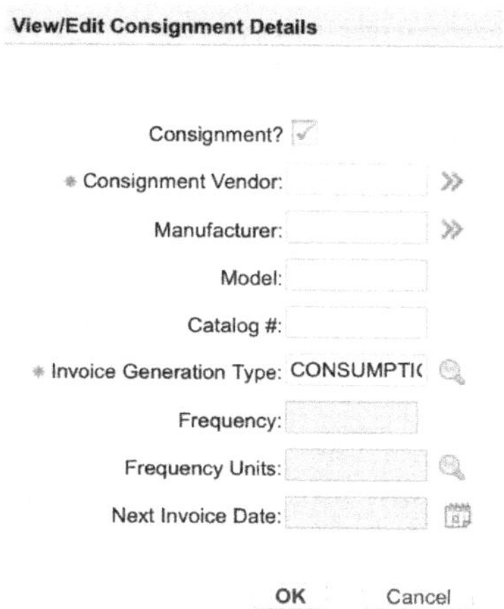

Figure 71 A Consignment Details Dialog

In *Organizations* application, the option **Maximum Number of Lines for a Consignment Invoice** in the action **Purchasing Options/Invoice Options** defines how many lines will be included on each invoice.

To generate invoices automatically, the cron task *ConsignmentInvoiceCronTask* must be enabled.

Reservation Types

In *Work Order Tracking* application, tab **Plans/Materials**, there is a default type for Material reservation: *AUTOMATIC*. Importantly, when requesting materials for WO, please do not forget to update **Required Date** field as it defaults to today. Maximo will change the reservation internally either to hard (APHARD) or soft (APSOFT)—AP- stands for "automatic processing". This calculation is based on the required date of the item and the lead time to procure it. This process is controlled by the cron task *InvResResTypeUpdateCronTask*, which must be enabled and configured.

The user may also indicate directly that a *HARD* reservation is required. *HARD* denotes a firm request for the materials, such

as, "I need this for my work, please do not touch". If there is enough of stock, the available balance will decrease immediately. It can be then changed only manually. If the hard reservation cannot be satisfied, it will change into a *BACKORDER* reservation until new items are received.
The user can also choose a *SOFT* reservation, which is more a demand than a request.

The action **Add/Remove Reservations** in *Inventory* application allows the Storeroom Manager to manage the material reservations. **Reservation Type** or **Required Date** can be changed and even the whole reservation may be deleted as long as there is no related Inventory Usage transaction.

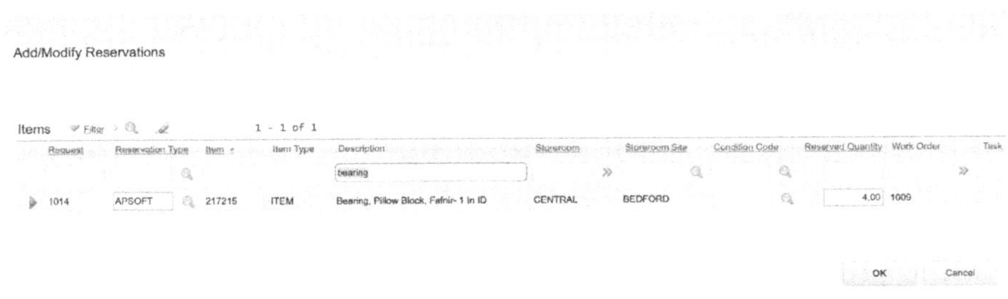

Figure 72 An Add/Remove Reservations Dialog

Automatic Reorder

This feature can greatly improve the availability of vital materials in the storeroom. However, setting up this mechanism requires a prior analysis to answer the following questions:

- When to order? What is the minimal quantity that equals the Reorder Point (ROP)?
- What to order? What is the Economic Order Quantity (EOQ)?
- Where to order? Who is the preferred vendor for this item?
- How to order? The reorder mechanism can automatically create PR or PO (depending on the setting in *Organizations* application, **Inventory Options**, **Reorder**

dialog). You have to define proper settings depending on the customer's purchasing processes.

After answering these questions, *ReorderCronTask* should be configured properly. It is important to specify the storerooms it should process in the parameters section.

Physical Count

To maintain accurate inventory, customers perform periodical checks: someone has to go to the storeroom and count the items. Then any differences are reported to adjust the balances. To avoid counting all the items in the storeroom, Maximo supports 'ABC Analysis' method, which defines the rules to count only a subset of inventory in a specific storeroom. The idea is based on grouping items by value and turnover rate, and assigning ranks to them (from the highest): A, B or C. The items of 'A' type have the shortest count cycle of a quarter, 'B' items are counted twice a year and 'C' ones—only once a year (the customer may choose different frequencies).
You can define the count frequency in ***Organizations*** application, option **Inventory Options/Inventory Defaults**.
To perform the analysis and assign the types, run the report *Inventory ABC Analysis.* It will populate the fields **ABC Type** and **Count Frequency**.
NOTE: The type of the item can change over the time based on the current consumption. Make sure to run the report *Inventory ABC Analysis* regularly.
Once the type and frequency are defined, you can run the *Inventory Cycle Count* report, which shows the list of the items that are due for being counted in the following month (**Count Frequency** must be greater than *0*). Please note there is no information about the current balance—to make sure the person who makes the physical count will not just copy this value.

IBM®

Inventory Cycle Count

Storeroom: CENTRAL
Site: BEDFORD

Item	Description	Issue Unit	Condition Code	Bin	Last Count Date	New Count Quantity
XMP-3400	Seal- AA519, 1 In Dia	EACH		A-3-5	7/11/98	
217213	Plate, Stainless Steel	EACH		A-3-8	7/6/95	
XMP-3500	Cylinder, Hydraulic- AA267	EACH		A-4-1	7/11/98	
11453	Seal, Mechanical, Self Aligning- 1 in ID	EACH		A-4-9	2/27/03	
121115	Bushing, Bronze- 1-1/2 In OD X 1 In ID	EACH		A-5-1	7/11/98	
G23117	Carton Guide- Chain Wash Machine	EACH		A-5-1	7/11/98	
GLOVES	Gloves, Disposable Latex	BOX		A-5-1	7/8/95	
117041	Connecting Link - Repair	EACH		A-5-2	7/8/95	
0-7205	Valve, Needle- 1/4 In	EACH		A-5-7	7/7/95	
4-0030	Grommet- Chain Wash Machine	EACH		A-5-7	7/7/95	
230-00	Elbow, Street- 90 Deg, 1 In	EACH		A-6-2	7/7/95	
G22713	Bracket- Carton Machine	EACH		A-6-2	7/7/95	

Figure 73 Report Inventory Cycle Count

IBM, Maximo 7.6 Report Booklet, accessed 7 December 2019, retrieved from https://www.ibm.com/support/pages/maximo-76-report-booklet

Once the inventory sheets are populated, the balances must be adjusted. To change the balances, find in the storeroom only the items you want to update and open the action **Inventory Adjustments/Physical Count**. A warning window will appear:

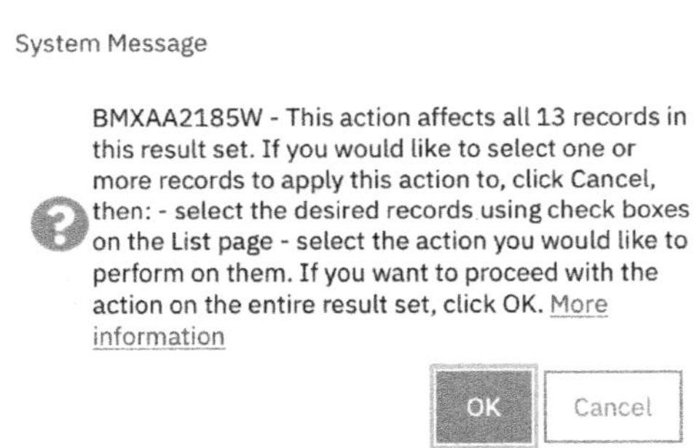

System Message
BMXAA2185W - This action affects all 13 records in this result set. If you would like to select one or more records to apply this action to, click Cancel, then: - select the desired records using check boxes on the List page - select the action you would like to perform on them. If you want to proceed with the action on the entire result set, click OK. More information
OK
Cancel

Figure 74 Physical Count Warning

After clicking OK, a window to enter the adjusted balances will appear and the user must enter new values:

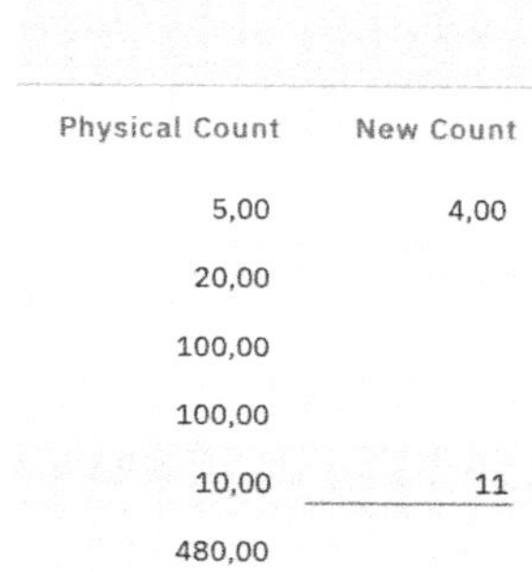

Physical Count	New Count
5,00	4,00
20,00	
100,00	
100,00	
10,00	11
480,00	

Figure 75 Adjusted Balance Values

There is no need to re-type values which are the same. Once the above window is closed, a message will confirm the changes:

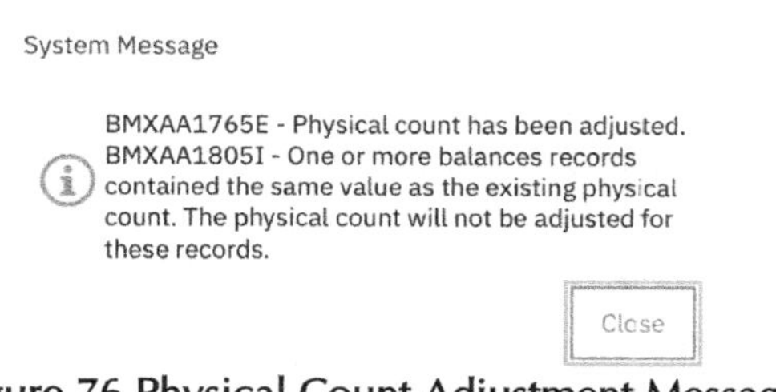
System Message
BMXAA1765E - Physical count has been adjusted.
BMXAA1805I - One or more balances records contained the same value as the existing physical count. The physical count will not be adjusted for these records.
Close

Figure 76 Physical Count Adjustment Message

To conclude the process, the action **Inventory Adjustments/Reconcile Balances** must be executed. Again, the warning message will appear to remind that some records will be updated but then the changes will be saved.

NOTE: You can also change the balance for only one item using the above two actions.

Alternatively, a mobile application can be used to support this process.

Saved Queries

This shows only non-zero balances, so I usually use it as a default condition in this application:

> *status != 'OBSOLETE' and exists (select itemnum from invbalances where curbal > 0 and invbalances.location*

= inventory.location and invbalances.itemnum = inventory.itemnum and invbalances.itemsetid = inventory.itemsetid)

Application Inventory Usage

The decision to use this application must be preceded by answering the question of what inventory management model is used at the customer's site. Is it self-service or a traditional storeroom with one person issuing materials? Is it used in all the storerooms? What about the materials stored in the service vehicles?
Maximo can support both the models:

- self-service in *Work Order Tracking* application on **Actuals** tab, on which the users can report the materials used,
- the storeroom manager can use *Inventory Usage* application.

And both the options can be used at the same time but if the storeroom manager is personally responsible for the balances in their storeroom, then it should not be possible for workers to issue or return the materials in *Work Order Tracking* application. You can then remove the buttons **Select Materials**, **Select Reserved Items**, etc. from the screen or conditionally hide the records for the storerooms operated by storeroom managers. Additionally, you may remove the access to **Issue Current Item** option in *Inventory* application and to **Issue Items from Storeroom** option in *Assets* application to prevent issuing the materials without creating item transactions.

When the customer decides to use *Inventory Usage* application, you can save the storeroom manager's time by enabling, in *Organizations* application, action **Inventory Options/Inventory Defaults,** option **Automatically create usage documents for new reservations**. This setting will automatically create a transaction (a pick list) whenever a worker reserves the materials for a Work

Order and the status is changed to *APPR*. The storeroom manager will then only approve this transaction when issuing the materials without entering all the details.

Issue and Return of Items and Tools

To issue materials and tools, create a new transaction with **Usage Type** *ISSUE* and choose the storeroom from which the item/tool will be issued. At the line level, choose the **Usage Type**: *Issue*, choose the item and provide charging information and then change the status to *COMPLETE*.
NOTE: If this is a rotating item/tool, you need to choose a specific asset which will be issued in **Rotating Asset** field—the same rule applies also to returns. Rotating items require separate transaction lines for each item with **Quantity** = 1.

If the bins are used and you have specified a bin in the transaction, then, while changing the transaction status to *COMP*, Maximo will check if there is enough material in this place. If not, Maximo will show **Split Usage Quantity** dialog asking the user to choose another bin to issue the material from. Alternatively, you can rely on **Auto-Split** button.

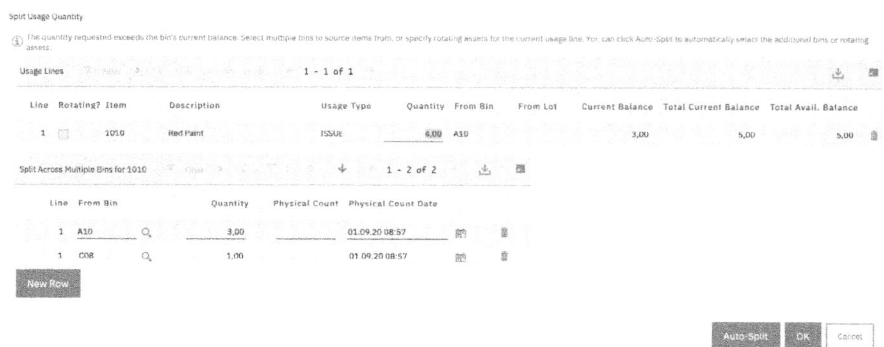

Figure 77 Split Usage Quantity

The details of the bins used can be checked with **View Transactions** action.

To return the unused materials or tools, create a transaction with **Usage Type** *ISSUE* and choose the storeroom to which the item/tool will be returned. At the line level, choose the **Usage Type:** *Return*. The button **Select Items for Return** can help identify the corresponding issue transaction—this will automatically populate the charging information for you. NOTE: Do not forget to change **Quantity** field.

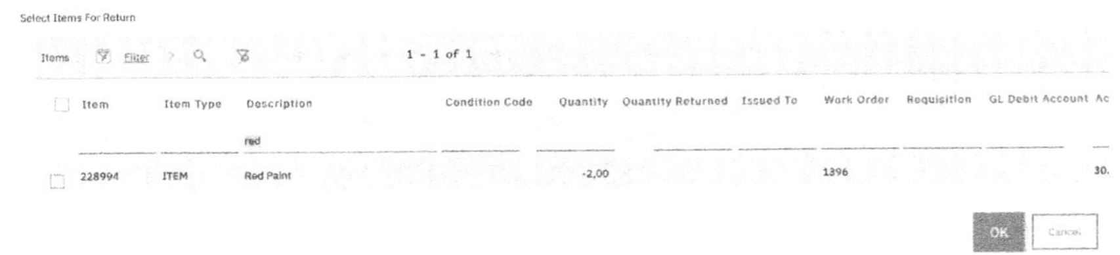

Figure 78 Select Items For Return

Then change the status of the transaction to *COMPLETE*.
You can also prepare the return transaction manually, pick the material, enter charging information.

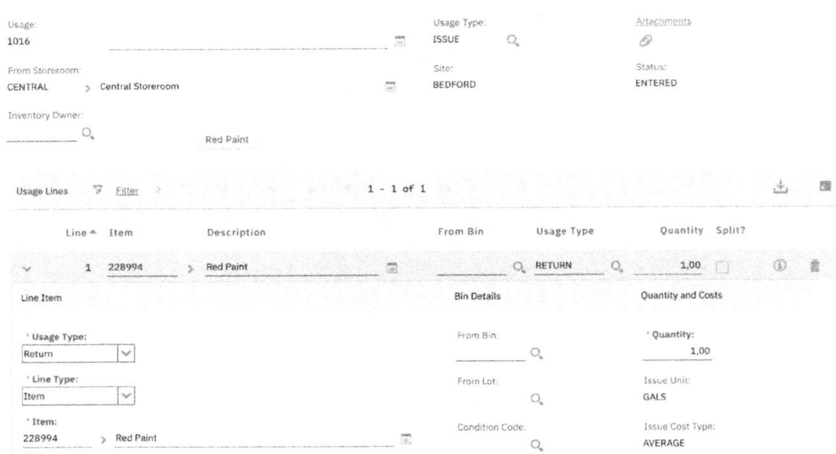

Figure 79 The Return Transaction

While saving this transaction, Maximo will display a message saying that it has found a corresponding issue transaction. Select **Keep Current Quantity** checkbox, save the record and change the status to *COMPLETE*.

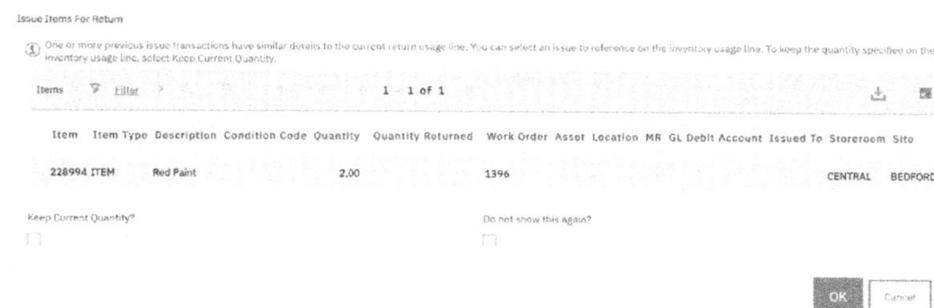

Figure 80 Issue Items For Return

Transfer Between Storerooms

Issue and return transactions are usually performed immediately but the transfer between storerooms, especially, when they are situated in different locations, can take some time. To transfer the materials, you will create a new transaction with **Usage Type** *TRANSFER*, select the source (**From Storeroom**) and target storeroom (**To Storeroom**), and add the materials. When the package is ready and stored at a specific place (staged area), you can change the transaction status to *STAGED* and then the courier will pick it up. The next status is *SHIPPED* and the shipment information must be provided:

Figure 81 The Shipment Information

This is the last step for the shipping storeroom. Now, the package is in transfer and its receipt must be acknowledged by the target storeroom in ***Shipment Receiving*** application.

Figure 82 Shipment Receiving Application

NOTE: The transfer can be canceled in status *ENTERED* or *STAGED* only.

In ***Organizations*** application, you can define some additional properties for transfers using the action **Inventory Options/Transfer Options.**

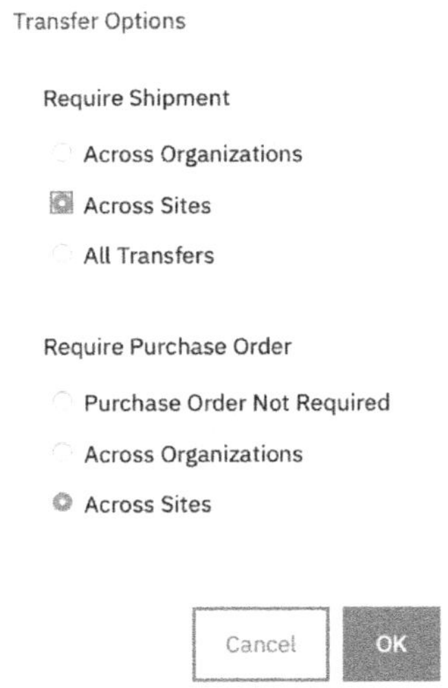

Figure 83 Transfer Options

Issue and Return Items and Tools to Labor Inventory Location

As mentioned before, Labor Inventory Location, which is the labor storeroom, can be created for each worker in ***Labor*** application. To issue or return items and tools to/from this storeroom, you need to create a new transaction with **Usage Type** *TRANSFER* and select the source (**From Storeroom**) and target storeroom (**To Storeroom**). If the item happens to be returned to the same location, you simply swap the location names:

- Issue:
    - From: CENTRAL, Central Storeroom,
    - To: HFINN, Huck Finn (Labor Inventory Location),
- Return:
    - From: HFINN,
    - To: CENTRAL.

Application Tools

Below are some examples of when tools functionality can be useful:

- the customer can control the content of the workers' toolboxes,
- the customer can track the tools in different locations,
- the costs of using external tools can be gathered,
- expensive tools can be monitored,
- tools (rotating items) can be maintained as other assets; tools (rotating items) can be maintained as assets: the measuring devices must be calibrated,
- verification of the required qualifications to operate tools can be enforced.

Known Issues and Initial Changes

The qualifications required to operate the tool can be defined either in *Tools* application in **Required Qualifications** table or in *Qualifications* application in **Tools That Require This**

Qualification table. However, Maximo only keeps this relation but no functionality is available, for example, to warn the operator that the assigned laborer has the required qualification. This has to be separately implemented.

Application Stocked Tools

The customer may want to control the issues and returns of the tools, and have one or several tool storerooms. ***Stocked Tools*** application will present the current balances of the tools in each storeroom. Standard actions allow for issuing/returning or transferring the tools (the same actions can be carried out in ***Inventory Usage*** application, too). The application also offers a Physical Count function (described before).

Module Planning

Application Job Plans

Job Plans are the main building blocks in maintenance and their main purpose is to support preventive maintenance. There are specific cases when the customer may create Job Plans to support the process of corrective maintenance. Sometimes, one cannot eliminate the failure but they can prepare a procedure to fix it quickly and efficiently. In the case of failures, you may also suggest preparing a Job Plan not to fix a failure but to investigate the root cause—what to check, how to find the error codes, etc.

The list of tasks in Job Plans can have multiple applications, not only guiding workers what to do but also reminding them about the most obvious tasks, such as:

- updating necessary documentation,
- testing the device/installation after reparation.

Having these small steps covered can improve the quality of work.

Tasks and Classifications

A Job Plan consists of a list of tasks, plus labor requirements/materials/tools/external services. This is a Job Plan with tasks:

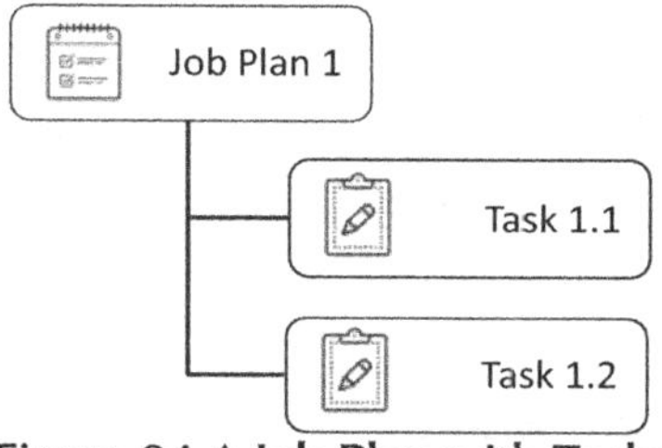

Figure 84 A Job Plan with Tasks

Let us check how this will be reflected as a Work Order:

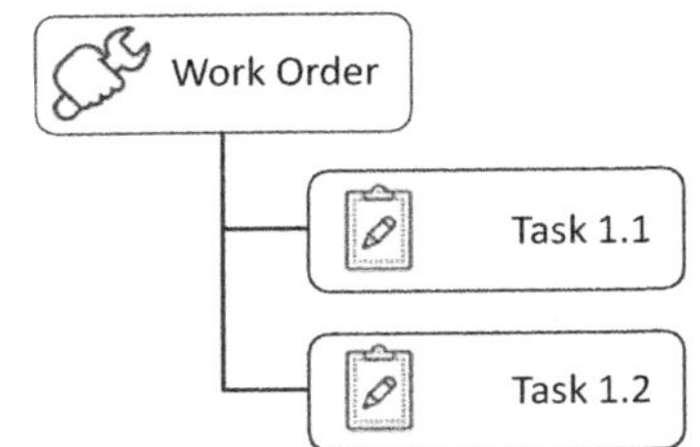

Figure 85 A Work Order with a Job Plan

Our Job Plan can also have a Classification with Attributes:

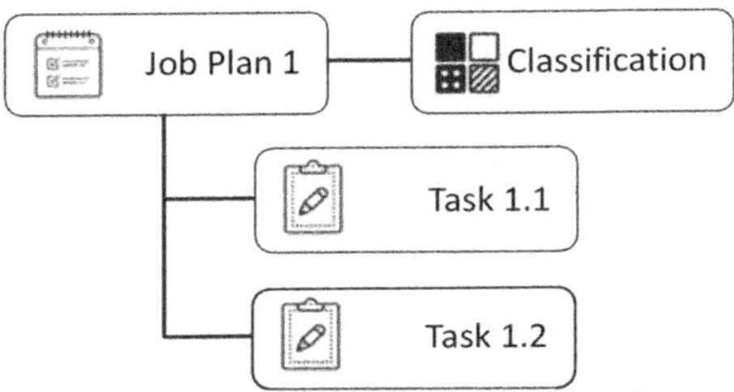

Figure 86 A Job Plan with Tasks and a Classification

If this Classification is defined for the use with *JOBPLAN* and *WORKORDER* objects, the Work Order will also inherit the same classification and its attributes.

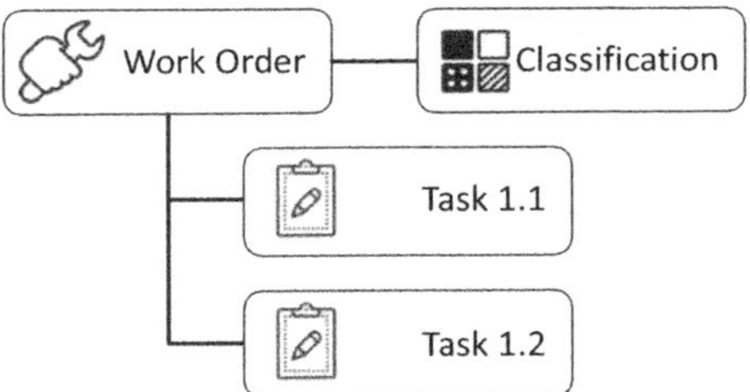

Figure 87 A Work Order with a Job Plan and a Classification

The Attributes in the Work Order can be used as a list of questions (or checklist) to collect the required information during the Work Order execution.
NOTE: If you want to assign a classification to tasks, it must be defined for the use with *JOBTASK* and *WOACTIVITY* objects.

Tasks and Meters

We can collect quantitative or qualitative information at the task level. In order to do this, a meter (of type *GAUGE* for quantitative information or *CHARACTERISTIC* for the qualitative one) should be added to the task:

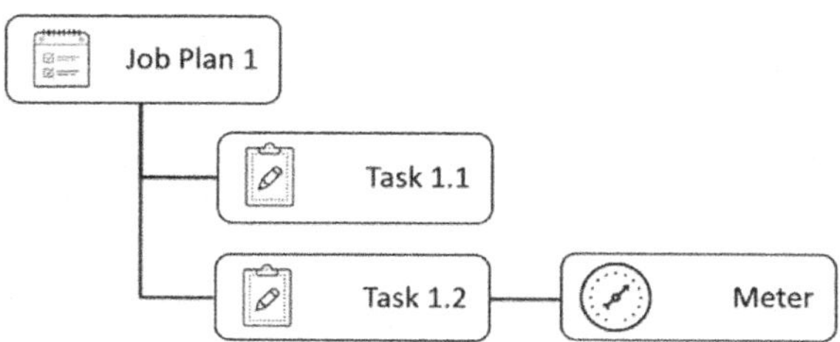

Figure 88 A Job Plan with Tasks and a Meter

In the Work Order object, we will get the task with a Measure Point:

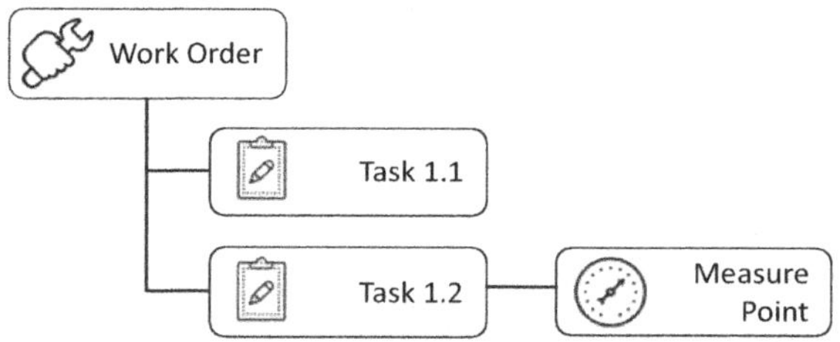

Figure 89 A Work Order with a Job Plan and a Measure Point

The Measure Point will only be visible if the object of the Work Order (Asset or Location) has the same meter associated. Additionally, in *Condition Monitoring* application, a new measure point for this meter and for this object must be defined. Users can then collect information, like the pressure or visual condition of the object. Using the above method, you cannot define the checklist to gather *CONTINOUOS* meter readings, such as the mileage or energy consumption.

Flow Control

This function allows you to define and control the order in which the Work Order tasks will be performed. There is already a field on the Job Plan Task record called **Sequence**, but it has no other function than sorting—users may still skip tasks or perform them in a random order.

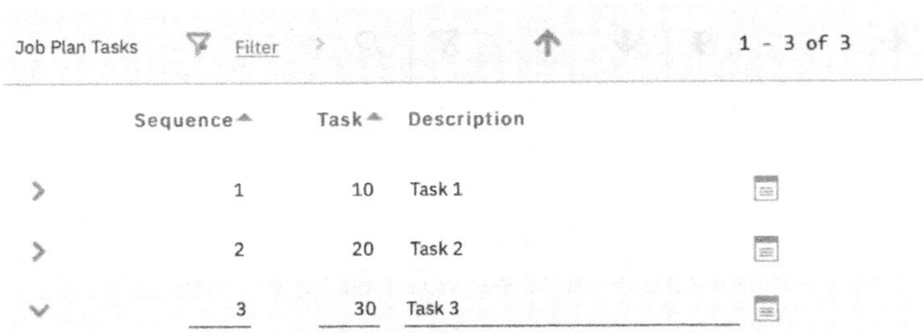

Job Plan Tasks Filter 1 - 3 of 3

Sequence	Task	Description
1	10	Task 1
2	20	Task 2
3	30	Task 3

Figure 90 Job Plan Tasks Sequence

To take control over the tasks you can define Flow Control for Job Plans. It will check that the sequence of tasks is maintained and change the status of the next task in the row.
The first step is to define when Flow Control will be in force; you will do that in ***Organizations*** application, action **Work Order Options/Work Type**. Expand the work type to control the flow and provide the start and end statuses, e.g. *INPRG* and *COMP* (remember this feature is for controlling the execution of the tasks and starting statuses like *WAPPR* or *APPR* makes no sense):

Figure 91 Flow Control Definition for Work Type

In the next step, create a Job Plan and select **Flow Controlled** checkbox. When defining the tasks, you will use **Predecessor** field to indicate that the tasks are interdependent, for example:

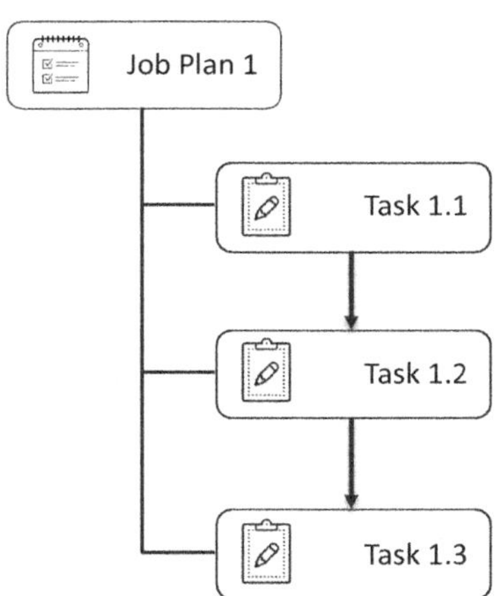

Figure 92 Flow Controlled Tasks

Task 1.2 has a **Predecessor**: *Task 1.1*, and *Task 1.3* has a **Predecessor**: *Task 1.2*. That means the technician must first execute *Task 1.1*, then *Task 1.2* and finally, *Task 1.3* (of course, you can define more complex scenarios like *Task 1.2* and Task *1.3* both can have *Tasks 1.1* as **Predecessor**).

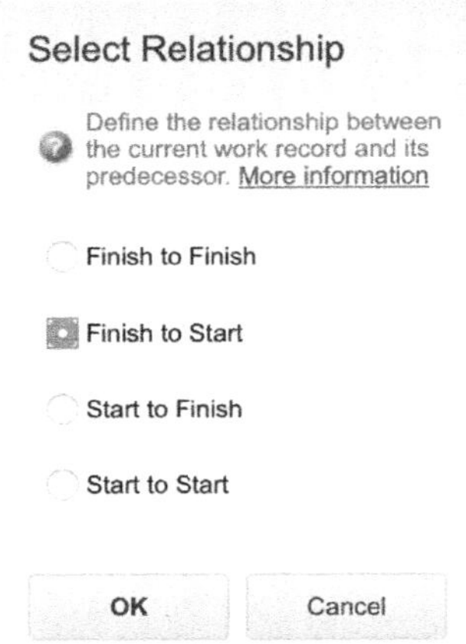

Figure 93 Flow Control Relationships

Also, the dialog to define the predecessor has more options to define not only *Finish to Start* relation but also other dependencies known from project management.

Once this Job Plan will be applied, WO and its tasks will have **Under Flow Control** checkbox selected, meaning Maximo will supervise the execution process.

The standard process will be as follows:

- WO will be approved and then the status will change to *INPRG*. This will update the status of the first task:

Summary	Estimated Duration	Status
Task 1.1	0:00	INPRG
Task 1.2	0:00	WAPPR
Task 1.3	0:00	WAPPR

Figure 94 Flow Control: Task 1.1

- Then, the first task will be finished, its status will be changed to *COMP*. This will update the next task:

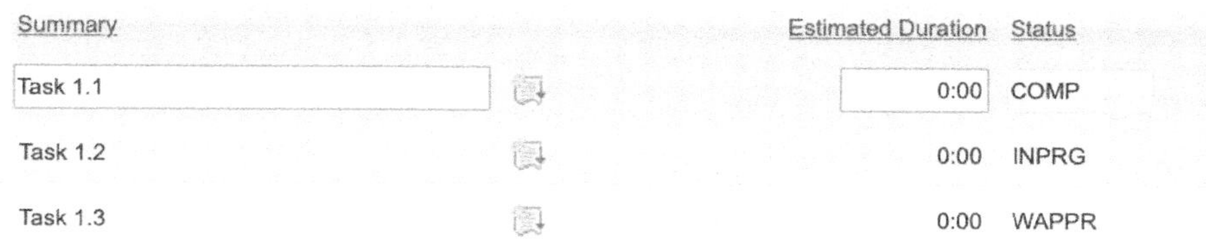

Summary	Estimated Duration	Status
Task 1.1	0:00	COMP
Task 1.2	0:00	INPRG
Task 1.3	0:00	WAPPR

Figure 95 Flow Control: Task 1.2

- The same sequence of events will be executed once the status of Task 1.2 will be changed to *COMP*:

Summary	Estimated Duration	Status
Task 1.1	0:00	COMP
Task 1.2	0:00	COMP
Task 1.3	0:00	INPRG

Figure 96 Flow Control: Task 1.3

The final change of the *Task 1.3* status to *COMP* will change the WO's status to *COMP*, too.

NOTE: Changing the WO status to *CLOSE* will NOT change the task statuses to *CLOSE*, you must close them separately.

Nested Job Plans

Until now, the result of our Job Plan configuration is just one work order, which can be assigned to a specific group or individual. What about more complex work, when we need to define multiple tasks for different groups, e.g. tasks for electricians and mechanics. In this case, we need to use Nested Job Plans (plans within plans). We must prepare separate Job Plans for both groups and then create another plan with Nested Job Plans for electricians (Job Plan 2) and mechanics (Job Plan 3).

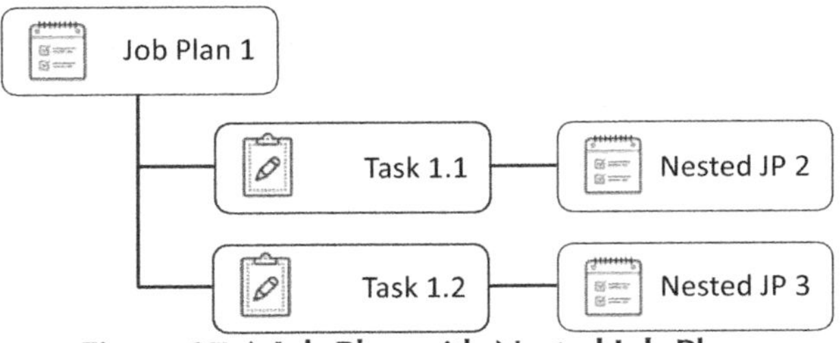

Figure 97 A Job Plan with Nested Job Plans

We will then have a hierarchy of Work Orders:

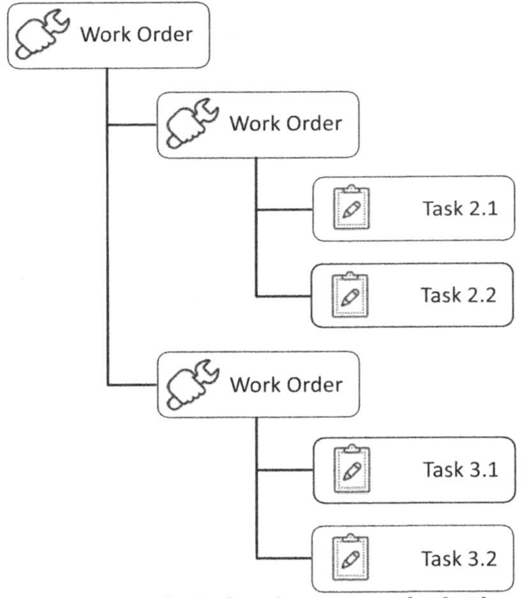

Figure 98 Work Orders from Nested Job Plans

Child Work Orders can be then assigned separately to each group of specialists.

Conditional Job Plans

The tasks and other Job Plan elements (Labor, Materials, Tools and Services) can be conditionally displayed. You must first enable this feature in *Organizations* application, **System Settings/Job Plans/Enable Job Plan Conditions**. The conditions are based on conditional expressions and allow, for example, for defining the tasks that will be included in the Work Order only during summertime.

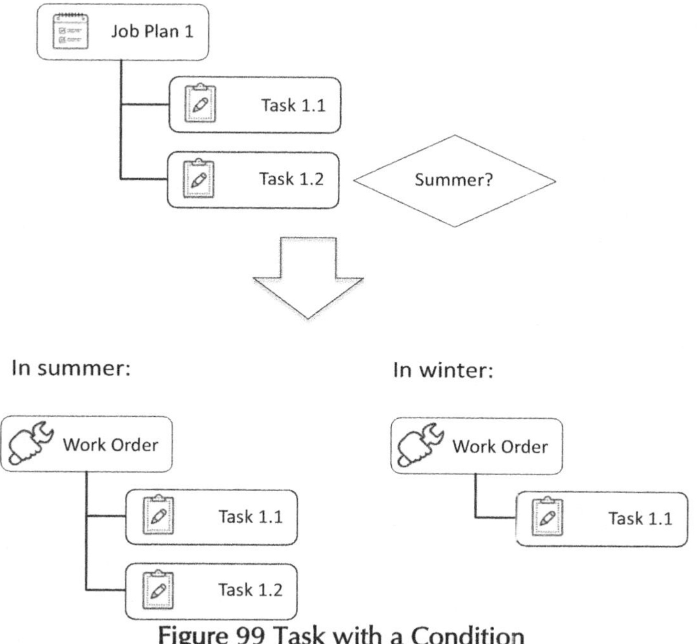

Figure 99 Task with a Condition

This feature can reduce the number of Job Plans and make them more flexible. To start using this feature, define the new condition and apply it to the task or resource.

Dynamic Job Plans

Finally, you can use the newest feature in Job Plans, i.e. Dynamic Job Plans. You can enable it by changing the System Property: *dynamicjobplan* to *1*. Then in ***Organizations*** application, **Work Order Options/Edit Rules** define when Dynamic Job Plan can be edited. You create a Dynamic Job Plan for a specific unit of work. For example, you can define the task duration and resources: the labor and materials needed to paint 10ft of a fence:

- Job Plan duration: 2 hours,
- Craft: *PAINTER*, 2 hours,

- Material: WHITEPAINT, 1 gallon.

There are different methods of calculation available:

- static,
- proportional (we will use this method in our Job Plan), level,
- linear assets.

In the Work Order, after applying this Job Plan, you will enter the actual length of the fence, e.g. 200ft.

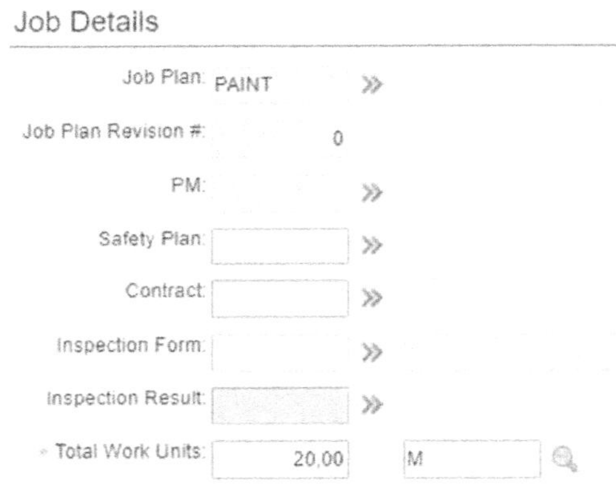

Figure 100 Units of Work on the Work Order

A Dynamic Job Plan will not change the list of tasks or resources, it will only re-calculate their quantity. Because I have chosen the *Proportional* method, that means: 200ft / 10ft = factor 20:

- Job Plan duration: 2x20 = 40 hours,
- Craft: *PAINTER*, 2x20 = 40 hours,
- Material: WHITEPAINT, 1x20 = 20 gallons.

The action **Apply Dynamic Job Plan** will then apply the calculation of the resources needed to the Work Order.

NOTE: you can use a Dynamic Job Plan in conjunction with a Route. The Route Stops have a field **Total Work Units**, which will re-calculate the planned material, labor etc., when the

Route will be applied to a Work Order with a Dynamic Job Plan.

Job Plans can be used for work standardization across the company; in that case, the **Organization** and **Site** fields should be empty. However, there are situations in which the plan must be location-specific because the specific machine type is available only on one site. In that case, the plans definition should include the site information.

Revision Control

More formalized planning departments may appreciate the Revision Control mechanism. This feature is enabled in *Organizations* application, option **System Settings/Job Plans/Revision Control for Job Plans.** Revisions allow creating a new version of the Job Plan, while the previous one in *ACTIVE* status is still valid and can be used in Work Orders. The new version can be then prepared and approved; only then the previous version will be deactivated (Status *REVISED*). Unfortunately, the revisions do not support (yet) re-activating one of the revised versions, only the last active plan can be used.

Craft vs. Labor

It is highly recommended to enter only the information about the required Craft, not Labor, in the Job Plan, because an engineer that prepares the plan may not know who will be available at the time of the Work Order generation. It will be the dispatcher who will assign people for each craft required. However, Maximo also allows Labor to be entered in the Job Plan. If you do it, then in the Work Order task you will see some information in the **Scheduled Start** and **Scheduled Finish** fields. This is a result of the Scheduler functionality being available in the Maximo code. Once the Job Plan is applied to the Work Order, it becomes a Work Plan and Labor is automatically assigned (check the **Assignments** tab).

If you want to prevent assigning Labor records to plans, simply remove **Labor** field from the application.

Creating Work Orders for direct request purchase items

On **Work Assets** tab, you can enter **Item** information. This will enable **Purchasing Details** section. You can then select **Create WO When Purchasing This Item** checkbox and choose an appropriate Work Type in **Work Type of Created Work Order** field.
This feature will automatically create a new Work Order when a Purchase Order for the above Item is approved. This Work Order will be generated regardless of **Inspection Required** checkbox in the PO.
NOTE: Work Order will only have the reference to the Job Plan, but no Asset or Location information. The link with the PO is a hidden attribute **GENERATEDFORPO**.

Known Issues and Initial Changes

The planner might want to deactivate one of the Job Plans, but during status change, there might be the following error displayed: *BMXAA4042E - The status cannot be changed for the selected records*. That means, this Job Plan is being used in one of the linked objects, but in which one?
To answer this question, you will need to add a new tab **Where Used** listing all the references to the Job Plan.
Job Plan can be used in ***Master PM***, ***Preventive Maintenance***, ***Routes***, ***Ticket Templates***, and ***Condition Monitoring*** applications. And there is one more place using Job Plans: ***Job Plans*** application, you use them as a Nested Job Plan.
Here is the list of sample relationships between **JOBPLAN** database table and other objects from the above list:

- Master PM (table **MASTERPM**)
    - *exists (select 1 from masterpmseq where masterpmseq.masterpmnum = masterpm.masterpmnum and jpnum = :jpnum)*
- Preventive Maintenance (table **PM**)

- o *exists (select 1 from pmsequence where pmsequence.pmnum = pm.pmnum and pmsequence.siteid = pm.siteid and jpnum = :jpnum)*
- Routes (table **ROUTES**)
    - o *exists (select 1 from route_stop where route_stop.route = routes.route and route_stop.siteid = routes.siteid and jpnum = :jpnum)*
- Ticket Templates (table **TKTEMPLATE**)
    - o *exists (select 1 from tktempltactivity where tktempltactivity.templateid = tktemplate.templateid and jpnum = :jpnum)*
- Condition Monitoring (table **MEASUREPOINT**)
    - o *lljpnum = :jpnum or uljpnum = :jpnum or exists (select 1 from charpointaction where measurepoint.pointnum = charpointaction.pointnum and measurepoint.siteid = charpointaction.siteid and jpnum = :jpnum)*
- Job Plans (table **JOBPLAN**)
    - o *exists (select 1 from jobtask where jobtask.jobplanid = jobplan.jobplanid and nestedjpnum = :jpnum)*

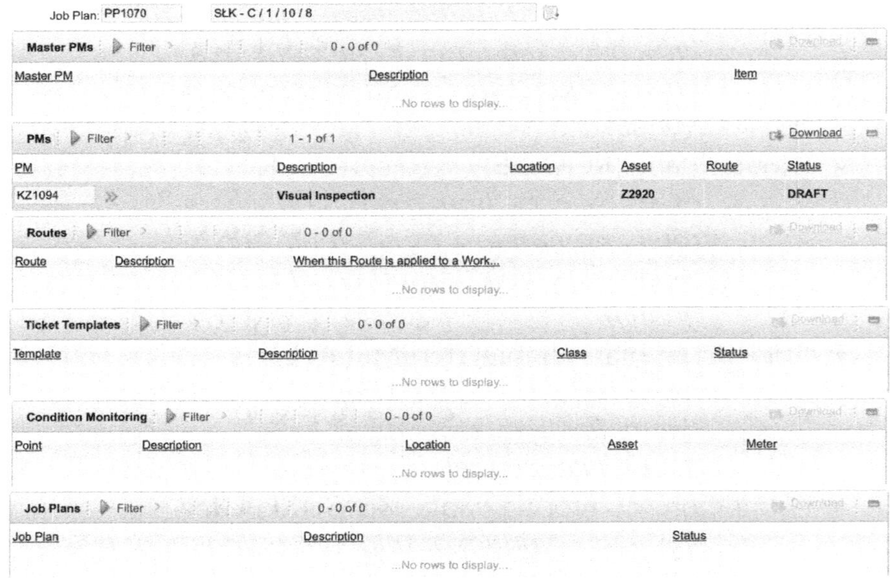

Figure 101 A Sample Where Used Tab

Please do not forget to enable the **Go To** action in each of the above tables. This will allow the Planner to go to the related record and remove the reference to the active Job Plan. Once this is done, the Job Plan's status can be changed.

In addition to the above configuration, you can also add a tab **Work Orders**, which will contain all work orders generated with this Job Plan information (use the relationship *PLUSCWORKORDER*).

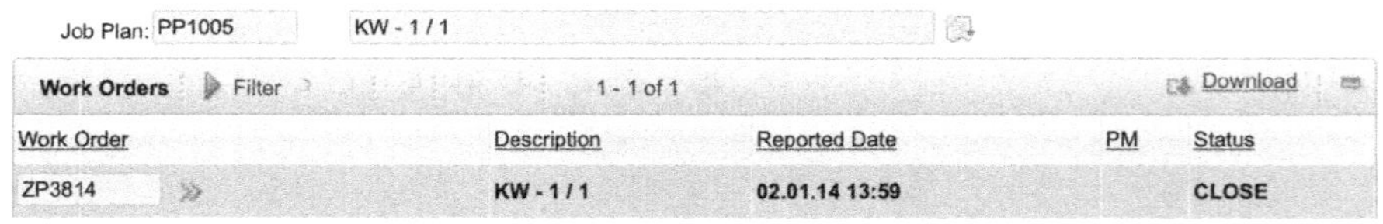

Figure 102 A Sample Work Orders Tab

Job Plans has a field **Template Type** with a domain **JPTEMPLATETYPE** which can be edited or extended. So far, this field has no specific function, you can only use it for grouping plans: *Maintenance, Activity, Process.*

The description of the Revision (**JOBPLAN.PLUSCREVCOM**) and its Long Description can be entered only when it is created. Afterwards, this field is read-only.

Figure 103 The Revision Description

We cannot expect that the planner who wants to update the existing Job Plan will have the list of changes they want to introduce upfront. I recommend making both the fields editable—this will give the planners a chance to describe in the Long Description all the changes which can be then used as Release Notes of the new Job Plan version.

If the planners work in a really high regulated industry, you may introduce for them a new field: **Review Date**, similar to the **Renewal Date** on contracts. This will indicate the date to review and possibly, create new revision of the Job Plan. An escalation or Result Set on the Start Center could remind the planner to do that.

Application Routes

Routes are a form of grouping assets and/or locations, and optionally, combining them with job plans.

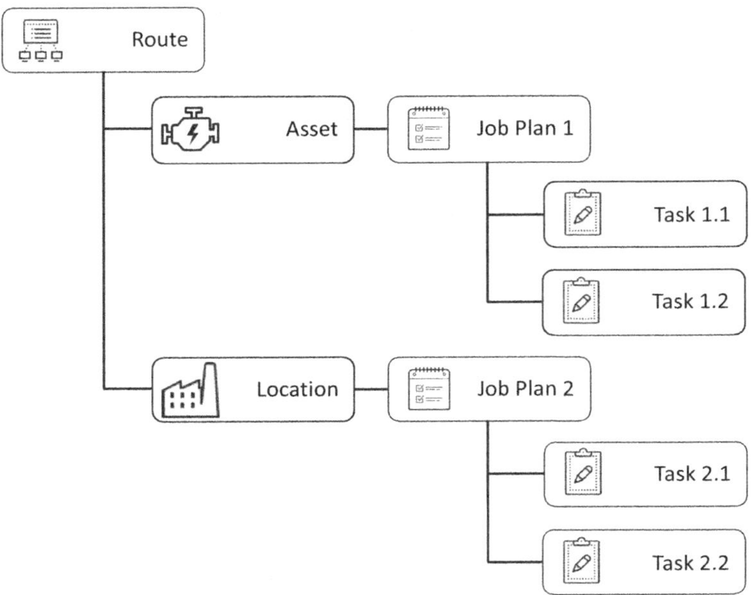

Figure 104 A Route with Job Plans

They can be used to present:

- the production/process lines: If you switch off one machine, the whole line is off, so it makes sense to do maintenance on all the elements at once. This route will include the Job Plans because each machine requires different handling.
- devices of the same type: A typical example of grouping the same devices is a campaign. It is the same list of jobs performed on a defined list of equipment. The jobs will be Work Orders, the list of equipment is a route. In the case of a car fleet, this could be winter/summer tire change for all the vehicles or the vendor's recall campaign. In the latter case, you may add a job plan with a list of the tasks suggested by the vendor. Another example of this route type is an inspection of elevators done by an authorized organization. One route for all the elevators in the company may reduce costs of the inspection because the inspector will come only once. This route may not have Job Plans.

- devices located at the same place: When the maintenance personnel have to visit multiple remote locations, it makes sense to perform the required actions for all the devices located there. This route will include the Job Plans because each machine requires different handling.
- one device which must be maintained by different specialists: If the machine has to be checked by various workers—an electrician and a mechanic—then the route for the same device with different Job Plans (for each specialist) can be created.
- measurement rounds: This is a list of the locations where the meters are installed; no Job Plans are attached. The list is an optimized path of how to walk and make the readings.

The assets/locations defined in the route are called route stops.

Routes are usually used in ***PREVENTIVE MAINTENANCE*** module but you can also apply the route to any work order using the action **Apply Route** in ***Work Order Tracking*** application.

The assets/locations defined in the route, when applied to the Work Order (by the PM or manually), can become:

- either Child Work Orders,
- or Records in **Multiple Assets, Locations and CIs** table on the Work Order,
- or Work Order Tasks.

Let us check how our sample route will be presented in ***Work Order Tracking*** application for each of the above scenarios:

Child Work Orders

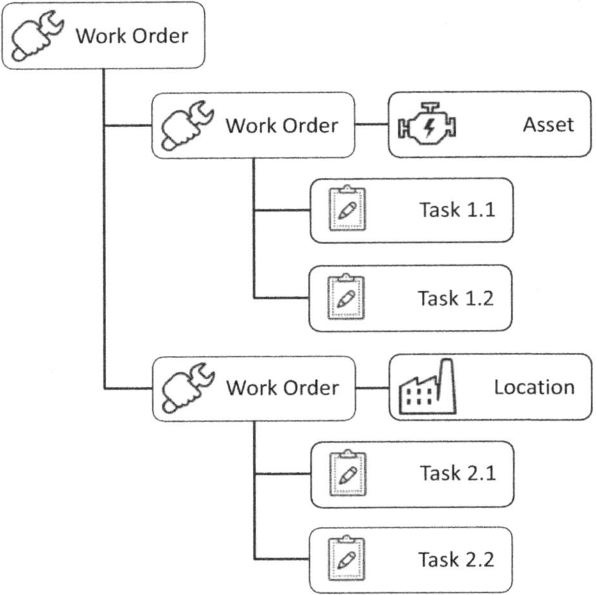

Figure 105 Child Work Order with Tasks

The result of applying the route is the hierarchy of Work Orders. Each work order has the corresponding object inherited from the route stop. The Child Work Orders have also the job plan assigned from the route stop and they will have the list of tasks (plus the materials, labor, tools and services) deriving from these job plans. When the route stops do not contain the job plan information, Maximo will generate the following structure:

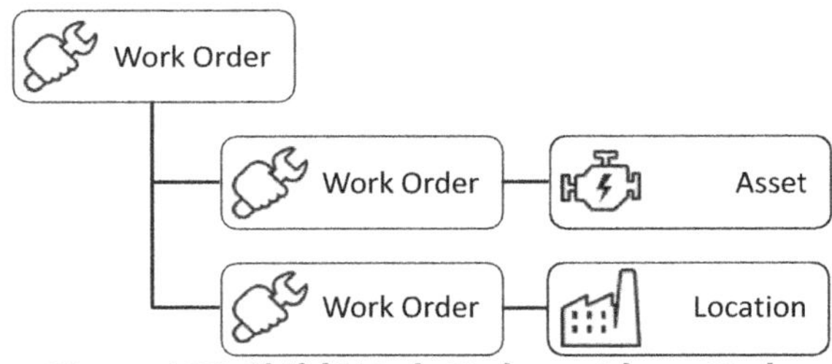

Figure 106 Child Work Orders without Tasks

We can have another scenario: a Work Order with tasks:

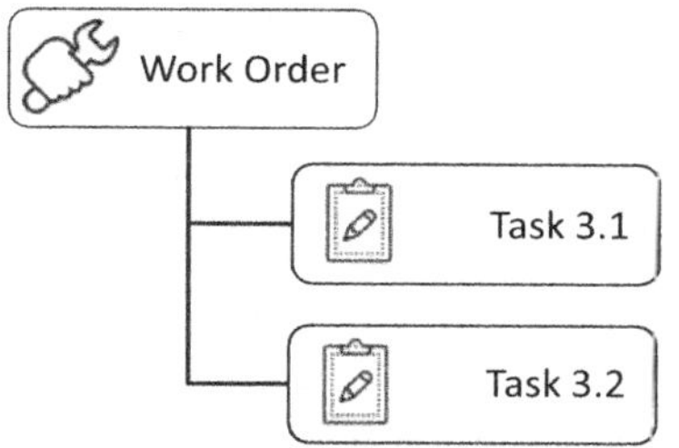

Figure 107 Work Order with Tasks

Then, we will apply our route with the objects WITH job plans. This way, we will get the following structure:

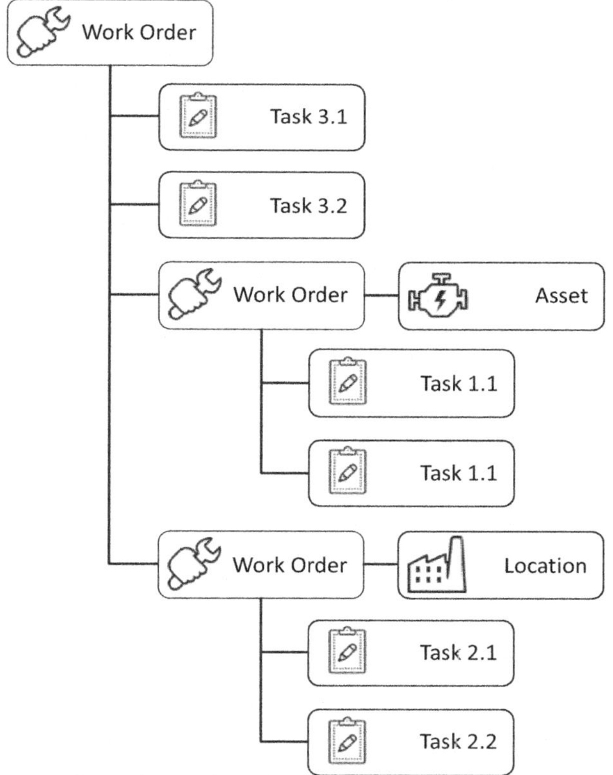

Figure 108 A Work Order with Tasks and Child Work Orders with the Tasks from the Route

Another variant is the same Work Order with the job plan but we will apply the Route with the objects WITHOUT job plans:

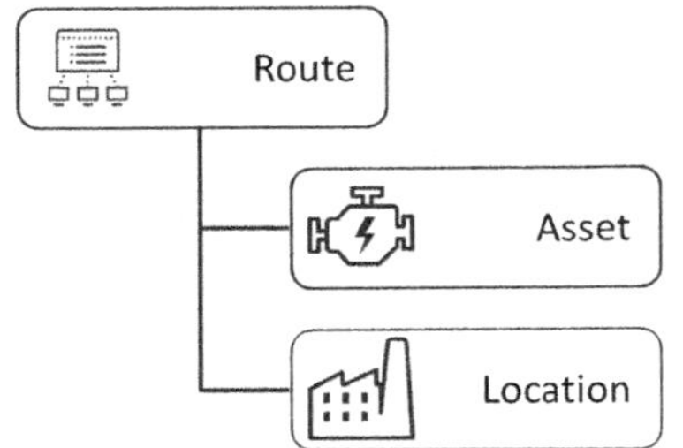

Figure 109 A Route without Job Plans

This will be the resulting Work Orders structure:

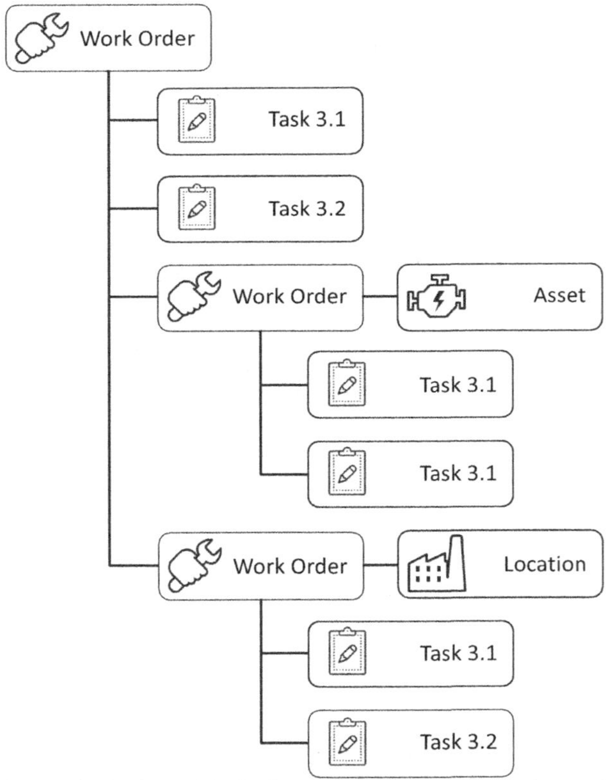

Figure 110 A Work Order with Tasks and Child Work Orders with the same Tasks

Please observe the differences between this setup and the previous one—which job plans are assigned to the child work orders.

Child Work Orders is my recommended setup for the routes. It allows to assign the child work orders separately and collect the costs for each of the assets in the route.

The two remaining options do not support the Job Plans for the route stops, so we need to prepare a simple list of objects only.

The second option is: the records in **Multiple Assets, Locations and CIs** table on the Work Order.
The result of applying the route to the work order is the same record but with the entries in **Multiple Assets, Locations and CIs** table.

Multiple Assets,Locations and CIs   Filter   1 - 2 of 2

Asset	Location	Configuration Item	Target Description	Sequence	Mark Progress?	Inspection Form	Inspection Result
00001					☑		
00003					☐		

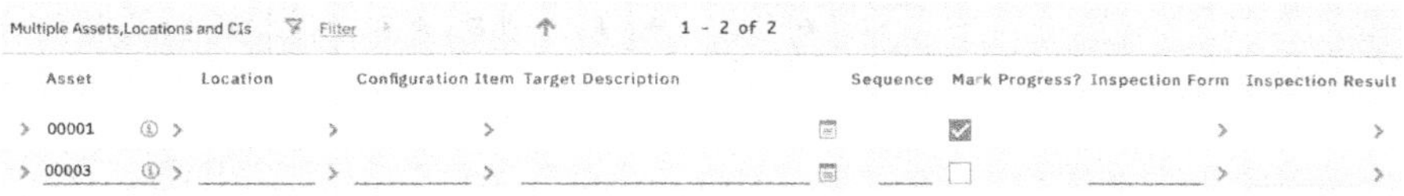

Figure 111 The records in Multiple Assets, Locations and CIs Table

This setup is best for the inspections of multiple objects since you can mark the records already visited (see, the column **Mark Progress**). However, you cannot allocate the work orders costs to the objects. Instead, you will assign to that work order either the location (the parent object for all the objects in the table) or GL account to collect the costs.

The last option is: Work Order Tasks.

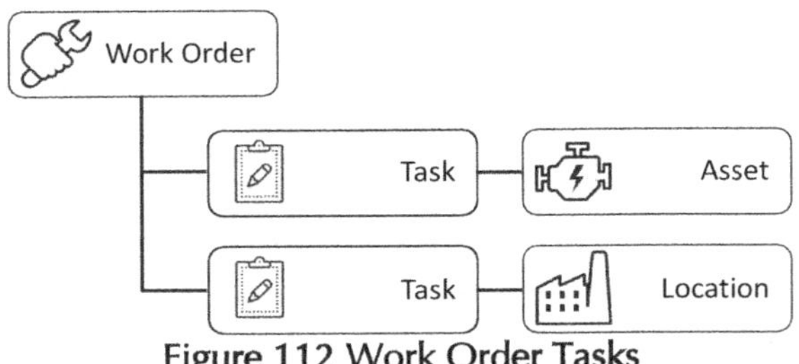

Figure 112 Work Order Tasks

If you apply to the Work Order both the Job Plan and the Route (defined as Work Order Tasks), you will get a very interesting structure:

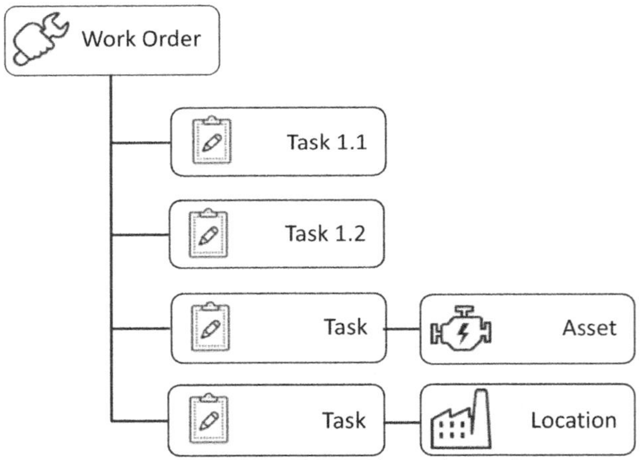

Figure 113 A Work Order with Tasks and a Route

First, you will get the lists of tasks from the Job Plan; then, Maximo will create the tasks for each of the Route Stops.

The structures from the option *Work Order Tasks* do not support the cost collection per asset. You may use this feature when the workers are assigned to tasks and not to work orders.

Known Issues and Initial Changes

In the table **Route Stops**, please add a column **Status** that shows the status of the asset/location. In Application Preventive Maintenance chapter, I describe the errors resulting from the fact that the PM for a route cannot generate Work Orders because one or more assets/locations is not active. Having this column will help the operator identify the inactive records and either change their status or remove them from the route.

Saved Queries

To quickly identify all the above routes with inactive elements, you can use this query:

> *route in (select route from route_stop where assetnum in (select assetnum from asset where status != 'OPERATING')) or location in (select location from locations where status != 'OPERATING'))*

Sub-module Safety

Applications Hazards and Precautions

Hazards and Precautions result from the local regulations and the customer may consult the organizations, like *OSHA* to prepare this information. In case no such a list is available, I include some samples to start from.
Hazards are equal to the risks that a worker may encounter while working. Precautions are measures to minimize these risks.

Sample Hazards:

- animals,
- microorganisms,
- noise,
- high voltage,
- dust,
- UV radiation,
- confined spaces,
- slippery surfaces,
- toxic chemicals,
- corrosives,
- static electricity,

- high temperatures,
- low temperatures,
- traffic,
- IR radiation,
- explosives,
- vibrations,
- smoke,
- work at height,
- work in excavations,
- blades and rotating elements,
- abrasive surfaces.

NOTE: You can add Hazardous Materials to the Hazards, too—they will be listed on **Hazardous Materials** tab in ***Safety Plans*** and ***Work Order Tracking*** applications.

Sample Precautions:

- safety glass,
- face shield,
- welding shield,
- hard hat,
- safety shoes,
- gloves, for example, heat resistant ones,
- insulated tools,
- protective clothing,
- safety belt,
- earplugs.

But precautions also embrace things such as:

- safety training,
- seat belts,
- work permits.

Hazards and precautions may not only support Occupational Safety and Health but also prevent environmental accidents and spills. As an example, a Hazard can be defined: *Engine oil spill* and the corresponding Precaution will be: *Spill pads.*

Application Lock Out / Tag Out

Lockout/tagout (LOTO) procedures result from the Standard Operating Procedures. They are always associated with specific assets/locations and serve as a guide of how to turn off (and later, turn on) machines—this is why, they have the **Apply Sequence** and **Remove Sequence** fields. LOTO procedures can be also used in ***Hazards*** application; they can then be presented as risk mitigants.

Figure 114 A Sample Lock Out / Tag Out Procedure

Application Safety Plans

You can group together: Hazards, Precautions, Hazardous Materials and Lock Out / Tag Out procedures for an asset or location in a Safety Plan. This plan can be then added to the Job Plan and when applied to the Work Order, it will populate the **Safety Plan** tab in the ***Work Order Tracking*** application.

Module Preventive Maintenance

Application Preventive Maintenance

This application can generate Work Orders based on the elapsed time or usage, e.g. miles driven or both (whichever comes first).

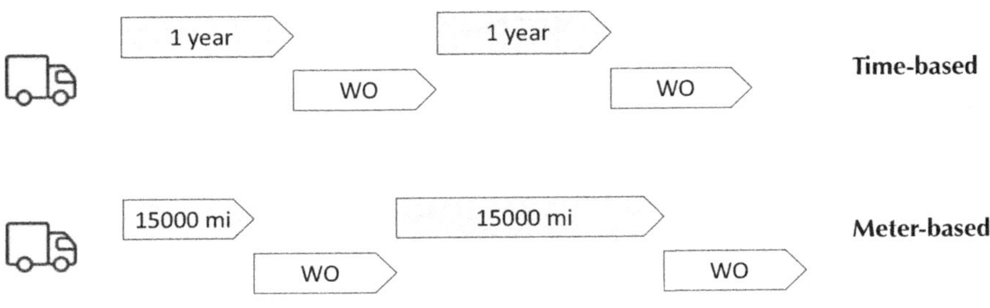

Figure 115 Time- and Meter-based Preventive Maintenance

In this chapter, I abstract from the theoretical definition of preventive maintenance. I focus on *Preventive Maintenance* application in Maximo, which offers an option to run certain actions periodically. My aim is to give you some ideas of how to use this mechanism best for the customer's benefit.

PM can be any repetitive action (not necessarily related to any asset or location):

- overhauls,
- inspections,
- lubrications,
- cleaning,
- regulations,
- measure readings, e.g. energy/gas usage,
- calibrations,
- external inspections, e.g. of elevators,

- painting,
- training,
- re-certification,
- registration or insurance renewals,
- report generation,
- procedure reviews.

Why should preventive maintenance be performed?

- Vendors may require some maintenance activities to keep the warranty valid.
- Periodical maintenance keeps the machines up and running.
- It makes them live longer.
- It is necessary to fulfill the official local or industrial obligations, like inspections.
- It releases people from remembering what and when should be done— Maximo will take care of everything.
- Sometimes, it may be a workaround to prevent a major failure. For example, a certain airplane model had an issue because of being powered continuously for 248 days. It could have lost all its electrical power due to the generator control unit going into failsafe mode. This would have caused the loss of power during a flight. The workaround was to reset the control unit before the *248th* day, so PM with a frequency of *246* or *247* days helped.
- PM keeps spare parts in good shape. For example, conveyor belts may be turned at intervals. Please do not forget that in the storeroom, there are also some rotating items = assets, which may require maintenance, too. Instead of creating PM for each device, the customer can have one generic PM for each storage location: *Maintain the spare parts in storeroom XYZ.*

PM can also be used to define one-time events, like:

- A Work Order to decommission an asset after reaching the end of the expected service life based on meter readings (for example, production cycles)—simply enter the maximum number of cycles as **Frequency** on **Meter Based Frequency** tab.

- A Work Order to perform the initial maintenance, for example, after the first month of service or after the first *500* hours. We cannot use the standard function of the PM because the frequency will always repeat the task. We need to add a new checkbox to ***Preventive Maintenance*** application: **One Time** to break the cycle. Then you will define the required frequency for this one-time job (can be time-based or meter-based) and mark the above checkbox. Additionally, you must create a new escalation. It should find all the PMs with **One Time** checkbox checked and **Counter** equal to *1*, and trigger the action changing the status of the PM to *One Time* (new status, synonym of *Inactive*). Once the PM reaches the defined threshold for the first time, the **Counter** will be updated from *0* to *1*, which will deactivate the PM.

In my opinion, wisely used PMs can change the way maintenance departments work, reduce the workload and frustration and move them to the next level on the maturity curve. Please pay attention to this feature and do your best to convince the customer to use PMs as much as possible.

Fixed and Floating Schedule

The time-based frequency for generating Work Orders can be either fixed or floating.

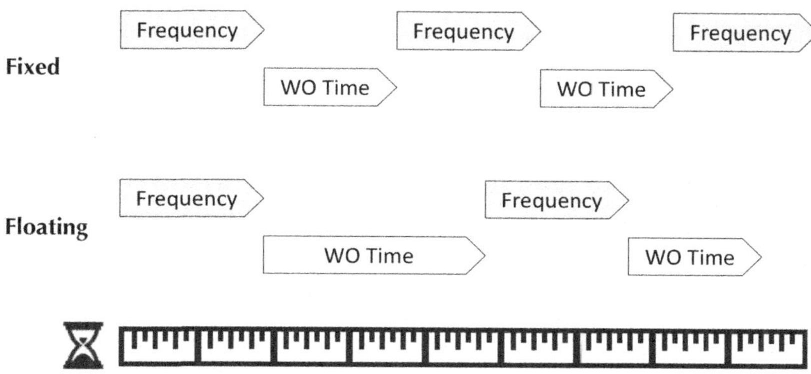

Figure 116 Time-based Schedules

In the case of a fixed schedule, the Work Orders are generated with the defined frequency based on **Target Start** date of the last work. For example:

- Frequency: *1 Month,*
- **Target Start** date of the previous Work Order: *February 11,*
- Maximo will generate next Work Orders on: *March 11, April 11* and so on.

A floating schedule depends on **Actual Finish** date of the previous Work Order. This date is populated when the Work Order reaches the status *COMP* or *CLOSE.* Let us take the same example:

- Frequency: *1 Month,*
- **Target Start** date of the previous Work Order: *February 11,*
- but the work order was completed just on February 27,
- Maximo will generate next Work Order on: *March 27*; we cannot determine further dates because they will be calculated on the fly.

To define the schedule type, use the field **Use Last Work Order's Start Information to Calculate Next Due Date** on

Frequency tab. Checkbox selected means: fixed schedule, cleared—floating.

PM Alerts

The purpose of this feature is to group the planned maintenance and other work (probably, the corrective one). When a Work Order is open to fix the failure and the PM for the same asset/location is due soon, the Work Order from this PM can be generated and both the jobs will be done in one go, without shutting down the machine twice.

First, we need to define WO status, which will generate the alerts; they are triggered only when Work Order Status changes to the chosen value. We can define this value in ***Organizations*** application, **PM Options/ Generate PM Alerts for Assets When Corrective Maintenance Work Order Status** is, e.g. *APPR*. NOTE: This option will not work for the initial status, like *WAPPR*.

We can now enter the values in ***Preventive Maintenance*** application on **Frequency** tab: **Alert Lead (Days)** for the time-based PMs and **Alert Lead** for the meter-based PMs. When the following conditions are met:

- for the time-based PM: **Next Due Date** – **Alert Lead (Days)** <= today
- for the meter-based PM: **Next Meter Reading** – **Meter Reading** – **Alert Lead** <= *0*,

and we change WO Status to *APPR*, **View PM Alert Information** dialog will be displayed with a list of all the PMs due soon.

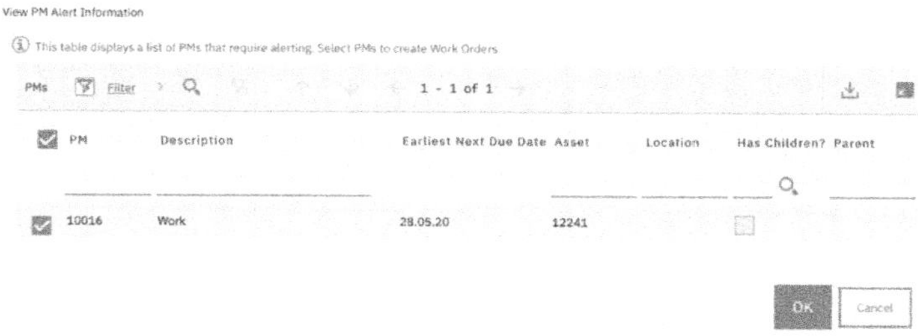

Figure 117 View PM Alert Information Window

We now have the option to choose one PM or more, which will be then generated for us immediately.
NOTE: This function will work only when the PM have not generated the Work Order yet.

Job Plan Sequence

One PM can have more than one Job Plan but only one JP may be used to generate the Work Order. You can add multiple maintenance procedures for one asset and define the order in which they will be launched.

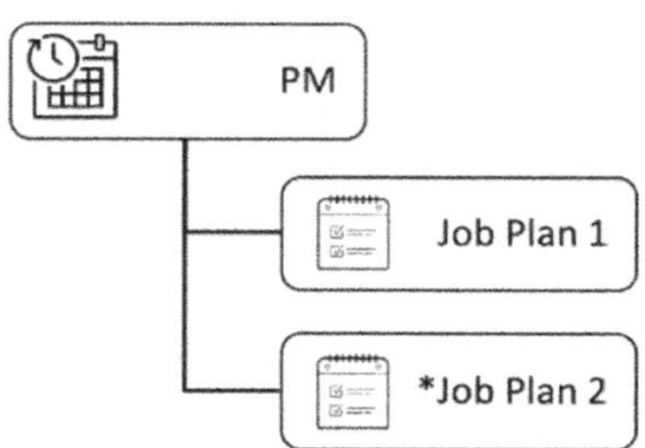

Figure 118 A PM with a Job Plan Sequence

In the above example, Job Plan 2 is due. The result of a Job Plan sequence is always one Work Order with a list of the tasks from the Job Plan which is now due:

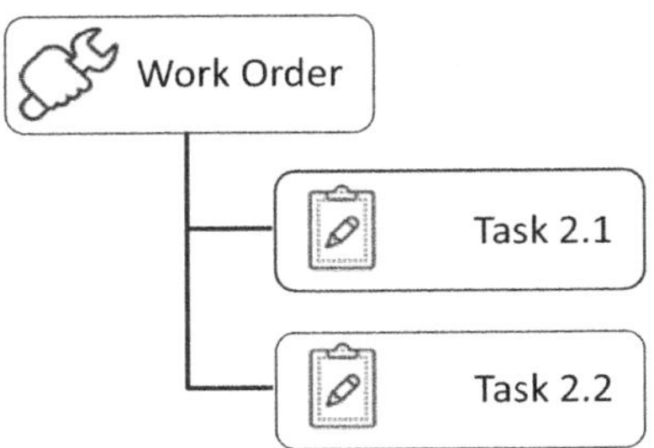

Figure 119 A Work Order from a PM with a Job Plan Sequence

Maximo calculates which Job Plan is due using **Sequence** field. For example, there may be quarterly, semi-annual and annual maintenance for an asset. First, we need to define what will be the frequency of our PM. The smallest common divider for all the three plans above is three months. Then, we will define when each plan should be triggered:

- quarterly—every *3* months, i.e. every *1* occurrence of the PM → Sequence: *1*,
- semi-annual—every *6* months, i.e. every *2* occurrences of the PM → Sequence: *2*,
- annual—every *4* months, i.e. every *4* occurrences of the PM → Sequence: *4*.

When the fourth occurrence is due, we should theoretically have three Work Orders: one with Quarterly maintenance, one with the semi-annual and one with the annual. However, in such a situation, Maximo will take the Job Plan with a highest sequence. In this example, the annual maintenance wins.

Sequential Job Plans can have a separate list of tasks or the Job Plans can include a list of the tasks from the previous instance. Let us take the previous example:

- Quarterly plan, **Sequence** *1*
    - Task 1
    - Task 2
- Semi-annual plan, **Sequence** *2*
    - Task 1 (from Quarterly plan)
    - Task 2 (from Quarterly plan)

    - Task 3—Semi-annual specific
- Annual plan, **Sequence** *4*
    - Task 1 (from Quarterly plan)
    - Task 2 (from Quarterly plan)
    - Task 3 (from Semi-annual plan)
    - Task 4—Annual specific

You can achieve a similar result with multiple Work Orders. You will need to create three PMs with three Job Plans for the same asset with the same start date.

- PM 1, every 3 months—just one WO will be generated.
    - Task 1
    - Task 2
- PM 2, every 6 months—two WOs will be generated: one from the 1-month schedule and one from the 3-month schedule.
    - Task 3
- PM 3, every 12 months—three WOs will be generated: one from the 1-month schedule, one from the 3-month schedule, and one from the 12-month schedule.
    - Task 4

It is very unlikely that a new PM with a Job Plan Sequence will always start with an initial plan. Rather, Maximo implementation will happen in the middle of the cycle for most assets. In that case, it should be possible to adjust the plans sequence. On the main tab of the PM, there is a field **Counter**, which informs what the current sequence is, for example:

- *0*—means a Job Plan with Sequence number *1* is due,
- *1*—next is a Job Plan with Sequence = *2*, etc.

We can change this number using the action **Set PM Counter**. Let us go back to my example with Quarterly, Semi-annual and Annual Job Plans. If we want to start our PM with a Semi-annual plan, we must enter *5* as a new value for the **Counter**. For an Annual plan, we need to change the value to *11*.

On the PM, there is a similar (hidden) field **LTDPMCOUNTER—Life to Date Counter**. It is increased by *1* whenever a new Work Order from this PM is created. You can put it on the screen to show how many Work Orders in total were generated.
NOTE: If you change **Counter** field, this will not update **Life to Date PM Counter**.

PM Hierarchy

You can organize active PMs in hierarchies, for example, to plan a complex overhaul of the production line (top-level PM is the whole project name; child PMs are for the elements of this line). It will then generate the Work Order structure if any of the PMs in the hierarchy is due, as long as the checkbox **Use this PM to Trigger PM Hierarchy** is marked for the child PMs). My recommendation is not to define the frequency at the child level at all but keep it only at the top PM level—data maintenance will be easier.
Child PMs will have an object assigned: asset or location, but the top-level PM must have either the top location or GL Account entered. As long as the PM is in the hierarchy, you cannot delete it but you must first remove it from the structure.
PM Hierarchy is similar to the route with Job Plans for each element (see, ***Routes*** application); however, it has one important difference: a Route stop can have only one Job Plan while a child PM can have its own Job Plan Sequence (a star means this Job Plan is now due):

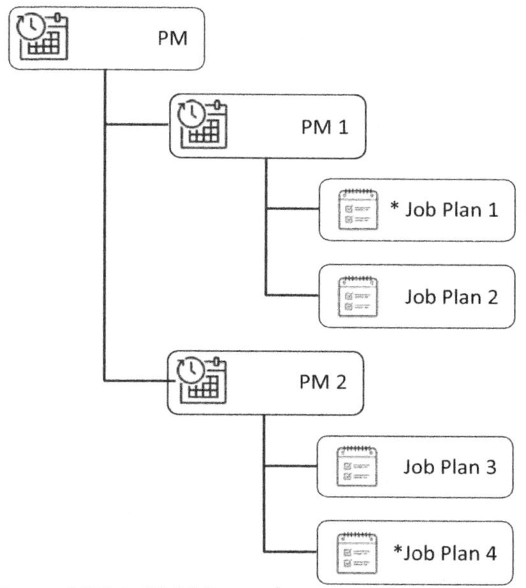

Figure 120 A PM Hierarchy with Job Sequences

This PM Hierarchy will generate the following Work Orders:

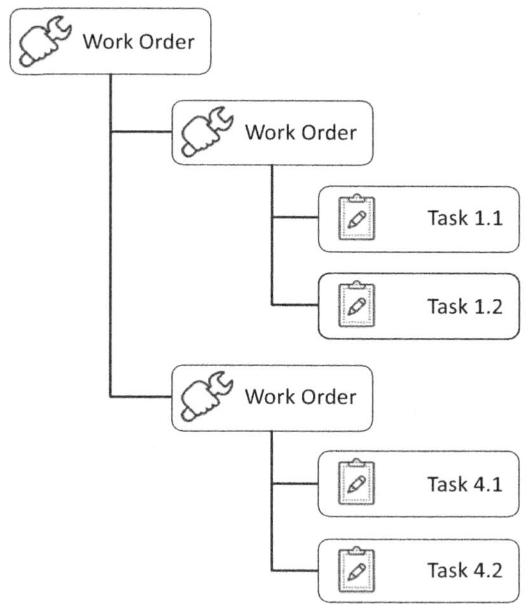

Figure 121 Work Orders from the PM Hierarchy

Please observe which Job Plan was used for the child Work Orders. PM Hierarchies will check the Job Plan sequence for each child object; therefore, the tasks will be always generated according to the individual schedule.

Forecasts

From the planning perspective, it is important to review the future dates of the planned maintenance to schedule the activities. To support planning, Maximo offers an option to generate the planned dates for each active PM without generating Work Orders (it applies to both: time- and meter-based PMs). A forecast can be generated either manually (action **Generate Forecast**) or automatically (cron tasks *PMForecastCronTask* must be enabled and the checkbox **Include this PM in the Forecast** must be selected).
While generating the forecast, you must enter the number of days for the forecast window, for example: *2920* for the next *8* years. The planner can extend the forecast dates simply by entering a new, bigger value for the forecast window and re-generating the forecast.

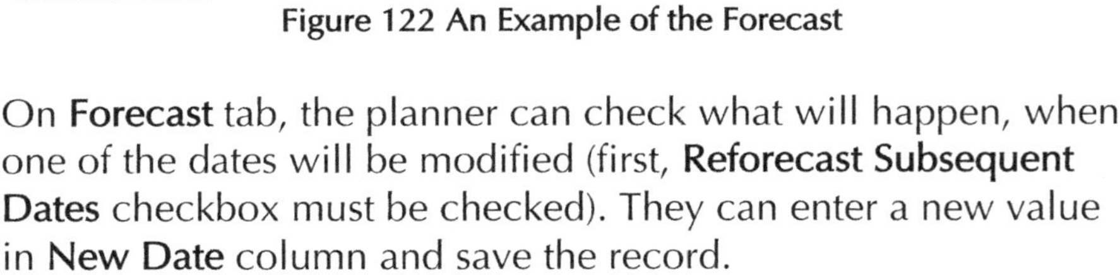

Forecast Details Filter 1 - 4 of 4

Forecast Date	Job Plan	New Date	Changed By	Changed Date	Remarks	Reforecast Pending?
01.05.20						
03.08.20						
03.11.20						
03.02.21						

Process Pending Reforecast

Figure 122 An Example of the Forecast

On **Forecast** tab, the planner can check what will happen, when one of the dates will be modified (first, **Reforecast Subsequent Dates** checkbox must be checked). They can enter a new value in **New Date** column and save the record.
NOTE: Only one date at a time can be changed.

The tab **Forecast Cost** is also available, which will calculate the costs of the planned jobs (manually: button **Calculate Cost** or automatically: cron task *PMForecastCostCronTask).* If the PM is using Job Plans sequence, the planner may observe changing costs of different plans.

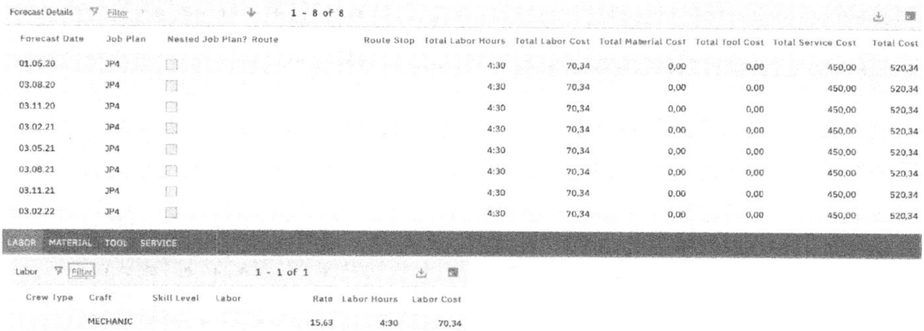

Forecast Details   Filter   1 - 8 of 8

Forecast Date	Job Plan	Nested Job Plan?	Route	Route Stop	Total Labor Hours	Total Labor Cost	Total Material Cost	Total Tool Cost	Total Service Cost	Total Cost
01.05.20	JP4				4:30	70,34	0,00	0,00	450,00	520,34
03.08.20	JP4				4:30	70,34	0,00	0.00	450,00	520,34
03.11.20	JP4				4:30	70,34	0,00	0,00	450,00	520,34
03.02.21	JP4				4:30	70,34	0,00	0,00	450,00	520,34
03.05.21	JP4				4:30	70,34	0,00	0,00	450,00	520,34
03.08.21	JP4				4:30	70,34	0,00	0,00	450,00	520,34
03.11.21	JP4				4:30	70,34	0,00	0,00	450,00	520,34
03.02.22	JP4				4:30	70,34	0,00	0,00	450,00	520,34

LABOR   MATERIAL   TOOL   SERVICE

Labor   Filter   1 - 1 of 1

Crew Type	Craft	Skill Level	Labor	Rate	Labor Hours	Labor Cost
	MECHANIC			15,63	4:30	70,34

Figure 123 Forecast Cost Tab

You can generate the Forecast and its costs for one year. Assuming the PMs are defined for all the planned work, the summary of these costs for all the objects will give you a value which is a yearly budget of the planned maintenance or at least an approximation of it. You can find the total cost in the field **PM.GRANDTOTALCOST** and the details in the following tables:

- PMFORECASTLABOR,
- PMFORECASTMATERIAL,
- PMFORECASTSERVICE,
- PMFORECASTTOOL.

Only one thing is missing here today: we cannot see the forecasts for multiple PMs on one screen, there is also no report which could present such a combination of records or a summary of the costs. You may need to prepare a custom application for planners to achieve that effect or a new report.

NOTE: Changing the daily average for the meter or changing the PM frequency (in PM from Master PM) or generating WOs from the PM will delete the existing forecast.

Seasonal Dates Tricks

PMs in Maximo are very flexible. Below you will find some examples of how to configure the schedule to generate Work Orders for specific days.

- a PM on the first day of the month:
    - o You can easily configure Maximo to achieve this result. All you need to do is to define the **Seasonal Dates** for each month and set both **Start Day** and **End Day** to *1*. Then define the frequency of *25* days (it must be less than a month to generate WOs) and the schedule is ready.

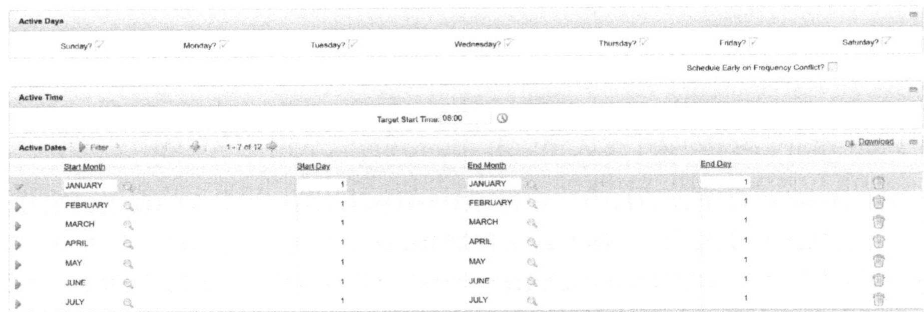

Figure 124 Seasonal Dates for PM on the First Day of the Month

- a PM on the last day of the month:
    - o This is a very similar scenario. Define the **Seasonal Dates** for each month and set both **Start Day** and **End Day** to *30/31* or *28* for February (unfortunately, there is no support for leap years). The frequency should be again *25* days.

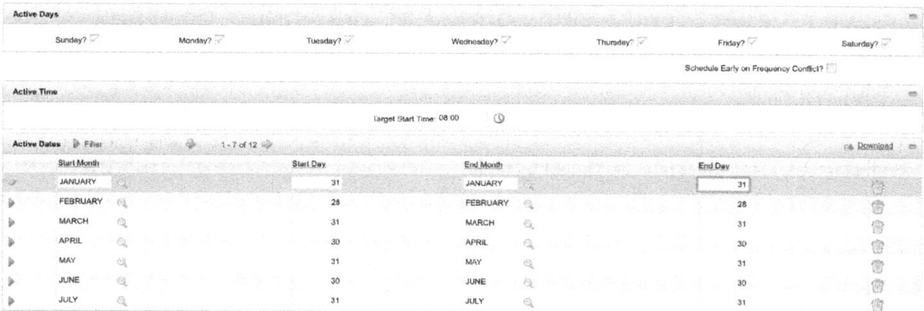

Figure 125 Seasonal Dates for PM on the Last Day of the Month

- a PM on the first Monday of the month:
    - This one requires unchecking of all the **Active Days**, except **Monday**, setting the frequency to *1* day and defining the **Seasonal Dates** for each month, and setting **Start Day** and **End Day** to *1* and *7*, respectively. Replace **Monday** with any other weekday.

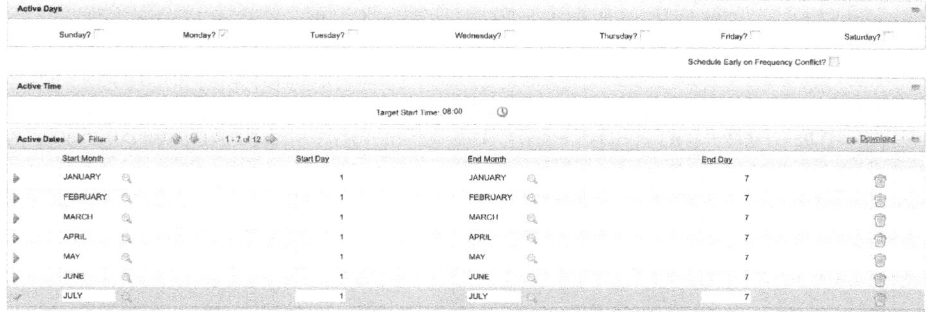

Figure 126 Seasonal Dates for PM on the First Monday of the Month

NOTE: **Estimated Next Due Date** field on **Frequency** tab must be also set according to the above rules.

Cancelling PM Work Orders

Not always the planned work runs as expected: it may happen that there are no resources available or that the subject of the work is not there, for example, the truck to be overhauled did not arrive. We can then cancel a PM Work Order, which can have an effect on the originating PM, depending on whether the WO is the last (or only) active Work Order generated from the PM record.

If the Work Order is the last one, then you will get the following message:

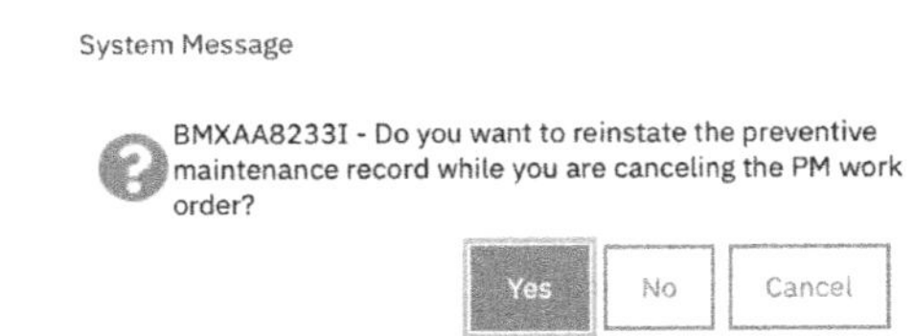
System Message
BMXAA8233I - Do you want to reinstate the preventive maintenance record while you are canceling the PM work order?
Yes
No
Cancel

Figure 127 Reinstate the Work Order Message

Reinstating means that Maximo will cancel the Work Order and roll-back **Counter** field on the PM record to the previous value. This is important when the PM has an active Job Plan sequence, because it will generate the next Work Order with the same Job Plan as the canceled WO. If you do not agree to reinstate, the new Work Order will have the next Job Plan in the sequence. Let us take an example:

PM has three Job Plans with the following sequences:

- JP1 Sequence 1
- JP2 Sequence 2
- JP3 Sequence 4

So far, Maximo has generated the Work Orders with the following Job Plans and the **Counter** will change as follows:

- WO 1001 JP1 Counter: 1
- WO 1002 JP2 Counter: 2
- WO 1003 JP1 Counter: 3
- WO 1004 JP4 Counter: 4

We need to cancel Work Order *1004*. Choosing the option to reinstate the PM will reset the **Counter** to *3*, which means that a new WO will have the same Job Plan (*JP4*) as WO *1004*.

A negative decision will leave the **Counter** equal to *4*, meaning that the new WO will become the next Job Plan in the sequence: *JP1*. In that case, one Job Plan: *JP4* will be skipped. NOTE: After canceling the Work Order, you may need to adjust the next due date using **Extended Date** field on PM record.

In case there are multiple Work Orders generated from the PM:

- WO 1207 JP1 Counter: 1
- WO 1267 JP2 Counter: 2
- WO 1299 JP1 Counter: 3

and we try to cancel WO *1207*, the following message will appear:

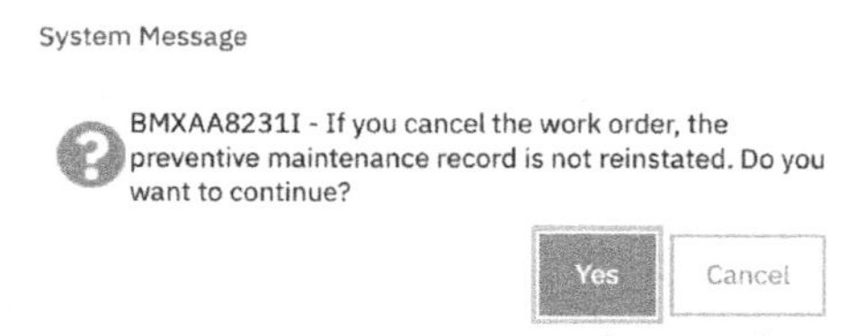

System Message
BMXAA8231I - If you cancel the work order, the preventive maintenance record is not reinstated. Do you want to continue?
Yes
Cancel

Figure 128 Cannot Reinstate the Work Order

It is impossible to reinstate the PM because **Counter** field was already updated twice.

Known Issues and Initial Changes

On **Seasonal Dates** tab, set the **Target Start Time** to something meaningful, like *08:00,* instead of *00:00.*

PMs do not use calendars (so far), so if the customer wants holidays to be considered, they must be defined as seasonal dates. It is therefore a good practice to define a PM template (without frequency or subject) just with seasonal dates and working days (e.g. Monday to Friday) to be used for new PM definitions.

NOTE: Seasonal dates must exclude holidays! For example, to define *December 25* as a holiday, you would need to define

Start Month and **End Month**: *December*, **Start Day**: *1*, **End Day**: *24* and another line: **Start Month** and **End Month**: *December*, **Start Day**: *26*, **End Day**: *31*.

NOTE: When PM frequency is set to *0* and PM has **Extended Date** set up, this may result in Maximo generating thousands of Work Orders. I have also seen Maximo generating thousands of Work Orders for PMs with the meter-based frequency when the average value of the meter was negative. Probably, there is an issue in preparing an average value for meters with the calculation method set to *ALL*. The workaround is to change the **Average Calculation Method** to *SLIDING-READINGS*, after which the average values should be calculated properly.

Sometimes the customers have problems defining **Lead Time (Days)** value. The easiest rule they can use is to set it to *10%* of the frequency. For example: frequency *6* months = *180* days, lead time: *18* days.

The list of PMs misses one important information: when the PM is due. To fix this, just add the field **Estimated Next Due Date** (**NEXTDATE**) to the record list. If the floating schedule is used, I suggest adding **Last Completion Date** field (**LASTCOMPDATE**), too–it will show when the last work order was completed.

There is popular customer request to assign the PM to a specific vendor. However, the **Responsibility** section on the PM record has only reference to internal groups or individuals. If you want to assign, for example, calibration PM to the vendor, you must add a new field **Vendor** in the above section and prepare a crossover domain to copy this information to the Work Order record. One of the customers wanted to add this vendor information to the Job Plan, but you should follow the rule that a Job Plan should be as generic as possible. It should be only a re-usable block of actions without any reference to people or companies. Only PM is more specific and therefore my recommendation is to add vendor information here.

A lot of people get confused by the fact that when Maximo creates a hierarchy of work orders from a PM (with a route or a nested Job Plan), only the top Work Order has the reference to the PM record. It works as designed but users expect all WOs generated by the PM to share the same information. You can populate the missing information in child Work Orders in different ways: an escalation, crossover domain or extension of the Java class that generates the WOs. You can choose your preferred method.

You can face an issue that the customer is not able to use Maximo for the time-based and meter-based PMs for a specific asset or assets. The issue results from the fact that Maximo requires the frequency factor to be the same for both the methods. But, for example, in the case of rolling stock, this may not be true. Imagine the following schedule:

- Job Plan 1 executed every 1 year or 150,000 mi
- Job Plan 2 executed every 2 years or 300,000 mi
- Job Plan 3 executed every 4 years or 600,000 mi
- Job Plan 4 executed every 8 years or 1,200,000 mi

These Job Plans are built gradually, i.e. Job Plan 2 is a copy of Job Plan 1, plus additional tasks, Job Plan 3 is a copy of Job Plan 2, plus additional tasks, and so on.

This is the ideal situation because the divisor for all of the plans is the same: *2*:

- 2÷1 year = 2 and 300,000/150,000 mi = 2
- 4÷2 years = 2 and 600,000/300,000 mi = 2
- etc.

This allows for using the Job Plan sequence in PM. The frequency for the time-based part will be *one year*, and for the meter-based part—*150,000 mi*.

Now consider this schedule:

- Job Plan 1 executed every 30 days or 9,000 mi
- Job Plan 2 executed every 200,000 mi
- Job Plan 3 executed every 6 years or 400,000 mi
- Job Plan 4 executed every 28 years or 3,200,000 mi

Please observe JP number 2—there is only one frequency type! This fact, and also the missing common divisor for dates and mileage, prevent using the Job Plan sequence. What are the options then?

Check with the customer if it is possible to change the maintenance plan. This would remove the cause so it is worth checking. At the same time, it is not very likely because the vendor or official agency provide an official maintenance instruction that the customer has to comply with.

Create separate PMs for each Job Plan with the separate frequencies. This is not a perfect solution but at least it automates some parts of the schedule. In the above example, this could look as follows:

- PM 1 with Job Plan 1 executed every 30 days or 9,000 mi
- PM 2 with Job Plan 2 executed every 200,000 mi
- PM 3 with Job Plan 3 executed every 6 years or 400,000 mi
- PM 4 with Job Plan 4 executed every 28 years or 3,200,000 mi

This PM list may generate two or more Work Orders for the same asset at the same time—this is the price of not having one PM with a Job Plan sequence. If such an overlap happens, the operator must cancel the WOs which have the tasks of lower importance. For example, if PM 2 and PM 3 generate WOs at the same time, the operator should cancel the WO created by PM 2, because Job Plan 3 includes the same tasks as Job Plan 2 does but has also some additional work to be done. This rule corresponds with the previous manual procedure, so the customer should accept it.

WOs are not generated

This is a very basic question: Why is the PM module not generating WOs? (expect for some very obvious reasons)

- *PMWoGenCron* cron task is not active.
- PM generation is not active for the site (**Organizations** application, **PM Options**).
- Admin mode is on.
- There is a missing frequency or next date in PM definition.
- Asset/Location is not active.
- Invalid **GL Account** has been entered.

There might be another cause: blocked *maxadmin* account or other account associated with the PM cron task.

Saved Queries

This query will list all the PMs that have some issues: the frequency was not defined, there is no next date, or the work object is missing or is inactive.
NOTE: If any record is found, it must be fixed immediately because it is generating a lot of entries in the logs. This query is not very efficient and it should not be run frequently.

> *status = 'ACTIVE' and (nextdate is null or (location is null and assetnum is null and route is null) or frequency is null or frequnit is null or nextdate is null or (location is not null and assetnum is not null and route is not null) or (assetnum is not null and assetnum in (select distinct assetnum from assetmeter where average < 0)) or (location is not null and location in (select distinct location from locationmeter where average < 0)) or (assetnum is not null and assetnum in (select assetnum from asset where status != 'OPERATING')) or (location is*

not null and location in (select location from locations where status != 'OPERATING')))

Application Master PM

You can call it "PM template", this is the place where you can define standardized maintenance plan for assets of the same type. This is important for companies having multiple copies of the same machine, for example 15 packing machines. Instead of creating manually a PM for each machine, we can use the concept of rotating assets and create PM template for the rotating item only.

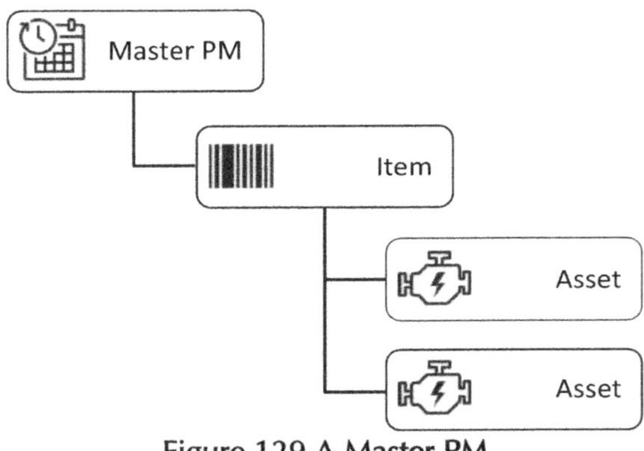

Figure 129 A Master PM

A Master PM can create 15 PMs for us (action **Create Associated PMs**).

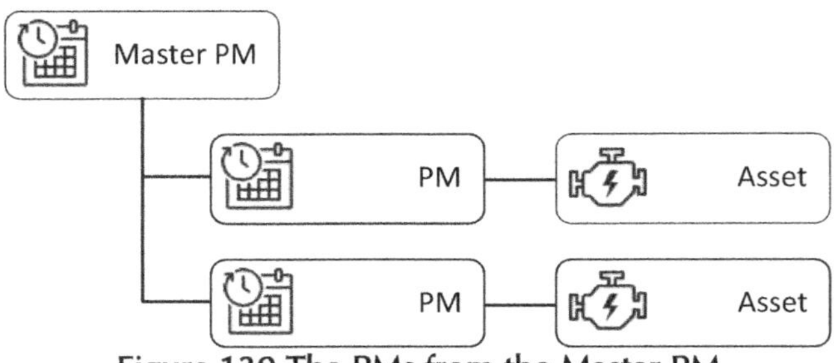

Figure 130 The PMs from the Master PM

In the template, you can specify, among others: the frequency (time- or meter-based), seasonal dates, a job plan (or a job plan sequence), and Work Order information, like Work Type, Status and Priority. You can even define the start date for the PMs (field **Next Due Date (Used During PM Create Only)**), but in the case of any existing cycles, the start date for individual machines may be different. Therefore, after creating PMs for the packing machines, you have to open each PM record and set the start date, and then change the status to *ACTIVE*.

A Master PM can not only create multiple PMs but also update the existing ones. The planner may want to shorten the maintenance frequency for packing machines based on the vendor's recommendation. Using the Master PM, it is enough to change the frequency there and use the action: **Update Associated PMs** to replicate this change to all the associated PMs.

Because the asset inventory changes constantly, new assets with the same rotating item might be purchased. To quickly create an associated PM for the newly acquired assets use the action **Create Associated PMs**. In the dialog, you will find new records without PMs.

Known Issues and Initial Changes

The first question I hear from the customers who see *Master PM* application is: where is the list of the just created PMs? Unfortunately, there is no such a tab, so you must build your own tab with a table (use *PM* relationship).

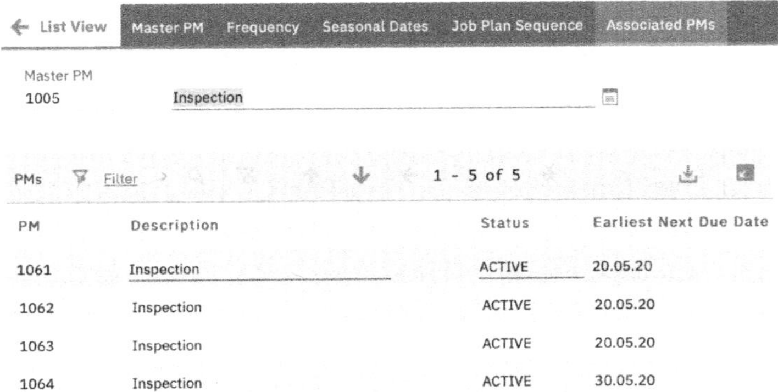

Figure 131 A Sample Associated PMs Tab

Module Purchasing

Supply Chain Processes

Purchasing applications in Maximo offer extensive support for ordering materials and services to support Work Management process. It is essential for the important or urgent jobs to have the required materials in place. The process can start with a self-service requisition, through Purchase Requisition and Purchase Order. It is possible to get the best offers from the market using Request for Quotation. Finally, invoices can be entered in Maximo to calculate the costs of materials and services.
Three-Way Match procedure is fully supported: the system checks the amount and value from Purchase Order, Receiving and Invoice, and will alert the user when there is an unexpected difference.
The full history of the purchase is maintained. One of my clients is always proud to present the purchase functionality of Maximo to his new business partners. At any moment, he is able to find when the parts for the Work Order were ordered, who requested them and how much was paid.

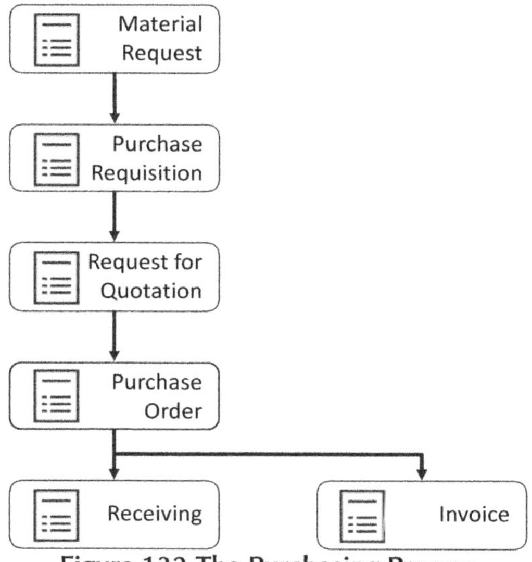

Figure 132 The Purchasing Process

Application Companies

It is very likely that the list of companies will come from ERP system. If this is true, then probably the whole application can be available solely in the read-only mode (define the access rights in *Security Groups* application, accordingly). You should also assign the companies to the correct Company Sets.
A financial system may contain thousands of companies which are not relevant for maintenance. Think about filtering out the source data to avoid the planner seeing the legal services company on the list.
As part of the Vendor Management process, the customer should use **Disqualified Vendor** checkbox to indicate the partners, which should not be considered in the future purchase transactions. Some customers may ask to add several additional fields to this screen to evaluate the performance of the vendors, like the average order value, or the average delivery time. Those values could be automatically calculated based on the Purchase Order information from Maximo.

Known Issues and Initial Changes

Many customers have problems with **Company Type** field. By default, it has only several values: *M—Manufacturer, V—Vendor, C—Courier*. But what about the cases when the company is both the vendor and manufacturer? You can either add more values to *COMPTYPE* domain or create a new tab with a table containing multiple entries for one company.

Application Purchase Requisitions

Purchase Requisition is a request to purchase materials or services. It is an internal document that is addressed to the purchasing department. There are two types of purchase requisitions:

- external, to purchase materials/services from the vendor,
- internal, to transfer materials between storerooms.

External PRs will be converted into Purchase Orders, but at this stage it is not required to enter the **Vendor** information yet. Besides, centralized purchasing can prevent users from choosing the vendor. Instead, Purchase Department will vet the potential suppliers and choose the best offer. Therefore, you may even remove **Vendor** field from the application to support this business process. Purchase Requisition must be then approved. In the next step, all the lines or only the selected ones can be copied to the Purchase Order. The functionality of picking Purchase Order lines from different Purchase Requisitions can optimize the purchase costs because you can buy more items cheaper.

An internal request must have **Internal** checkbox selected and the source storeroom must be chosen. Then, at the lines level, you will pick the materials to be transferred and assign target storeroom.

NOTE: All the storerooms (the source and target ones) must have the checkbox **Use in PO/PR** selected in ***Storerooms*** application. The internal PR must be approved and Purchase Order must be created from it. Once the PO will be approved, it will automatically create Inventory Usage *TRANSFER* transaction between the storerooms. The actual transfer must be completed by Storeroom Manager.

Figure 133 An Internal Purchase Requisition

Purchase Requisitions can be also generated from **Inventory** application, either manually, while the Work Orders are waiting for the materials, or automatically, while the current balance is below the Reorder Point.

NOTE: To generate purchase documents, you must first define which type should be generated and when. Go to ***Organizations*** application, action **Inventory Options/Reorder** and choose between PR and PO.

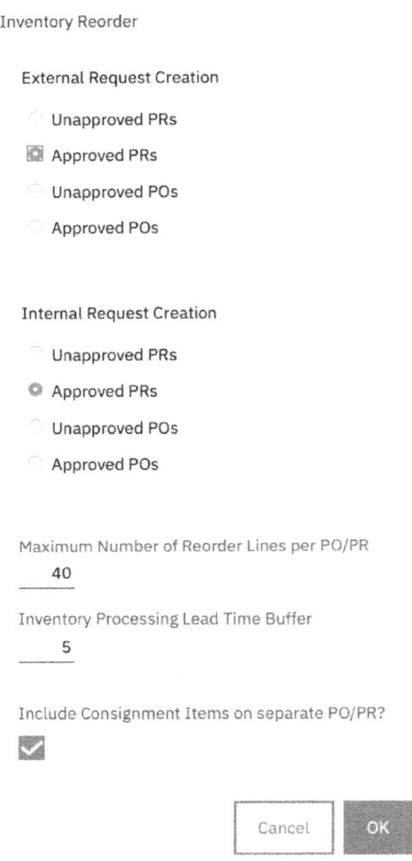

Figure 134 The Inventory Reorder

Known Issues and Initial Changes

To view the item's attributes on **Specifications** tab, the item classification must be defined for use with *PRLINE* object.

Applications Desktop Requisitions

Work materials can be requested also through material requests (desktop requisitions). There is a group of applications in *SELF SERVICE* module for creating Material Requests (MR):

- Create Requisition—is like a web-shop experience, with a wizard and cart to order items,

- View Requisition—to view the previous requisitions,
- View Templates—the user can save frequently ordered items in a template and order them from it,
- View Drafts—it is possible to save the request before submitting it to add more items later.

These applications are dedicated to the end-users with the Self-Service Requestor license only. In other words: the users who do not have an access to Work Orders and Purchase Requisitions, can still initiate an external purchase of items/services, or request the existing material from a storeroom with the use of Material Request.

The choice between issue and purchase request depends on the content of two fields on the material line in Material Request:

- Vendor
- Store Location

NOTE: Entering value in **Vendor** field will empty **Store Location** and vice versa.

If **Vendor** information is provided, then Maximo will generate Purchase Requisition and the process will continue with Purchase Order generation and material/services receiving.

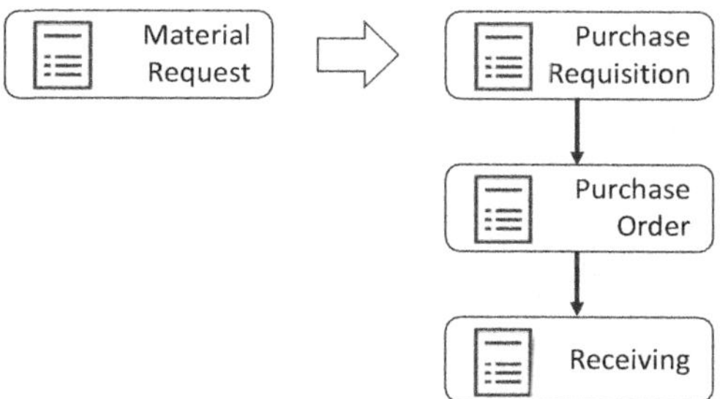

Figure 135 Purchase Requisition from Material Request

When you enter **Store Location**, Maximo will create Inventory Usage transaction to issue the ordered materials from the storeroom. Storeroom Manager has to complete the transaction.

Figure 136 Request Material from Storeroom

NOTE: Material Requests for a Work Order are by default not visible anywhere in *Work Order Tracking* application. Only the issued materials (on **Actuals** tab) will contain the information about the Material Request (field **Requisition**).

Application Request for Quotations

Before ordering materials, the buyer may want to use this application to ask the potential suppliers for their offers. The buyer will create a list of the items, choose the vendors and wait for their responses. They will present their terms for each of the items: prices and delivery times. Based on this information, the winner can be chosen to generate the Purchase Order.

Known Issues and Initial Changes

It may be required to prepare a custom report, with the customer's visual identification, layout and terms and conditions to print the request for a quotation.

Some customers may want to integrate this application with their existing electronic commerce platforms, like e-auctions.

Application Purchase Orders

Purchase Orders are official purchasing documents. They will be sent to the suppliers to purchase goods and/or services.
To avoid potential fraud through manipulation of the content of the POs, they are revision controlled. Any new version must be approved again.

Similarly to the Purchase Requisitions, Purchase Orders may also be external and internal. External Purchase Orders must always include **Vendor** information.

As mentioned in the chapter about Inventory Management, the consignment storeroom can generate Consignment Purchase Order to replenish the stock.

When the customer generates numerous POs and they often repeat themselves, you may propose introducing simple PO templates with all the vendors' details, lines, etc. to create one or more POs that will be frequently used, and keep them in *WAPPR* status. When an actual PO needs to be generated, the user will simply use **Duplicate Purchase Order** action to create a copy of the template, which will be then processed as usual.

Known Issues and Initial Changes

To view the item's attributes on **Specifications** tab, item classification must be defined for use with *POLINE* object.

It may be required to prepare a custom report, with the customer's visual identification, layout and terms and conditions to print the purchase orders.

Application Receiving

For the materials to appear in stock, they must be received. Also, the delivery of services must be confirmed. The application ***Receiving*** has two tabs for the above purposes. The user must choose the ordered items/services and confirm the quantity (or return or void the line).

In the *Item Master* and *Service Items* applications, it is possible to enter a value in the field **Receipt Tolerance %**. This parameter is important for the goods that are sold by quantity, e.g. by weight. It will be applied to the PO lines (can be changed there, too) and it will calculate the acceptable tolerance levels for:

- Items (quantity tolerance), or
- Service Items (amount tolerance).

Maximo will compare the received quantities with the PO line and the tolerance levels, and will warn the user if there is a mismatch between the values (i.e. received quantity is bigger than ordered quantity + tolerance).

Some materials and services may require an inspection on receipt, for example, of the condition of coatings or the completeness of the documentation. The **Inspection Status** of this line will be *WINSP* and **To Location** field will be the site's holding location. The user has to run **Change Inspection Status** action to approve the materials/services condition.

While receiving rotating items (**Inspection Status** is equal to *WASSET*), the action **Receive Rotating Items** must be executed. The user can click **Autonumber** button to generate the asset IDs and then serial numbers must be entered separately for each position. Additionally, the Item Assembly Structure can be applied to the assets to create the structure of components. NOTE: This dialog can be very problematic for customers, especially, if they are receiving tens or hundreds of assets. They may criticize the effort which is needed to create new assets and they can demand a more automated solution, like importing the assets from the spreadsheet.

Once an inspection and rotating items have been processed, the **Inspection Status** will change to *COMP*.
The status of the receipt is displayed in **Receipts** field. It will change from *NONE* to *PARTIAL* (when only some elements have been received) and, finally, to *COMPLETE* (when all the materials/services have been received).

There is a setting in ***Organizations*** application, option **Purchasing Options/PO Options/Enable Option to**

Automatically Close PO's on Invoice Approval which will close the Purchase Order automatically once the invoice for the PO was approved. You can also create an escalation to close the Purchase Order with **Receipts** field equal to *COMPLETE*. Purchase Orders with partially received items must be closed manually. Maximo will warn you that not all items have been invoiced, but you can close the PO anyway.

Returning Items/Services

Not always is buying materials or services unproblematic. You can receive some damaged parts or some pieces may be missing, or after several days you discover an item is incomplete. In any case, you should return the faulty part to the vendor. There is a button **Select Items for Return** (and **Select Services for Return** on **Service Receipts** tab). Having pressed it, enter the quantity of the items/services to be returned and save the transaction.

NOTE: using **Select Receipts to Void** button, you can undo a receipt made in error.

Known Issues and Initial Changes

Change the default filter on **List** view to exclude the completed deliveries.

Application Invoices

Before closing a Work Order, the outstanding external documents, like invoices for the services, should be processed. They will be ordered via Purchase Order, but not every invoice requires it; for example, you can register the invoices for the accommodation of the technicians or fuel purchases.

It is possible to define the tolerances for the users who process the invoices (application *Security Groups*, tab **Limits and Tolerances**).

NOTE: using this application, you can enter not only regular invoices, but also consignment invoices and credit/debit notes.

Invoice lines may not only relate to the purchased goods or services but also to the return of packages or the deposit paid. In that case, the number of the invoice line must be negative. Maximo does not allow to enter a negative price; instead, you will need to enter a negative quantity, e.g.

Line	*Description*	*Quantity*	*Price*	*Amount*	*Result*
10	Package Return	1	-500		**ERROR**
10	Package Return	-1	500	-500	**OK**

Sometimes, the invoice gets entered in error. There is an option to remove erroneous bookings. Run the action **Create Revers Invoice** and it will create a new invoice record that will reference the original one.

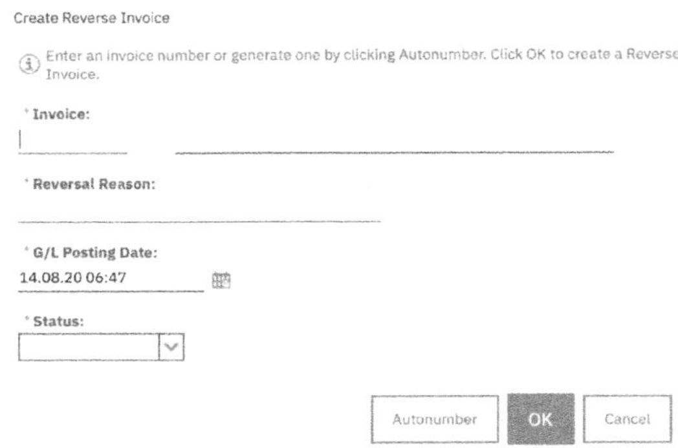

Figure 137 Create Reverse Invoice Action

For every invoice line there will be a corresponding one with an altered sign (see, the below example).

Line	Item	Description	PO	PO Site	Quantity	Unit Cost	Tax	Line Cost
1		> Container Return		>	-1,00	500,00	0,00	-500,00
2		> Transportation		>	7,00	150,00	0,00	1 050,00

Figure 138 An Original Invoice

Line	Item	Description	PO	PO Site	Quantity	Unit Cost	Tax	Line Cost
1		> Container Return		>	1,00	500,00	0,00	500,00
2		> Transportation		>	-7,00	150,00	0,00	-1 050,00

Figure 139 A Reverse Invoice

Known Issues and Initial Changes

The Work Order lookup on **Invoice Lines** tab has no information about the status of the WOs. You do not know which one was approved and you can pick the wrong one by mistake. You should either add a new column with the WO status or pre-filter this lookup to show the Work Orders only in *APPR, INPRG* or *COMP* status, or implement the both measures.

Application Terms and Conditions

In this application, you can save all the legal conditions and the sales ones: warranty, and payment and transport terms. They can be used in Purchase Requisitions, Purchase Orders, Request for Quotations and all the types of contracts.

NOTE: The terms and conditions are copied over between the applications; for example, they will be copied from Purchase Contract to Purchase Order.

Each condition has a code, and also short and long descriptions. When used in one of the above applications, it can be assigned a sequence number, too.

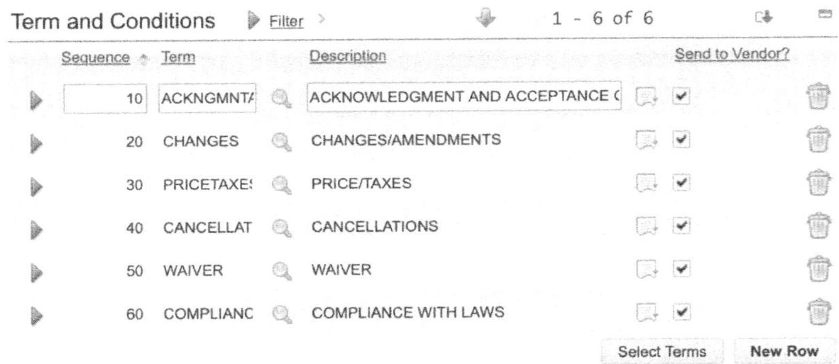

Figure 140 Sample Conditions

IBM, Maximo Asset Management 7.6.0 Preview Site, accessed 3 August 2019, retrieved from https://www.ibm.com/support/pages/maximo-asset-management-760-preview-site

This will allow you to create a ready to print/send document because you can include the long descriptions (with the necessary formatting) in the right order. You can select **Editable** checkbox to decide whether the conditions will be editable or not in the target application—this may prevent changing important paragraphs by the users.

NOTE: If you edit a condition in the target application, its code will be erased and only the description and long description will stay on the screen.

Another checkbox is **Default on PO**—this will simply copy all such conditions to new POs.

In ***Organizations*** application, the action **Purchasing Options/Contract Options** has a button **Associate Terms** to build a pre-defined set of conditions for each contract type, which will be applied to a new contract record.

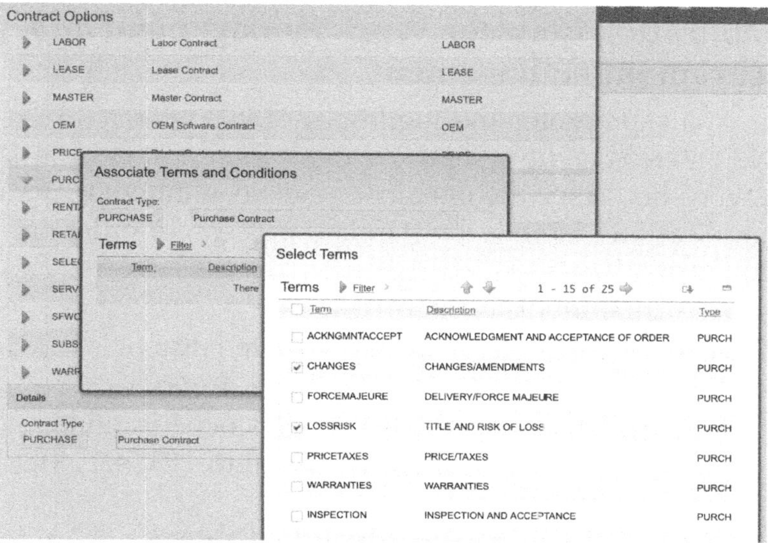

Figure 141 Contract Options

IBM, Maximo Asset Management 7.6.0 Preview Site, accessed 3 August 2019, retrieved from https://www.ibm.com/support/pages/maximo-asset-management-760-preview-site

The conditions can be provided and maintained by legal, maintenance and purchasing departments.

You can also use Terms for other purposes, for example, to populate the Job Task **Description** and **Long Description** from a template. This is particularly useful when the customer has a list of predefined tasks which can be used in multiple Job Plans and it is not always worth to duplicate the plan.
All you need to do is to populate **Type** field for terms with a predefined value, e.g. *JOBPLAN* (you can also add a domain with other values for **Type** field). Next, create a crossover domain to copy the **Description** and **Long Description** fields to the Job task record. Finally, you will add a new field to ***Job Plans*** application with the above domain, which will be used to select the Terms.

Collaboration between Work Management and Procurement Management

So far, I have presented the subprocesses that operate in individual areas of the system.

Now, you should see the interaction between different modules and applications. Here is the standard process for ordering materials for a Work Order:

- A Work Order is created;
- Materials are entered on **Plans/Materials** tab;
- The user changes the WO Status to *APPR;*
- Maximo checks if there is enough stock (if something is missing, the WO Status will change to *WMATL*, Material Status will be *NONE*);
- The user should run **Reorder/Reorder Items** action in ***Inventory*** application to create the Purchase Requisition;
- A standard purchasing process takes place:
    - The user changes Purchase Requisition status to *APPR*;
    - The user creates Purchase Order;
    - The user changes Purchase Order status to *APPR*;
    - The user receives materials in ***Receiving*** application and changes the receipt status to *COMPLETE*;
    - The user enters the invoice for the above Purchase Order;
    - The user approves the above invoice;
- The user issues the material to the Work Order in ***Inventory Usage*** application, status: *COMPLETE*;
- Maximo changes the WO status to *APPR* again, Material Status will be *COMP* (NOTE: When only some materials are available, the status changes to *PARTIAL*);
- The user can continue working with the Work Order and change the status to *INPRG*.

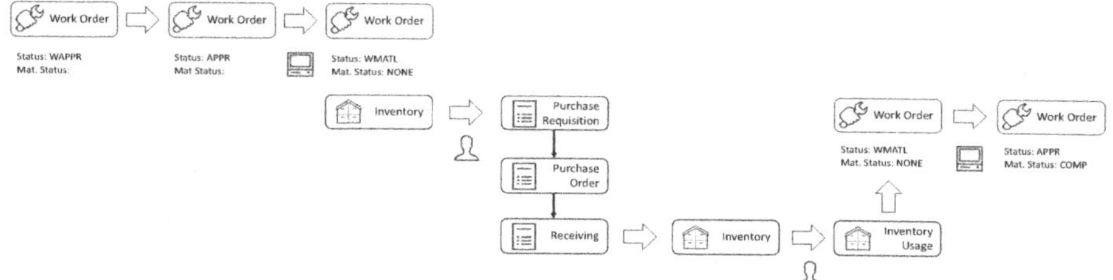

Figure 142 A Material Ordering for a **Work Order**

The above diagram shows the flow of goods through the storeroom, but materials for the order execution can also be acquired through the so called direct issue. The materials for the direct issue will be:

- in real life: purchased and delivered directly to the place of work, without going through the storeroom,
- in Maximo: issued immediately to an asset/location/work order upon receipt.

To define an item for the direct issue you will need:

- in MR: to leave the **Store Location** empty,
- in WO: to select **Direct Issue** checkbox,
- in PR/PO: to select **Issue on Receipt** checkbox.

The process to order materials for the direct issue has the following steps:

- A Work Order is created;
- Materials are entered on **Plans/Materials** tab;
- The user changes the WO Status to *APPR*;
- If there is an item marked as **Direct Issue**, Maximo changes the status of the Work Order to *WMATL*;
- The user should run **Reorder/Reorder Direct Issue Items and Services** action in *Inventory* application to create the Purchase Requisition;
- A standard purchasing process takes place:
    - The user changes Purchase Requisition status to *APPR*;
    - The user creates Purchase Order;

- The user changes Purchase Order status to *APPR*;
- The user receives materials in ***Receiving*** application and changes the receipt status to *COMPLETE*;

- The materials are automatically issued to the Work Order and the WO status changes to *APPR*;
- The user can continue working with the Work Order and change the status to *INPRG*.

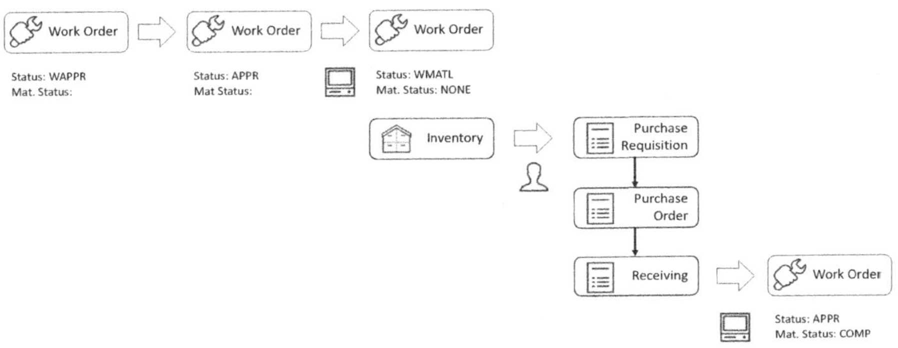

Figure 143 Material Ordering with Direct Issue

The interaction between Work Management and Purchasing Management is visible in this section on *Work Order Tracking* application.

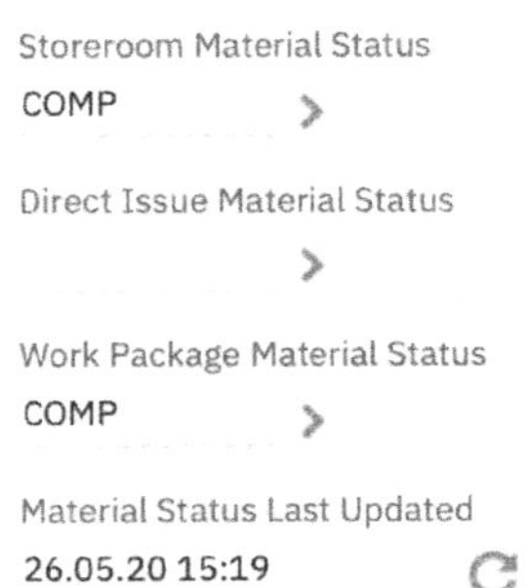

Figure 144 WO Material Status

To update the Material Status automatically you must enable the cron task *WOMaterialStatusUpdateCronTask*.

To order external services, the flow will be almost the same as for the materials:

- A Work Order is created;
- The services are entered on Plans/Services tab;
- The user changes the WO Status to *APPR*;
- The user should run **Reorder/Reorder Direct Issue Itms/Svcs** action in ***Inventory*** application to create the Purchase Requisition;
- A standard purchasing process takes place:
    - The user changes Purchase Requisition status to *APPR*;
    - The user creates Purchase Order;
    - The user changes Purchase Order status to *APPR*;
    - The user receives the services in ***Receiving*** application and changes the receipt status to *COMPLETE*;
    - The user enters the invoice for the above Purchase Order;
    - The user approves the above invoice—services costs will be visible on the Work Order;
- The user can continue working with the Work Order and change the status to *INPRG*.

NOTE: The above scenarios do not exhaust all the options for purchasing materials/services. Companies may buy not only spare parts but also printer paper, fans or gloves. I have also skipped the invoices to simplify the flow. Please take some time and test your own use cases in Maximo.

Integration with Financial Software

As Inventory and Purchasing modules exist at the interface of maintenance matters and the financial ones, these are the most likely integration points between Maximo and ERP system. The level of integration depends on the current customer processes. For example, the customer wants to have the whole purchasing module only in ERP.

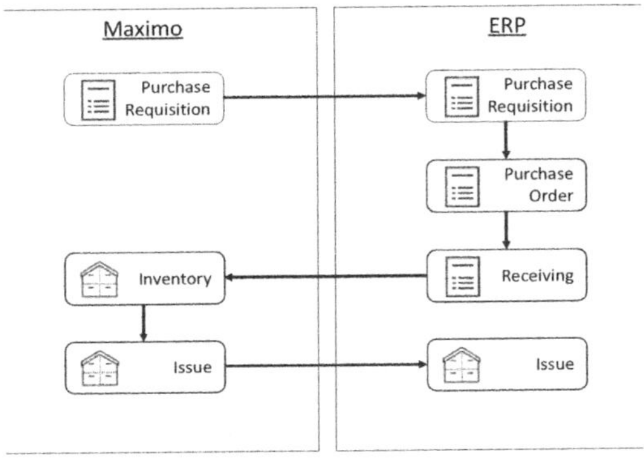

Figure 145 Maximo-ERP Integration 1

Maximo will only initiate the process with the PR and receive the materials. All the issue transaction must be reported back to ERP system to decrease the balance.

But a very common scenario occurs when ERP is 'issuing' the whole delivery after receiving (the transaction is written in the books), and from this moment on, ERP does not know where these materials will be used:

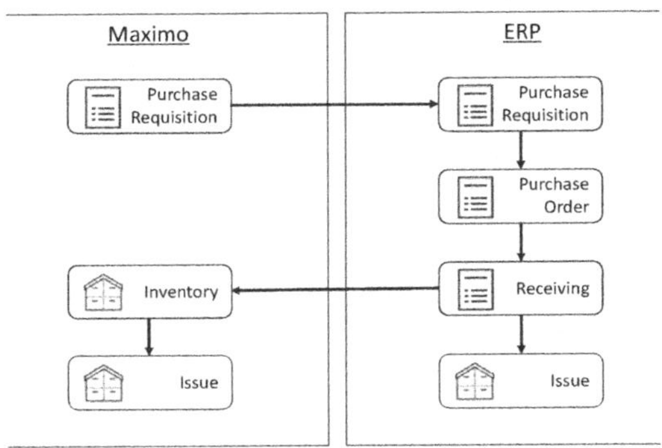

Figure 146 Maximo-ERP Integration 2

In this scenario, Maximo will receive the information about the purchased materials and issue them to the Work Orders. In the financial system, issuing is a purely accounting procedure.

You can also have any other variation of the above. For example, PR and PO can be both created in Maximo.

Some customers decide to use only Maximo for inventory and purchasing management (sometimes, also to buy pens, paper and other goods). In that case, you might only send a summary of the transactions to ERP:

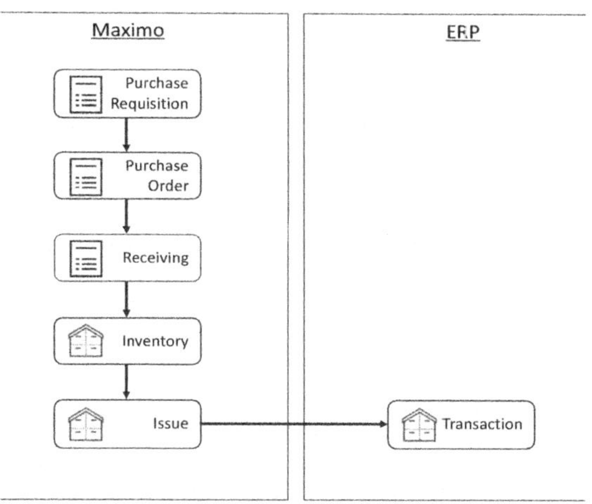

Figure 147 Maximo-ERP Integration 3

Please discuss in detail the role of each system: ERP, Maximo, and other systems, like contract management. Design clear flows of information between the systems. Pay special attention to reservations. If inventory is shared between ERP and Maximo, you will need to exchange the information not only about balances and issues but also about reservations, which complicates the whole picture.
This integration can significantly impact your timeline and increase the degree of system complexity.

Module Security

Application Security Groups

Known Issues and Initial Changes

When logging into Maximo as *maxadmin* for the first time, you will not have an access to every application and option in the system. You should go to ***Security Groups*** application and manually grant the access for *maxadmin* group to every application and every option in it (this does not apply to **Hide portlet** option in portlet applications because for *maxadmin* they should be un-checked). The same can be done in seconds using the SQL command below:

> *DB2 insert into applicationauth (app, groupname, optionname, applicationauthid) select app, 'MAXADMIN', optionname, next value for applicationauthseq from sigoption s where optionname != 'NOPORTLET' and not exists (select * from applicationauth a where a.app = s.app and a.optionname = s.optionname and a.groupname = 'MAXADMIN')*

While creating security groups, please do not forget that the security profile should correspond with the license type this group will use. This is especially important for *Limited* and *Express Use Users* licenses. Do not give the security group more access than defined by the license agreement. For example, *Limited Use Users* can access only three Maximo modules and the security group must reflect this limitation.

Security Profiles

To simplify management and increase readability of security profiles, I have developed a simple method to define security groups. It is based on defining several types of dependent groups:

- geographical,
- functional,

- report access,
- storeroom access,
- add-ons.

You can add your own types if necessary.

Let me explain this concept with the example presented below.

Sites:
- Baltimore,
- Dallas,
- Houston.

Roles:
- Planner—creates Job Plans and Preventive Maintenance schedules;
- Worker—executes Work Orders;
- Storeroom manager—issues materials from the storeroom;
- Manager—manages labor, checks the status of Work Orders.

Storerooms:
- Baltimore-Central,
- Baltimore-Small,
- Dallas,
- Houston.

The following reports are available:
- 2000-Inventory Balance in *Inventory* application,
- 2010-Work Order Details in *Work Order Tracking* application,
- 2011-Work Order Costs in *Work Order Tracking* application (contains sensitive financial information, so only managers should view it).

And there are the users:

- John, working in Dallas as a storeroom manager;
- Dave, working in Baltimore as a storeroom manager for Baltimore-Small;
- Steve, working in Baltimore as a worker and a storeroom manager for Baltimore-Central;
- Frank, working in Dallas as a manager;
- Peter, working as a country manager;
- Tom, working in Houston as a planner.

The idea of geographical groups is based on giving an access only to a specific site; therefore, we will create one group for each site:

- BALTIMORE,
- DALLAS,
- HOUSTON.

Standard users will be assigned to one group. Someone at a higher level in the hierarchy will be granted an access to multiple sites, i.e. they will be assigned to multiple geographical groups.

In my concept, functional groups give an access only to a specific application or applications; there is no site authorization. The role profile is built by combining multiple functional groups. In our example, there are the following Security Groups:

- WO-EDIT— an edit access to ***Work Order Tracking*** application,
- WO-READ— a read-only access to ***Work Order Tracking*** application,
- JP-EDIT— an edit access to ***Job Plans*** application,
- PM-EDIT— an edit access to ***Preventive Maintenance*** application,
- STORE— an edit access to the ***Inventory*** and ***Inventory Usage*** applications,

- LAB-EDIT— an edit access to ***Labor*** application; you should also authorize this group to edit labor (**Labor** tab in ***Security Groups*** application).

Report groups determine the access to specific reports, and we have the following groups:

- REP-INV-BAL—2000-Inventory Balance report in ***Inventory*** application,
- REP-WO-DET—2010-Work Order Details report in ***Work Order Tracking*** application,
- REP-WO-COST—2011-Work Order Costs report in ***Work Order Tracking*** application.

Finally, we need separate groups with storeroom authorization (**Storerooms** tab in ***Security Groups*** application):

- STR-B-CENTRAL—Baltimore Central storeroom,
- STR-B-SMALL—Baltimore Small storeroom,
- STR-DALLAS—Dallas storeroom,
- STR-HOUSTON—Houston storeroom.

Add-ons are meant to give to the selected users an extra access to certain application options, for example, to export data or edit historical work orders.

Now we are ready to build the security profiles for our users employing the 'LEGO blocks':

- John:
    - DALLAS,
    - STORE,
    - STR-DALLAS,
    - REP-INV-BAL.
- Dave:
    - BALTIMORE,
    - STORE,
    - STR-B-SMALL,
    - REP-INV-BAL.

- Steve:
    - BALTIMORE,
    - WO-EDIT,
    - REP-WO-DET,
    - REP-INV-BAL,
    - STORE,
    - STR-B-CENTRAL.
- Frank:
    - DALLAS,
    - LAB-EDIT,
    - WO-READ,
    - REP-WO-COST.
- Peter:
    - BALTIMORE,
    - DALLAS,
    - HOUSTON,
    - WO-READ,
    - REP-WO-COST.
- Tom:
    - HOUSTON,
    - JP-EDIT,
    - PM-EDIT.

As you can see, you can easily read profiles from the list of the groups assigned to specific users. For example, in Peter's case, we know that he has an access to all the sites and he can read Work Orders and run the cost report. This way, even a person without an IT background can manage the access rights. You can create a simple report for managers, who will be able to check if their subordinates have the correct access rights. This setup can be also used to create requests for the access to Maximo. The manager will simply mark what is needed for a specific person, and the user administrator will translate it in proper Security Groups. This request could look like this:

The access to sites (mark at least one row):
[ ] BALTIMORE
[ ] DALLAS
[ ] HOUSTON

The access to information (mark at least one row):
[ ] WO-EDIT or [ ] WO-READ
[ ] JP-EDIT
[ ] PM-EDIT
[ ] STORE
[ ] LAB-EDIT

The access to storerooms (mark at least one row, requires STORE):
[ ] STR-B-CENTRAL
[ ] STR-B-SMALL
[ ] STR-DALLAS
[ ] STR-HOUSTON

The access to reports (can be none):
[ ] REP-INV-BAL (requires STORE)
[ ] REP-WO-DET (requires either WO-READ or WO-EDIT)
[ ] REP-WO-COST (requires either WO-READ or WO-EDIT)

Please remember that this is just an example. You can change it according to your needs.

While defining the functional groups, please do not forget to authorize the groups to the actions related to the status change. It is not enough to give a permission for **Change Status** only—you should also give an access to (for example): **Approve**, **Cancel approve,** etc.

The Security Group that will be responsible for moving assets must have an access to GL components defined because it generates financial transactions in the background.

Functional groups obviously include also system administrators with *maxadmin* privileges. But for larger organizations, I suggest introducing two additional groups:

- user administrator,
- business data administrator.

The purpose of having a separate user administrator role is to split duties between configuring and monitoring the performance of the system and managing the users. The user administrator, in my concept, should have an access only to ***Users*** application with the option to add, deactivate, un-lock users and change their security group memberships. Please do not forget to use **Authorize Group Assignment** option to give the appropriate privileges to the user administrator; usually, with this role one should not be able to assign anyone to *maxadmin* group.
This role will not be needed in Maximo if the customer decides to use LDAP for user management. In that case, only detailed security group definitions will be kept in Maximo (and they must have the same IDs as the ones in LDAP). User records and the assignment of users to security groups will all happen on LDAP side. User management will be centralized for all the systems.

The business data administrator role is another attempt to reduce the load on the system administrator. It is also about encouraging business users to take responsibility for the system. The idea is that there will be one person or more in business departments who will manage business data, i.e. they will have an edit access to such configuration applications as ***SLA***, ***Failure Codes***, and ***Classifications***. You can also give this role an access to ***Domains*** application but only to the selected records, for example, only **QUALTYPE, ASSETTYPE** (this will require defining data restrictions for this group). All the other users will only use the data prepared by business data administrators. Of course, it is assumed that people assigned to this group will be trained to edit the information in these applications.

Ensure that the option **Can log In During Admin Mode** for ***Start Center*** application has not been granted for the groups other than system administrators. Users should not be able to work in Admin Mode because the system functionality at this moment is limited.

Data Restrictions

You have already seen some examples of data restrictions in the book. Restrictions define which records (or even fields) a specific group (or all users) can see or edit. Below are a few examples of restrictions I use in my projects:

Cost Management records are by default editable in *CLOSED* status. To fix this create a new condition:

:fcstatus = 'CLOSED'

Use the above condition in a restriction which will make the record read-only:
Object: *FINCNTRL*
Application: *FINCNTRL*
Type: *READONLY*

When you create a new Work Order manually, you can still choose the Work Type *PM* which should be reserved for planned work only. To hide unnecessary Work Types, create new condition:

:worktype in ('CM', 'EM')

And new restriction:
Object: *WORKTYPE*
Application: *WOTRACK*
Type: *QUALIFIED*

From now on you can only create corrective and emergency Work Orders.

Restrictions can be also applied to attributes, for example, this restriction changes the edit mode of a classification attribute to read-only when the Service Request is resolved:
Object: *TICKETSPEC*
Attribute: *ALNVALUE*
Application: *SR*
Type: *READONLY*
Condition: *:classstructureid = (select classstructureid from classstructure where classificationid = 'FLEET') and :class = 'SR' and :assetattrid = 'BUS' and exists (select 1 from ticket where status = 'RESOLVED' and ticketuid = :refobjectid)*

You can extend my groups model (geographical, functional, etc.) by adding new groups with data restrictions for example with an access to records with specific classification only. This will give you additional flexibility while defining security profiles for users.
NOTE: Please observe how the below restrictions work because this may be confusing:

- QUALIFIED— SHOW ONLY records for which the condition is met,
- HIDDEN—HIDE the records for which the condition is met.

Saved Queries

Run the below query to find the security groups which can log in in Admin Mode.

groupname in (select groupname from applicationauth where optionname = 'ADMINMODELOGIN')

Application Login Tracking

This application does not exist in Maximo but you should create one after you **Enable Login Tracking** in **Security Controls** dialog.

Log-in tracking tracks all log-in attempts and is usually required by IT security policies. A new application should be based on **LOGINTRACKING** table.

NOTE: The information stored in this table may not be 100% accurate because users may lose the connection with the server but this it is still the best source of information for security analysis.

NOTE: There is a standard dialog available in ***Users*** application (action **Manage Sessions**, tab **Login Tracking**) which can display the same information but a separate application is more easily accessible and allows to save queries (see, below).

Saved Queries

Having login tracking enabled, we are able to introduce some interesting queries.

The list of all the e-Signature events:

app = 'CONFIGUR'

The last successful and failed log-in attempts of the user. This query can be used on the start center in a portlet. Users can control unauthorized log-ins using their credentials.

logintrackingid = (select logintrackingid from logintracking where userid = :USER and upper(attemptresult) = 'FAILED' and attemptdate = (select max(attemptdate) from logintracking where userid = :USER and upper(attemptresult) = 'FAILED')) or logintrackingid = (select logintrackingid from logintracking where userid = :USER and upper(attemptresult) = 'LOGIN' and attemptdate = (select max(attemptdate) from logintracking where userid = :USER and upper(attemptresult) = 'LOGIN' and attemptdate < (select max(attemptdate) from logintracking where userid = :USER and upper(attemptresult) = 'LOGIN')))

Application Users

Known Issues and Initial Changes

Make **Default Insert Site** field mandatory because otherwise, the user will not be able to enter any record. Value for this field should be initially provided. If the user has an access to multiple sites, they could change it in the **Profile** window.

User settings are evaluated only after logging in. That applies to *maxadmin*, too. If you change *maxadmin's* time zone or locale, it will be used in the system only after the server restarts. This will affect all the mechanisms that use *maxadmin* account: escalations, cron tasks and notifications.

Users application has a nice feature: login IDs and users' IDs are separate fields, which allows for changing the login name without affecting the user's record. For example, the security policy in the company may change, and instead of numerical codes, email addresses may be used as logins.

While creating or changing the password for a user, you will see that the checkbox **E-mail Password to User** is selected and read-only. And, if your system is not yet configured to send the emails or the user does not have their email address, you will not be able to save the user's record because Maximo will try to email the password. Unfortunately, you cannot set the checkbox **E-mail Password to User** to be empty; the only available solution is to make it editable. You can do it in **Security Controls** window, go to **Automatic Password Generation** section, and change **Password Generation Display** to **Allow Generated Password to Be Displayed On Screen**. Then, in **Set Password** window, you will be able to deselect **E-mail Password to User** checkbox and save the password without emailing it.

Debugging User Permissions

Security Profile tab should be your first stop to verify users' permissions when they have no access to a specific site or application, or cannot perform an action. This includes Conditional UI not working for a user. **Security Profile** offers a comprehensive view of all the authorized applications, sites, restrictions, and limits.

Passwords

No, this is not another instruction how to create good passwords but some suggestions how to keep the system secure. The first one is to change the default passwords for all the system logins (*maxadmin, mxintadm, maxreg*) right after the installation.
The second one is to keep the passwords different in the production and test environments–especially, for system accounts. This can prevent potential issues, like importing test data into a production system.
NOTE: The passwords should be updated after each environment refresh (i.e. when production data are copied to a test server).

License Types

It is important that the customer checks their license compliance. You can use the field **Type** in *Users* application for that purpose. Out-of-the-box, it does nothing. All the users will be assigned *TYPE 1* value. You can change the domain *USERTYPE* and either change the descriptions of the existing values *TYPE 1, TYPE 2* or create your own values with custom IDs and names. You should at least define the values for the *Authorized, Limited Use, Express Use* and *Self-Service Requestor* licenses (you can extend this model to include licenses for add-ons, industry solutions or mobile applications). Then the customer can assign the appropriate license type to each user.

NOTE: Please remember to define the default value for this field in *Users* application.
After that, the existing report *User Type* or custom report can be run to verify the number of licenses used.
NOTE: Only active users should be included in the reports.

Block non-active users

Because the number of the owned Maximo licenses is usually limited, it is a good idea to deactivate non-active users (for example, those not active during the last three months). To do this, you have to create an escalation for **MAXUSER** table with the following condition (it requires log-in tracking to be enabled):

> *DB2 status = 'ACTIVE' and sysuser = 0 and userid in (select userid from logintracking where attemptresult = 'LOGIN' group by userid having days((select current timestamp from sysibm.sysdummy1)) - days(max(attemptdate)) > 90)*

This should trigger an action that will change the user status to *INACTIVE*.

Protect system

I have earlier described the situation when the PM generation might be affected because of *maxadmin* login being blocked. When one of the system logins is blocked, this could be a sign that someone has tried to hack the system and entered a wrong password too many times. To prevent that, create an escalation which will inform the designated person that the system login is blocked:

Applies to: *MAXUSER*
Condition: *userid = 'MAXADMIN' and status = 'BLOCKED'*

The escalation point can send a notification that the user has been blocked or restore the *ACTIVE* status automatically. And of course, you can do the same to protect other logins.

Saved Queries

Below are a few useful queries.

Users without a Security Group—something must be definitely wrong.

userid not in (select userid from group user)

Blocked users—this number must be minimal or zero, and this should be reviewed because when the user's account is blocked and the user is not complaining about it, it may be a candidate to be deactivated and his license granted to someone else.

status = 'BLOCKED'

Users with the same display name (potential duplicates).

status = 'ACTIVE' and (personid in (select personid from person where displayname in (select displayname from person group by displayname having count(*) > 1)))

Module Self Service

Application Create Service Request

Known Issues and Initial Changes

By default, the field **Site** is not populated in Service Request. That means someone has to enter this information later. I usually add a crossover domain to the field **Reported By** and copy the content of **Default Insert Site** field from **MAXUSER** table.

This screen usually requires a small configuration. First, the **Summary** and **Description** fields must be configured as mandatory because otherwise, someone can submit an empty request.

If it is required to define the affected asset but the customer is not using the User/Custodian feature, then every time the user opens the Assets dialog, it will be empty. This is because the list of assets is pre-filtered to include only the assets that are associated with the current user. To change it, you must modify the default value for the field **ASSETFILTERBY** in **SR** table to *!ALL!*.

Request Information from Users

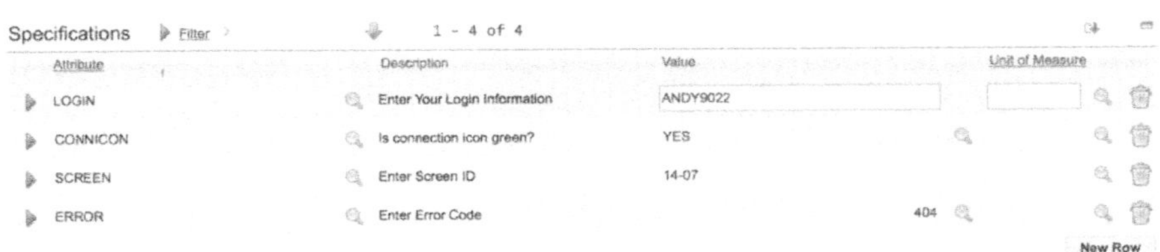

Specifications
Filter
1 - 4 of 4
Attribute
Description
Value
Unit of Measure
LOGIN
Enter Your Login Information
ANDY9022
CONNICON
Is connection icon green?
YES
SCREEN
Enter Screen ID
14-07
ERROR
Enter Error Code
404
New Row

Figure 148 Sample Attributes in Create Service Request

While reporting the failure of a specific machine, the engineer might need some specific information to find the root cause. A request for information can be easily represented in **Create**

Service Request application with the use of classifications. You will need to discuss with engineers what the cases are and when they need specific information, and then create the classifications for them. For each classification, you will then define a set of attributes = the questions that need to be provided. Use domains whenever possible in order to minimize the number of typing errors. Finally, click **Use With Object** icon and mark each of the attributes as **Mandatory** in **Create Service Request** application; also, make the classification field required. Now, the users will be forced to choose the classification and then to answer all the questions. This way, the quality of data will increase, and the time needed to determine the causes of a failure will be shorter.

Application View Service Requests

By default, ***View Service Requests*** application was designed for the users with a *Self-Service Requestor* license. Typically, it is used by the operators from production departments, who can submit problems with the machines they use. However, there are situations when, for example, the production site manager wants to have an access to ALL the requests submitted by his people. This exceeds the scope of the *Self-Service Requestor* license but the customer may decide to buy authorized licenses for site managers so they could see the other Service Requests. In that case, you can modify the default query for ***View Service Requests*** application in **MAXAPPS** table to work with both the use cases:

> *(reportedby in (select personid from maxuser where userid=:user and type = 'READ')) or (siteid = (select defsite from maxuser where userid =:user and type = 'AUTH'))*

The first part of the query allows the requestor to view only their records (and a *Self-Service Requestor* license is enough for that). The second one gives the production site manager an insight into all the requests from their site but, of course, an appropriate license is necessary (see, License Types).

Module Service Level

Application Service Level Agreements

SLA is a tool to manage suppliers but also monitor the maintenance department's performance against its obligations. That means you should define two types of SLAs: *CUSTOMER* and *VENDOR*. The first one should be applied to Service Requests and the second one to the Work Orders assigned to external companies. While defining commitments, at least the *RESOLUTION* type should be used. When the SLA is applied to Service Requests and/or Work Orders, it will automatically set the target dates (*RESPONSE* commitment sets **Target Start** while *RESOLUTION* sets **Target Finish** date). This is the foundation for establishing the monitoring of SLA. Usually, it includes defining the queries by comparing the current date and target date. They can be used on start centers to show the records that are close to the deadline or have reached target dates. The first option is better because it gives the manager some time to react and prevent problems. Another option is to create escalations which will send notifications that half the time has been reached, three-quarters of the time have been reached, and finally, that the SLA time has been breached. The best practice for SLAs says that the first reminders should be sent at least to the responsible person and the last one should also go to their manager.

An important part of SLA is ranking. It is used to determine which agreement should be applied in case there are multiple matching SLAs. In such a situation, Maximo will take the SLA with the lowest number. This is a method to define the desired processing path and conditions that are more important, for example:

Ranking 1: Work Type = *EM*
Ranking 2: Work Type = *CM*

Module System Configuration

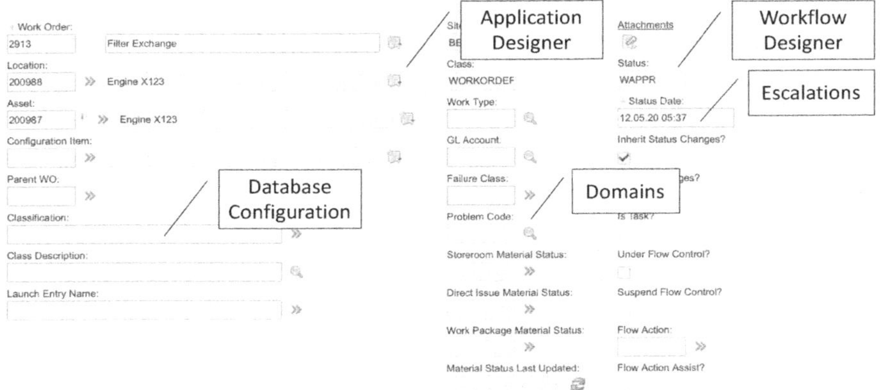

Figure 149 Configuration Options

When you open any Maximo application, there appears a screen with some fields. As a consultant, you can change the screen layout: move, delete or add fields—this can be done in *Application Designer* application. If you need to change the length of the existing field or add a new one, you will use *Database Configuration* application. Attaching a menu to a field is a task of *Domains* application and *Database Configuration*. You can control who can change the status and when, using the workflows defined in *Workflow Designer* application. Important dates can be monitored by SQL code from *Escalations* application and any delays can be notified by e-mail using the templates from *Communication Templates* application.
This is just a fragment of all the Maximo capabilities as there are also other applications which can help you to deliver the solution tailored to the customer's needs.

The configuration of Maximo requires experience. You can shorten the time to get it by reading articles on the Internet and analyzing the existing Maximo mechanisms or learning from your peers. A very good source of information are reports. You can analyze queries from reports to better understand the data structures and their relationships.

Always document your changes. It may sound silly but I have seen a lot of projects when this was forgotten and after a few months or even weeks, nobody was able to recall who and when had made it, and most importantly, why it had been implemented.
Fortunately, most of the configuration objects contain Long Descriptions: Escalations, Communication Templates, Actions, Roles, Cron Tasks, Workflows, Email Listener, Automation Script… Use a Long Description to provide some information about the purpose of the object, and who and when has created it. Add the information about the relations to other objects, pre-requisites, reference to RFC or requirement. Maintaining such an installation will be much easier. Do not forget to document Java code, reports and changes in XML files, like **LIBRARY.XML**.

Application System Properties

Below are a few examples of the system properties that are usually changed. The actual list can be longer.

- SMTP server related properties to send email notifications:
    - mail.smtp.host,
    - mail.smtp.user,
    - mail.smtp.password,
    - mail.smtp.ssl.enable.
- Attachments properties to define which file types are allowed and how big they can be:
    - mxe.doclink.doctypes.allowedFileExtensions,
    - mxe.doclink.maxfilesize.
- Performance related property:
    - mxe.db.fetchResultStopLimit—to limit the number of records returned. Please note that if this setting has a low value, it can virtually lock Migration Manager or affect statistical reports.
- System sessions:

    - mxe.webclient.maxuisession—defines the maximum number of sessions allowed on the server,
    - mxe.enableConcurrentCheck—equal to *1* allows only one session per user, value *0* means that multiple sessions are allowed.
- Layout (version 7.6):
    - mxe.webclient.tabBreadCrumbs—in version 7.6 changing the value to 0 will make the tabs visible while on **List** tab,
    - mxe.webclient.skin—*iot18* is 7.6.1 layout, *tivoli13* is 7.6 layout, *tivoli09* is 7.5 layout,
    - mxe.webclient.systemNavBar—shows/hides the navigation bar (*1/0*),
    - mxe.webclient.verticalLabels—value *1* shows the labels above the field, *0* – on the left of the field.

Observe **Live Refresh?** flag of the property. If it is not set, Maximo server must be restarted to change this.

Have you noticed **New Row** button in the application? With this button you can add missing properties or create your own ones; for example, you can define here a URL to the external system instead of hardcoding it in your scripts, or define a threshold for KPI definitions.

Application Domains

This is one of the simplest features in the system: providing dictionary values for the fields. Domains should be widely used because they ensure data integrity and standardize input; only the data from the list can be entered. This applies not only to alphanumeric domains but also to numeric domains and numeric range domains—you do not need to write any validation classes as domains will do this work. Numeric domains can contain integer values (priority *1, 2, 3*...) or decimal values (fuel tank fill: *0.25, 0.50, 0.75, 1.00*). Numeric range domain *0* to *8* can be used to report working hours (a worker can report the maximum of *8* hours per shift).

There is a special domain type: crossover domains. People are often confused about how they work. They should be attached to the field that triggers an action, not to the field that is the target of the action.

NOTE: Multiple crossover domains are already defined in the system to copy information between different applications. Before creating your own domain, please check—maybe you could extend the existing one by adding a new line with the source and target fields. For example, if you need to copy more information from an asset into a Work Order, use *ASSET2WO* crossover domain and add your fields. The crossover domains cannot be used for date fields.

Table domains add a lookup functionality to the fields. For example, you may have cloned ***Work Order Tracking*** application to prepare a special application for instrument calibration. You may then create a new table domain and link it to **Asset** field to limit the number of the assets displayed in the dialog only to those with the classification equal to *M&TE*. You will use **List Where Clause** in table domain to define this condition.

Domains are re-usable; for example, a domain with *Yes/No* values can be used in any place where only two values are allowed.

And you should think about domains also in terms of potential integration points. In larger implementations, some domain values may be imported from another system, such as, SCADA or ERP.

Known Issues and Initial Changes

Keys in domains are not multi-language enabled, only the description can be provided in different languages. Therefore, some customers decide to have the keys as either English words (assuming this is the official language in the whole company) or as numbers: *1—high priority*, *2—medium priority*, etc. In the latter case, you will only add the value description in the local language.

Several domains require your action during the initial setup because they are either empty or standard content may not be applicable:

- DOWNCODE (downtime codes),
- EMAILTYPE,
- PHONETYPE,
- QUALTYPE,
- USERTYPE (license types).

You will probably also edit status domains, such as, **SRSTATUS, WOSTATUS, POSTATUS** and **FCSTATUS,** and add new statuses required by the customer's processes.

You can define conditions for one or more domain values which can hide/unhide them. If your condition refers to some variables in an application, e.g. *:status = 'COMP'*, you must always enter a value in **Object Name** field; otherwise, Maximo will not know how the variable should be evaluated.

Application Communication Templates

Known Issues and Initial Changes

Predefined email communication means that the message will have a standard content but also a logo, social media icons and legal disclaimers, which are part of the customer's visual identification. If you want to include logos and other graphical elements in the templates, then they should either be saved on the application server or available as links (or use the below trick).

Notifications are sent in the *maxadmin* context, which means that all the numbers/dates are formatted according to these account settings and the time is always presented in *maxadmin's* time zone. If the system is used across multiples time zones, users might get confused about the dates. To avoid this, set the *maxadmin's* time zone to *GMT* or *EST*, and add in all the templates information about it, e.g. *:reportdate GMT.*

HTML format has been available in Communication Templates for years, but I can still see most of the notifications in plain text and even the record URL is not inserted.
If you do not know HTML, ask someone for help, as applying even some basic tags can change the appearance of the message dramatically. Please compare the two messages below:

A plain text version:

New Work Order 1023 was entered
Description please change the valve #16-leak
Asset 1345 Compressor
Location 1509 Room #121

The same text with some formatting:

New Work Order Notification

Work Order	1032	please change the valve #16-leak
Asset	1345	Compressor
Location	1509	Room #121

Click here to open the WO

Your Maintenance Team

The second message uses really basic tags: bold, italic and a table. I have also used the link to the WO record. Here is the source code:

```
<h2>New Work Order Notification</h2>
<table style="width: 60%;">
	<tbody>
		<tr>
```

```
                <td><b>Work Order</b></td>
                <td>:wonum</td>
                <td>:description</td>
            </tr>
            <tr>
                <td><b>Asset</b></td>
                <td>:assetnum</td>
                <td>:asset.assetnum</td>
            </tr>
            <tr>
                <td><b>Location</b></td>
                <td>:location</td>
                <td>:location.description</td>
            </tr>
        </tbody>
</table>
<br />
Click <a
href="https://<server>/maximo/ui/?event=loadapp&value=wotra
ck&additionalevent=useqbe&additionaleventvalue=wonum=:w
onum">here</a> to open the WO
<br />
<br />
<b>Your Maintenance Team</b>
```

Now it is your turn: use your imagination, add some extra text, formatting (but not too much), and pictures to make the message attractive and informative.

Embed pictures in notifications

Thanks to HTML format of the notifications, we can embed the official logo and/or social media images directly in the body of the Communication Template.

The first step is to convert the image (I suggest taking small size pictures) into the text string using Base64 encoding. You can find numerous Web sites which can do this conversion.

NOTE: The size of the result will be greater than the original file!
The encoded binary file will look like this:

data:image/jpeg;base64,/9j/4AAQSkZJRgABAQAAAQAB AAD/2wBDAB....

Copy this text to a clipboard. In Communication Template record click the icon **View HTML Source** in the toolbar of **Message** field. This will switch the editor to HTML source code mode. Now, you need to add the tag: *<img src=„">*, paste your encoded text between quotation marks, and save the record (you can extend the tag, for example, by adding width and height parameters). Your picture will be visible in the emails sent from the system.
You can use HTML source code editing mode to add tables and other formatting, too.

Rich Text

If you want to use rich text in long descriptions and you are in a multi-language environment, consider using *UTF-8* as encoding. To do this, set the following system properties:

mxe.email.charset = *UTF-8*
mxe.email.content.type = *text/html; charset=UTF-8*

Application Cron Tasks

When configuring cron tasks, it is important to check if all the parameters are correctly defined. For example, reorder cron task runs only for some specific sites and storerooms. Also, cron tasks are triggered in the context of a specific user, so their privileges must be sufficient to perform the planned actions.

Do not rely on out-of-the-box cron tasks only. You can add new ones with the help of a skilled Java programmer, for example, integration cron, or tasks which will delete historical data, like old workflow assignments.

Saved Queries

The below query allows for checking the last run time of cron tasks (it should be run in the database tool).

select taskname, lastrun, lastend from taskscheduler

Application Escalations

Escalation is one of the most powerful mechanisms in Maximo and most importantly, it can be configured without programming. Escalations can send notifications or perform actions; they can be used for different purposes:

- to inform the manager about delayed Work Orders,
- to deactivate Maximo users who have not logged into the system during the last 30 days,
- to close completed Work Orders automatically,
- to close completed Purchase Orders,
- to close related work orders when the Cost Management Project is also closed,
- to remind the buyer that a purchase order still has not been received,
- to inform the manager that the worker's qualification is about to expire,
- to notify the buyers about the expiring contracts.

Escalations have a very powerful, two-level filtering mechanism. You can define the initial filter in **Condition** field but then add further conditions in **Escalation Point Condition**. A typical usage would be:

- **Condition**—find all the open Work Orders with **Priority** 2;
- **Escalation Point Condition 1**—*4* hours after the reporting date; and/or
- **Escalation Point Condition 2**—*8* hours after the reporting date.

Do not forget that the **Elapsed Time Interval** may be negative. This option can be used to define proactive actions, for example, for Work Orders with the target dates determined by the SLAs. The escalation points can be defined as *-4* hours before **Target Finish** date to send a reminder to the assigned person, and as *-2* hours before that date to send a reminder to the assigned person and the department manager. You can also create such conditions that will calculate a half and three-quarters of the SLA time.

> *DB2 nvl(100*(timestamp(current timestamp) - timestamp(reportdate))/(timestamp(targetfinish) - timestamp(reportdate)),0) > 75*

The customer may want to see on the start center all the Work Orders for which the first (-4 hours) and second (-2 hours) escalation points have already run. This can be easily configured:

- to the Work Order table add two new integer fields: **XESCPNT1** and **XESCPNT2**;
- for each of the above escalation points define an action that will set the field value to *1*;
- finally, on the start center portlet's **Display Options**, define **Color Parameters**:
  - **Condition Attribute: XESCPNT1, Expression:** *Equal To,* **Expression Value:** *1*, **Color:** *Yellow,*
  - **Condition Attribute: XESCPNT2, Expression:** *Equal To,* **Expression Value:** *1*, **Color:** *Red.*

Conditions can be used not only to filter records out but also to prevent an escalation from running at night or on weekends. For example, this SQL clause allows the escalation to run only on Wednesdays, Thursdays and Fridays between 8 AM and 4 PM:

> *DB2 dayofweek_iso(reportdate) between 3 and 5 and hour(reportdate) between 8 and 16.*

Be careful using **Repeat** flag. It is not selected by default. The action/notification for the found record(s) is executed only once.

If you set it to *Yes*, each time the escalation runs and the same record is found, the action/notification executes again.

You can define escalations not only for the most obvious objects, like Service Requests or Work Orders, but also for Work Log—to notify someone there is a new entry in the log (the tables **WORKLOG, COMMLOG**) or when the Owner of the WO has changed (the table **WOOWNERHISTORY**).
NOTE: you can use any Maximo table in the escalation, it only has to be marked as **Main Object** in *Database Configuration* application.

Sending notifications may result in an error because the email address may not exist. You can configure Maximo to re-send the notifications with the usage of a standard *SEND_FAILED* action, but when the address is missing, it will not help. It is better to include the following condition to check for not empty email address:

> *owner is not null and exists (select emailaddress from email, person where person.personid = owner and email.isprimary = 1 and email.personid = person.personid)*

Escalations are controlled by a cron task *ESCALATION*.

Known Issues and Initial Changes

The **Condition** field, as well as **Escalation Point Condition**, has the length limit. The queries can be up to *2000* characters long. It happened to me several times that the condition was so complicated that it exceeded the above-mentioned limit. In that case, you may try to divide the condition between both condition fields or use short aliases for long database tables names in subqueries to save some space.

Saved Queries

The below query will list all the escalations which have **Repeat** flag set to *1*.

> *active = 1 and escalation in (select escalation from escrefpoint where repeat = 1)*

Application Workflow Designer

Before designing a workflow, you should document the expectations. You can use a UML State Machine Diagram to document the workflow:

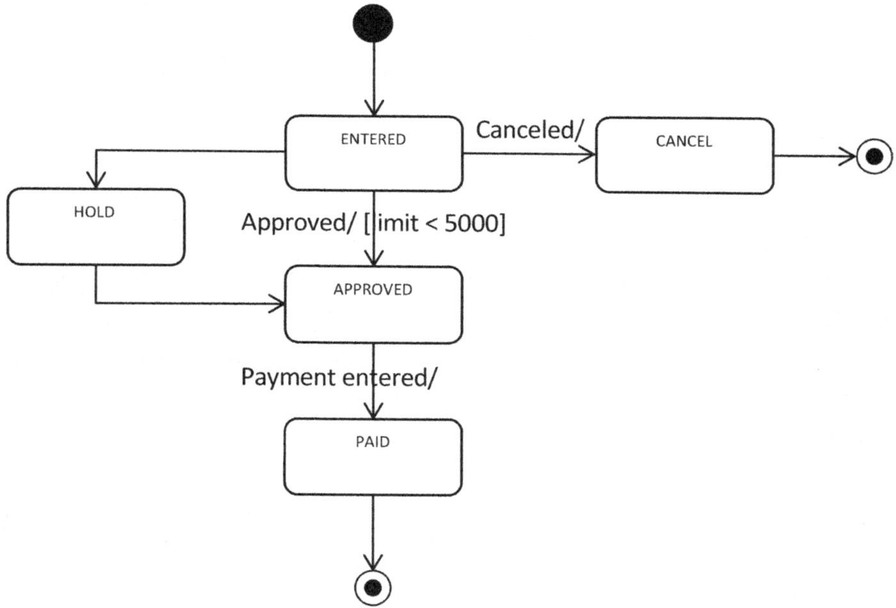

Figure 150 A Sample State Machine Diagram

Put all the statuses on the page, mark where the process starts (the black circle) and which statuses are final (circles with dots). Then, connect the statuses with transition lines. Transitions can have a description which consists of trigger/[guard]/effect, e.g.

Approve/ [limit < 5000] /Payment type->Transfer

'Trigger' is the cause of the transition, for example, a change of the status in the related record or manual action. 'Guard' defines conditions which the trigger must meet. Finally, 'effect' is an action triggered as a result of the transition.

A state diagram helps you to observe interactions with other processes and lets you check if all transitions are in place, or if there are not too many connections (spider's web).

Disabling Status Change

When you create a workflow for an application, manual status changes should be disabled; otherwise, the records will be never fully controlled. Maximo has two predefined actions to disable/enable status changes:

- NOSTATUS,
- OKSTATUS.

NOSTATUS will block status changes and to do that you should put this action at the beginning of your workflow, for example, on the first arrow after Start node. The record will be then added to **EVENTRESPONSE** table (the column **VALIDATEACTIONID** will have the value *PVSTATUS*). Status changes will be blocked until *OKSTATUS* action is called or the workflow process for this record stops.

NOTE: *NOSTATUS* blocks status changes for everyone, including the workflow. If you need to change the status in the workflow, you have to do that in the following sequence:

- Action OKSTATUS—enable status changes;
- You action to change the status e.g. to *INPRG*;
- Action NOSTATUS—disable status changes again.

All the above steps should be grouped in a new action of *Action Group* type.

Here is a sample workflow that uses the *NOSTATUS* and *OKSTATUS* actions:

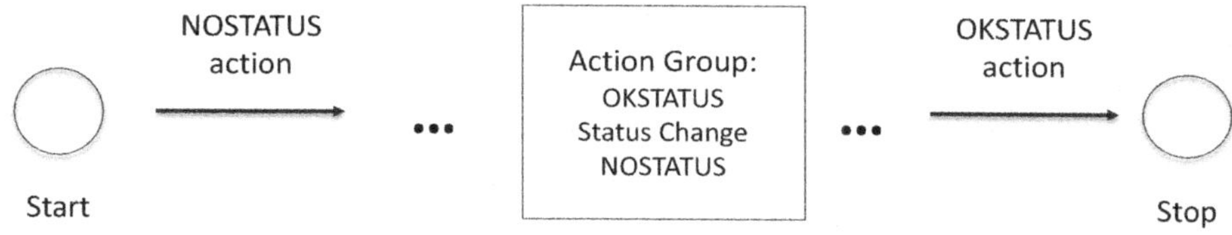

Figure 151 A Workflow with NOSTATUS, OKSTATUS Actions

It may happen that the record will remain in a blocked status. You can unlock it manually in the database using the following command (this example will unlock the Work Order record number *1000* in site *DEMO*):

> *delete from eventresponse where validateactionid = 'PVSTATUS' and sourceid = (select workorderid from workorder where wonum = '1000' and siteid = 'DEMO') and sourcetable = 'WORKORDER'*

Known Issues and Initial Changes

Workflow does not allow for routing more than one record at a time while **Change Status** action can be applied to multiple records. The customer may ask to change the standard behavior of the system, and some consultants try to customize Maximo to meet the customer's expectations. In my opinion, this is a wrong decision because the foundation of a workflow is the flow of information between different people: a person opens the records, reads the content and takes appropriate action. Moving records in bulk has nothing to do with this process; rather, it is an action. Either the customer does not need the workflow functionality for this application (and **Change Status** should be enough) or perhaps, an escalation could help.

Sometimes, you may discover that the status changes of the records run by the workflow are not saved in the history. This is a result of using the wrong action type in a workflow. The action that changes the status and leaves a record in the history should be of the type **Change Status**. However, **Set Value** action can also change the status but no historical entry will be created.

There is a very useful practice in workflow which requires that whenever the action is negative (*Reject, Cancel…*), the decision-maker should explain why they have decided so. In Maximo, you have two options to record the explanation:

- **Memo** field in **Route Workflow** dialog,
- Work Log entry.

The first method is easier—it requires only a global restriction for the object **INPUTWF** to make the attribute **MEMO** required, based on the following condition:

> *:actionid in (select distinct actionid from wfaction where instruction = 'CANCEL' and processname = 'XSR').*

The length of **Memo** field is limited only to 50 characters, which might not be enough to store the explanation. I suggest developing a custom dialog that will ask the user to enter the explanation, and then it will save it in a new work log record.

Alternative method of workflow programming

The standard approach to defining a workflow is the use of assignments and **Inbox/Assignments** portlet, but you can use an alternative method. This workflow will be always triggered and finished after someone presses **Route Workflow** button—there are no assignments. The record is in the workflow only temporarily, during its execution. The workflow can check some initial conditions, such as, whether the user is a member of the proper group. If they are not, an error message displays, and the workflow quits. Then there can be separate conditions for the current status, followed by actions. The user can click **Route Workflow** numerous times and the workflow will always re-evaluate the conditions. Usually, I use this workflow with Result Set portlets on the start center which display the records in a specific status.

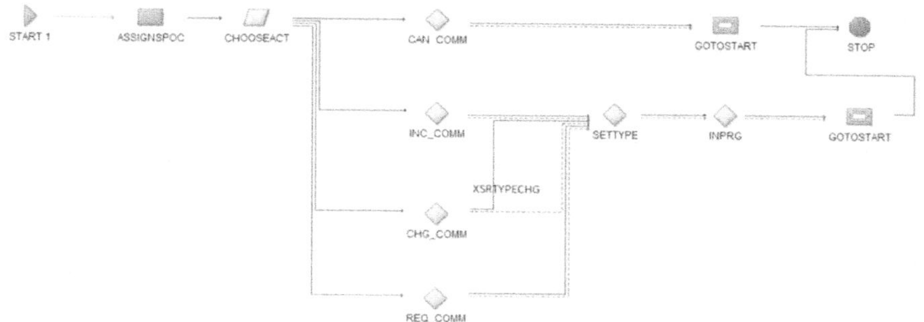

Figure 152 A Sample Workflow

Pseudo-workflow

When the customer decides that workflow is too complicated, you can propose the standard status changes flow but supported by conditions. The condition will check which transitions are defined, and present the users with a list of the statuses allowed in the flow. In the above state diagram there are the following transitions:

ENTERED -> CANCEL
ENTERED -> APPROVED
ENTERED -> HOLD
HOLD -> APPROVED
APPROVED -> PAID

To force the flow you will need to assign conditions to status values in the status domain (like *SRSTATUS* or *WOSTATUS*):

Status	**Condition**
ENTERED	*:status not in ('HOLD', 'APPROVED', 'CANCEL', 'PAID')*
CANCEL	*:status = 'ENTERED'*
APPROVED	*:status in ('ENTERED', 'HOLD')*
HOLD	*:status = 'ENTERED'*
PAID	*:status = 'APPROVED'*

The conditions say, 'From which statuses can I move to this status?' When the condition is false, it will hide the status on the list.

Because in the conditions we refer to the variable **:status**, make sure that you always enter **Object Name** for the condition; otherwise, Maximo will not understand the context of the variable and will throw an error.
The conditions for *CANCEL* and *HOLD* statuses are identical, you can re-use the condition.

You can add extra elements to the conditions when required, for example, checking if we are in the context of a specific application or if the user belongs to a specific group.

Application Automation Scripts

Automation scripts are supposed to complement the Java code. You can use simple scripts, like the below one, to create an action to take ownership of the record.

mbo.ownership()

Alternatively, you can use more sophisticated scripts, for example, for date formatting:

from java.util import Date
from java.text import SimpleDateFormat
tempStr=SimpleDateFormat(„MM-yyyy").format(DATETIME)

Also, you can write really complex scripts but in this case you should determine whether Java class will not be a better choice. You can use scripts in actions, conditions and validations, but not in cron tasks or integrations.
The scripts seem to be simple but still require programming skills and a deep MBO knowledge. They may also affect the system performance, so you should carefully consider when to use scripts and when to write a Java code.

Application Designer

My first advice for working with applications is to maintain consistency of the layout and functions. This statement is related to Development Standards, mentioned in Part I, in which all such requirements must be saved. Each application should follow the standard Maximo layout, i.e. it should have all the necessary menu buttons, search functionality (including **Where Clause**), standard Signature Options (including **Run Reports**), attachment control, etc. It is also about having a consistent approach to several configuration issues (NOTE: The list of options per issue may not be complete):

- records filtering—Maximo offers multiple options to filter records:
    - in the application: define at the application's **Presentation** level;
    - in the database: **MAXAPPS** table, column **RESTRICTION**;
    - tables on **List** tab can have **Default Value** control with a condition;
    - in the bean classes;
    - in *Security Groups* application in the form of **Global Restrictions**;
- sorting the order of the records:
    - you can define it at the application's **Presentation** level;
    - it can be defined in the table definition in **Order By** field;
- making the fields required:
    - you can do it at the database level: **Required?** flag;
    - you can make it required in the application definition (**Input Mode**: *Required*);
    - you can use the Conditional UI to force a mandatory entry of the field;
- setting the default value of the field:
    - at the database level: you can use system constants, like *&SYSDATE&*, *&AUTOKEY&*;

- use **Default Object** control in ***Application Designer*** application or add following tag in application XML: *<defaultvalue dataattribute="**ATTRIBUTE**" id="**UNIQUEID**" value="**VALUE**"/>*;
- insert a record in **APPFIELDDEFAULTS** table (*DB2 insert into appfielddefaults (app, siteid, username, defaultvalue, objectname, attributename, appfielddefaultsid) values ('ASSET', 'SITE', 'MAXADMIN', '1', 'ASSET', 'PRIORITY', nextval for appfielddefaultsseq)).*

Each mechanism has its own purpose and they cannot be used interchangeably. You should agree with the team about when to use each method and what the standard approach is.

I have observed that it is quite common to forget about replicating field changes in **Advanced Search** window (adding new fields or removing not used objects). Please add this topic to the discussion about application changes during the workshops.

The Power of Multi-part Textbox

Usually, this control can present a pair of a code and description, e.g.

Figure 153 The Asset Information

The customer may also need a description of the field with a domain. For example, a domain **XLOCPRIORITY** with values: *1—High, 2—Normal, 3—Low* is added to **Priority** field for Locations. Then, you need to build a new relationship **XPRIODESC** to **NUMERICDOMAIN** (or **ALNDOMAIN** when the lookup contains text values), e.g.

value = :locpriority and domainid = 'XLOCPRIORITY'

Now, use a new relationship name in the second part of the multipart textbook by entering **XPRIODESC.DESCRIPTION** in **Attribute** field.

But this control has absolutely no limitation of what part 1 and part 2 could be. You can use even non-related items; in ***Labor Reporting*** application we can prepare the field to display standard working hours and the overtime:

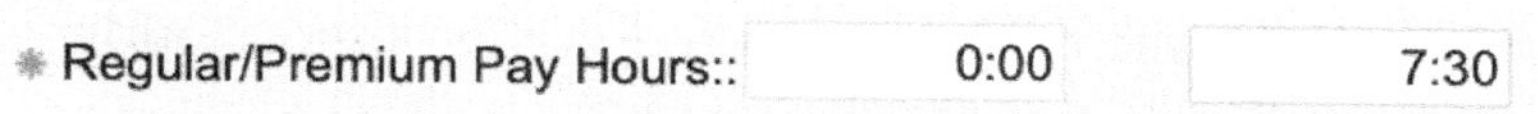

* Regular/Premium Pay Hours:: 0:00 7:30

Figure 154 Unrelated Fields in Multi-part Textbox

Both parts can have their own lookups; see, another example:

Work Type

IN ACON

Figure 155 Unrelated Fields with Lookups

You can use this control when your screen is busy, and you need to pack more content or group two fields logically—try today!

Changing Standard Labels

Do not translate standard system labels without a REALLY good justification. This is a typical approach of the companies that replace their legacy systems with Maximo. The users want to see the old terminology in the new system, e.g. replace Maximo's 'Location' with 'Place'.
But this is not as simple as you may think. You must change this label in all the applications where it is used. And what about **Advanced Search** window? What about the dialogs and reports? Should they also be changed?

Instead of making local changes, you can make them global by changing the labels in *Database Configuration* application.

Keep in mind that a new definition may seem to be out-of-context in some applications. And what about the Signature Options names? Should they be updated too?

What will happen after the upgrade? A new application may come with the original labels. Who will review the differences? What about translating the labels to other languages? Who will be responsible for this?

And the list of questions goes on and on... Finally, has this terminology change been considered in the original budget and schedule? Who will pay for the changes?
Probably, it would be easier to prepare a good training for the users, including a dictionary of the 'old' to 'new' terminology.

Conditional User Interface

Do not be afraid to create new Signature Options. This is part of the Conditional UI mechanism. Usually, this new option will be assigned to *maxeveryone* group in order to make sure that everybody uses the same mechanism.
NOTE: Do not forget to re-log in after creating a new Signature Option to make sure the security profile has been refreshed.
NOTE: Do not forget to authorize the security groups for the newly created Signature Option in other environments: TEST, PROD! This is one of the most common mistakes that are made during the implementation.

You can create flexible hide/show switches that can, for example, hide the attachment controls in a certain record status, hide sensitive (financial) information for certain user groups, hide the whole tabs for specific users, or show the field to be populated only when the record is waiting for the approval.

Conditional UI is often used to attract the user's attention. For example, in ***Work Order Tracking*** application, you can change the color of **Work Log** tab to red if there are any records saved. This will save the user some mouse clicks to check if there are any comments. The same mechanism can be used for **Safety** tab to indicate there is some important safety information. This is a sample condition that may be used:

> *:wonum in (select wonum from wosafetylink where siteid =:siteid).*

NOTE: Pay attention to national/cultural specifics. For example, in some countries, the percentage of people who are color blind to red may be significant. In that case, a boldface font should be used.

And one more thing: Conditions are evaluated only at the record level. This means you cannot use them on **List** view; especially, for hiding one of the columns.

Tables

From the functional point of view, the tables in Maximo are very important, because almost every application has a List View table and other tables with related information. IBM has equipped the tables with multiple properties, to define how they work. These properties can be used to meet many users' expectations, for example: to show the table filled out or to see the records in tables sorted.

General | Advanced

Control ID: sparepartsform_sub_assemb

Label: Subassemblies

Input Mode:

Select Mode:

Bean Class: psdi.webclient.beans.asset.SparePartsBean

Order By:

Data Source ID: sparepartsform_sub_assemb

Business Object:

Parent Data Source ID:

Relationship: ASSETCHILDREN

Width:

Description:

Title Attributes:

Start Empty?

Filterable?

Collapsed?

Figure 156 Standard Table Properties

The configuration starts with the **Relationship** property—it will determine which records will be visible in the table. Enter the name of the relationship between the current object and the other database table. Remember to pick the relationship which can return multiple records, not just one.

Use the **Label** field to name your table, in a multi-language environment, you may need to visit the table again and enter the translation.

Data Source ID—it is a good practice to name all new objects using a naming convention. I use always the prefix *X*, e.g., *XPRTABLE*.
This ID can be then used to create related tables. For example, you may want to add in the ***Work Order Tracking*** application a new tab with the list of all Purchase Requisitions created for the Work Order. Below the PRs list, there should be another table with a list of Purchase Orders for the selected PR record. To meet this requirement, create two tables, one for the requisitions

(**Data Source ID** *xwopr*) and one for the purchase orders (**Data Source ID** *xwopo*).
You will need also two relationships: between **WORKORDER** and **PR** database objects (*XWOPR*) and between **PR** and **PO** (*XPRPO*). To link both tables, enter the data source of the first table in the **Parent Data Source ID** field in the second one.

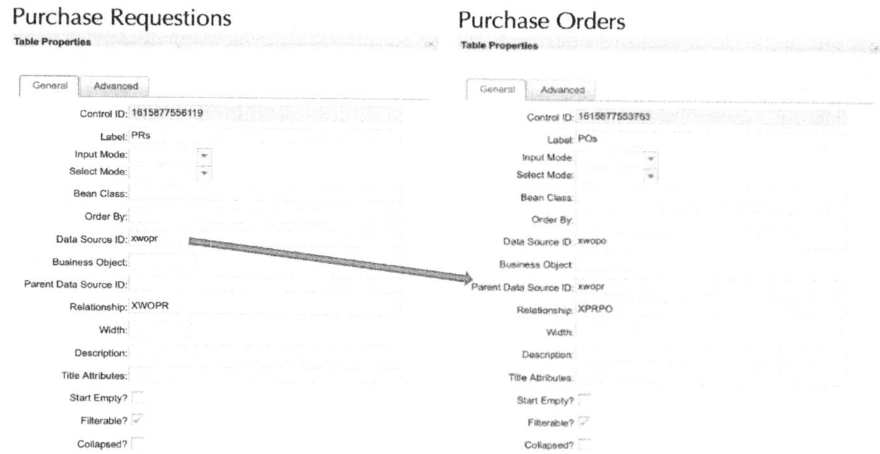

Figure 157 The Definition of Related Tables

Now, the second table will present the Purchase Orders related to the selected Purchase Requisition only.

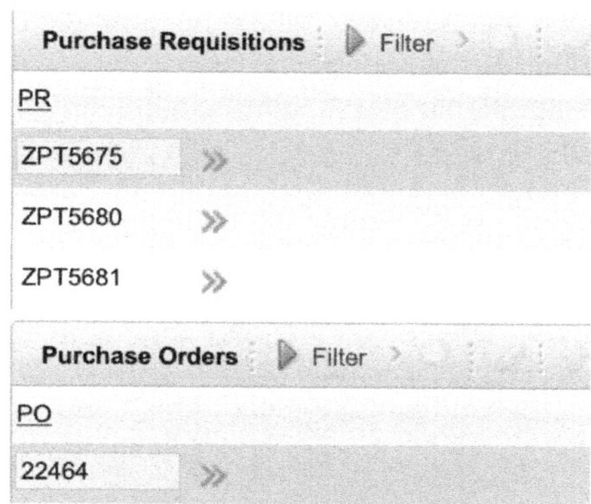

Figure 158 The Related Tables

There is only one detail missing here. The users may not be sure from which Purchase Requisition comes the PO in the bottom table. To solve this issue, and explicitly bind the two objects, you will add a parameter *{0}* to the Purchase Orders table title (you can add more parameters too: *{1}*, *{2}*...). To define the parameters, edit the XML source of the application and add the parameter and the section:

```
<table datasrc="xwopo" id="1615877553763" label="Purchase
Orders for {0}" parentdatasrc="xwopr" relationship="XPRPO">
        <sectionheader id="xwopo_sectionheader">
                <paramvalues id="xwopo_params"
property="label">
                        <paramvalue dataattribute="prnum"
datasrc="xwopr" id="xwopo_param_1" position="0"/>
                </paramvalues>
        </sectionheader>
<tablebody id="1615877553841">
        ...
```

The result will be a clear reference to the Purchase Requisition:

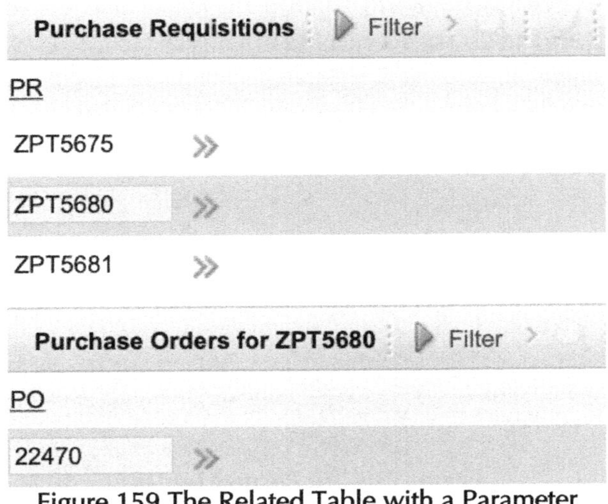

Figure 159 The Related Table with a Parameter

NOTE: because you are adding parameters to the titles, you must provide the translation including the parameter(s) for every language installed.

Order By property defines the default sort order for this table. You can sort by one or more fields, ascending or descending. You can even force Maximo to sort ascending and descending by multiple fields at the same time e.g., *COMMODITYGROUP DESC, ITEMNUM ASC*. This is only the default sort order; the users will be able to change it as they want.

Most of the auto-numbered records like Work Orders, Purchase Requisitions, etc. have the type *UPPER*, which means they contain text and are sorted alphabetically. This can return unexpected results because the Work Orders numbered: *1, 2, 3, 10, 20, 30, 100, 200, 300* will be sorted in the following order:

1

10

100

2

20

200

3

30

300

Figure 160 Standard Sorting Order

To fix this, you can use the **Order By** property and convert the text to numbers using the following function:

DB2 *cast(wonum as int)*

This setup will present the records in the expected order:

Figure 161 The Records Ordered by Numbers

NOTE: the column with the record identifier must contain only digits, otherwise, you may get an error.

Sometimes, you may be forced to save some space on the busy screen. In that case, select the checkbox **Collapsed**. This will display the table in a closed section.

Most of the tables have the **Start Empty** checkbox not selected. That means the table is filled with the rows when the current record is open e.g., ***Labor Reporting*** application. This has an effect on the system's performance, because every time the user opens the application, a database query is executed. **Start Empty** property means Maximo will display the table, but the user must initiate the search then.

The tables have also additional properties, but first, you need to run **Toggle Show All Controls** action. This will reveal *tablebody* section with the following options:

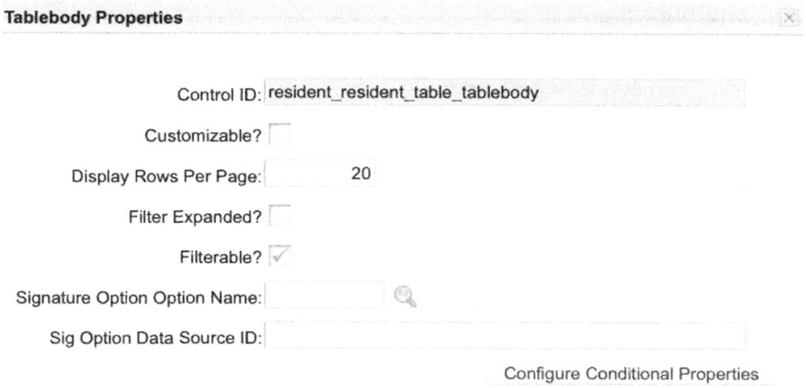

Tablebody Properties

Control ID: resident_resident_table_tablebody

Customizable?

Display Rows Per Page: 20

Filter Expanded?

Filterable?

Signature Option Option Name:

Sig Option Data Source ID:

Configure Conditional Properties

Figure 162 The Tablebody Properties

Here, you can decide if the table should have the filter line expanded by default: property **Filter Expanded**.

You can also define how many rows will be displayed in the table: **Display Rows Per Page**. This property can help you to better use the available space on the screen because computer screens are getting bigger and more content can be seen, but a lot of tables in Maximo show only a few records, causing the rest of the screen to be empty.

To define a standard filter for a table, add the **Default Value** control to the same section where the table is located. Enter the attribute to filter by in the **Value** field. You can define here one or multiple values to search for (comma separated). You can use also the operators available: *>, <, =,* etc. as well as the wildcards *%*. Set the **Default Type** to *Query*.

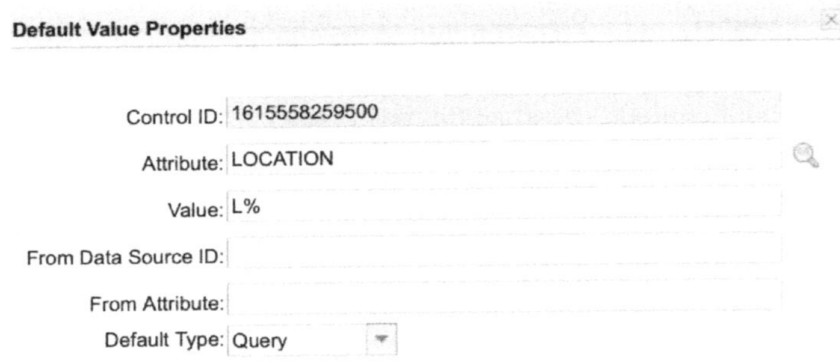

Figure 163 The Default Value Control for a Table

Similarly, to the default sort order setting, the users may remove or change this filter.

If your table has a details section, it will be shown only when the user will expand it. If you want the details to be always visible, then you will need to add in the XML file, in the table property, following clause:

rowdetailsexpanded="true"

As with other interface elements, the appearance and behavior of tables can also be controlled using Conditional UI. You can make the table read-only or use the colors to bring the user's attention to a specific row or cell in the table.

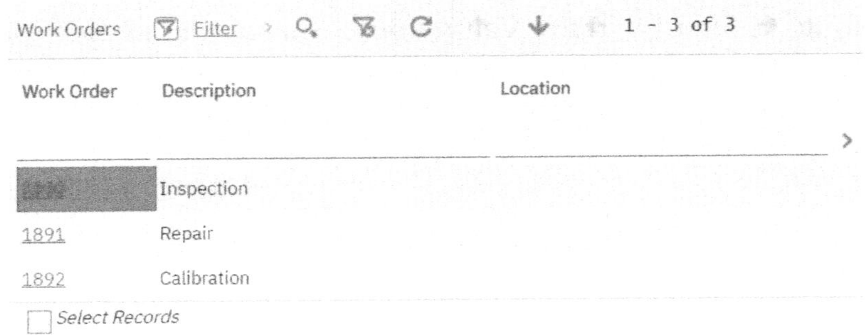

Figure 164 A Sample Conditional Formatting of a Table

Conditional User Interface allows creating complex queries checking multiple database tables. It also allows you to color the separate cells, but if you need to change the color of the whole line based on just one attribute you can use the trick from Chon Neth (InterPro Solutions). Chon has described some years ago the use of the *displayrule* section in the application's XML file. There are two types of display rules:

- Checking for the exact value of the attribute,
- And, checking if the value is in the specified range.

In the first example, the Work Order list will be colored based on the **Work Type** attribute. All emergency Work Orders will have a red background, all lines for Corrective Maintenance will be yellow.
Insert the following section in the **WOTRACK**'s XML, in the **List** table, directly before the *</tablebody>* tag.

```
<displayrule id="WOTypeExact"
dataattribute="worktype">
        <exact id="WOTypeEM" value="EM"
classname="bgred" />
        <exact id="WOTypeCM" value="CM"
classname="bgyellow" />
</displayrule>
```

Please, enter unique names in id tags. In the *classname* tag, you can use all the available styles: *txtbold, txtblue, bgorange…* And here is the result:

[illegible]	Failure	1068	WAPPR	EM
2032279	Flat tire	1000 ⓘ	WAPPR	CM
2032280	Filter exchange	1001 ⓘ	WAPPR	PM
2032284	Oil check	1002 ⓘ	WAPPR	IN

Figure 165 Colored List of Work Orders

You can use the second option (checking for the range) in the ***Job Plans*** application to highlight the **Labor** records based on the **Quantity** field. For example, **Quantity** between *2* and *4*— yellow background, *5* and above will be orange.

Insert the following section in the **JOBPLAN**'s XML, in the **Planned Labor** table, before the *</tablebody>* tag.

*<displayrule id="QuantityRange" dataattribute="**quantity**">*

*<range id="Quantity_2_4" lower="**2**" upper="**4**" classname="**bgyellow**" />*

*<range id=" Quantity_5_99" lower="**5**" upper="**99**" classname="**bgorange**" />*

</displayrule>

Now, the planner will have a visual indicator, that multiple workers are required.

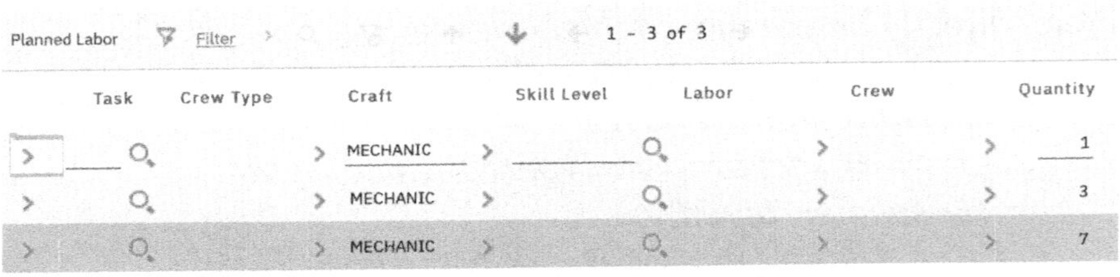

Planned Labor Filter 1 - 3 of 3

	Task	Crew Type	Craft	Skill Level	Labor	Crew	Quantity
>			MECHANIC				1
>			MECHANIC				3
>			MECHANIC				7

Figure 166 Colored List of Planned Labor

You can use the tables to:

- view the data (change the **Input Mode** of the whole table or columns to *Readonly*),
- edit the data,
  - o directly in the table as for example in the ***Job Plans*** application, in the **Tasks** table,
  - o in the **Details** section of the table,
- add new records (add a *buttongroup* control to the table, name the button **New Row** and enter *addrow* as an **Event**, you can also define it to be a default button),
- delete the records (add a column with an **Event** *toggledeleterow*).

XML files

While editing any XML file, do not forget to add it to your software version control system. Also, do not use Notepad program for editing because it may corrupt the file and you will get an error *BMXAA0931E—Content is not allowed in prolog* while importing such a file; use programmer's editors instead.

You will probably edit **LIBRARY.XML** file to edit dialogs. Please do not forget to name the new controls uniquely—use the convention described in Development Standards chapter. If you want the changes you have made to this file to appear after importing it, you will need to re-start the server to re-load the cache.

Another frequently edited XML file is **LOOKUPS.XML**. I have already mentioned several times that to improve Maximo's functionality, you should add new columns to the existing dialogs. For example, in ***Assets*** application, you should add the column **SERIALNUM** to **ASSET** and **ROTATINGASSET** dialog.

I have met a few customers who did not want the users to have the option to export records to a spreadsheet because of potential security breaches. You can remove this functionality globally by editing **CONTROL-REGISTRY.XML** file and replacing the line:

```
<property name="download" />
```

with:

```
<property name="download">
        <default-value>false</default-value>
</property>
```

Then you should re-build and re-deploy Maximo.

In **MENUS.XML** file, there is a very interesting section, *menu id="HELP"*, which gives you control over the entries in **Help** menu.
You can, for example, remove irrelevant items, such as *IBM Electronic Support*, or add links to the customer's internal procedures.

You can also edit **WEB.XML** file in order to change *<session-timeout>* tag. It defines the automatic log-off time in minutes. By default, it is set to *30* minutes but some customers may ask you to increase this time.

Applications Cross Reference

Here is my best practice to link two applications. Whenever one application allows to define the relation to another app, this other app should at least show the same reference. If the functionality permits, the other app should allow defining a reverse relation.

The example is *Person Groups* application, which allows for adding records from *People* application. However, in *People* application you cannot even see the groups associated to the person. My approach is to allow viewing this information by adding a new tab **Person Groups** in *People* application (for details, see the chapter about the application *People*). Of course, Person Group record must have **Go To** action to open the corresponding item to view details. Theoretically, you could also add **New Row** button to define a new Person Group for the person record. This may not be possible, though, because of the agreed design: the decision could be made that Person Groups for people are only defined in *Person Groups* application—in that case solely a read-only view will be permitted in *People* application.

History Tab

In all the applications that have e-Audit enabled, I suggest adding a new tab called **History**.

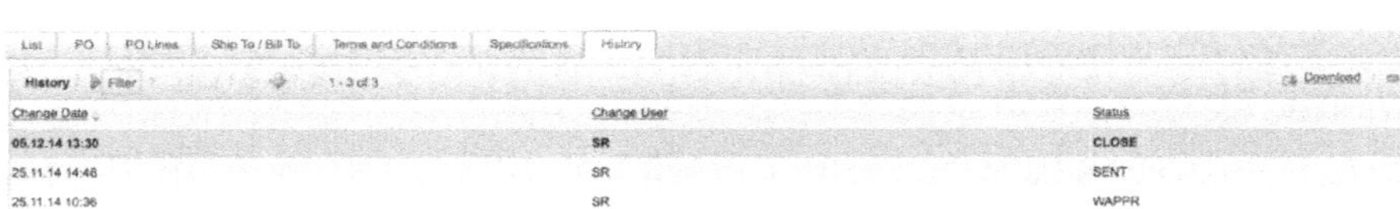

Figure 167 A Sample History Tab

It should contain a read-only table with the details from **A_** table that are related to the current object and contain all the fields being audited. Usually, it is sorted by **Change Date** in descending order.
NOTE: A new relationship to **A_** table will be required. For example, for **WORKORDER** object, a new relationship **XAUDIT** to **A_WORKORDER** table must be defined *wonum = :wonum and siteid = :siteid.*

Application Database Configuration

Known Issues and Initial Changes

I have once implemented a Help Desk system which had a very nice feature: each new custom table defined by the user had already some predefined content:

- Unique identifier,
- Status,
- Short Description,
- Create Date,
- Created By,
- Modified Date,
- Modified By,
- ...

Particularly, the last four fields are interesting because then you can easily identify when the record was created and when it was modified (a very common question in the production environment). In Maximo, you can find similar fields but the system is not consistent: not all the fields are present and they are named differently in different tables: **ENTERBY, ENTERDATE** or **CREATEBY, CREATEDATE** or **CREATEDBY, CREATEDDATE.** I wish this could be fixed one day but if you want to change it now, please create new fields (use the same names across all the tables!) and assign default values using the variables *&USERNAME&* and *&DATETIME&*.

While searching for a table, please remember that a default query in *Database Configuration* application has a standard clause, *internal = 0,* which will prevent system tables from being displayed. You have to edit the 'where' clause if you want to see them.

In theory, Maximo 'masks' the database underneath but there are still some differences between the databases. For example, database functions may be different or the data types are not identical, which causes such issues as a case sensitive search of Long Descriptions fields in DB2, while other databases offer a case insensitive option.

Relationships

One of the foundations of Maximo's flexibility are relationships between database tables. They allow us to use fields from one application in another application. We do not need to replicate this information, hence saving disc space; we only present related information on the screen. A typical example is displaying a description of the related field. This requires defining a simple relationship **XWOCOMP** between two tables, e.g. between **WORKORDER** and **COMPANIES**:

company = :vendor

and then, referring to **Name** field, using the relationship name, e.g. **XWOCOMP.NAME**.

With the help of relationships, we can also get the description from a domain attached to a field. In my previous example, there is a lookup attached to **Priority** field in *Locations* application. We need a relationship **XLOCPRIO** between **LOCATIONS** and **ALNDOMAIN**

value = :locpriority and domainid = 'XLOCPRIORITY'

then, we can access the description with the usage of dot notation: **XLOCPRIO.DESCRIPTION**

But we can have also more sophisticated relationships; for example, an asset which belongs to the Classification *CAMERA* might have an attribute *ATEX Certified*. We may want to add this attribute to the Work Order record, using the relationship to **ASSETSPEC**:

> *assetnum = :assetnum and siteid = :siteid and classstructureid = (select classstructureid from classstructure where classificationid = 'CAMERA') and assetattrid = 'ATEX'*

A relationship can return not just one record but a list of records; for example, we can add a new tab in ***Preventive Maintenance*** application to show who and when has changed some important parameters, such as PM frequency. This will require a relationship **XAUDIT** between **PM** and **A_PM** tables:

> *pmnum = :pmnum and siteid = :siteid*

Now, you will enter the above relationship name in the table on the new tab in order to display the login, date and changed values: **EAUDITUSERNAME**, **EAUDITTIMESTAMP**, **FREQUENCY**, **FREQUNIT**.

But we can do a lot more, for example, adding the next PM due date (**NEXTDATE**) to the asset record. We need a new relationship between **ASSET** and **PM** objects: **XNEXTPM.**

> *DB2 assetnum = :assetnum and siteid = :siteid and status = 'ACTIVE'*
> *and nextdate = (select min(nextdate) from pm where assetnum = :assetnum and siteid = :siteid and status = 'ACTIVE' and group by assetnum, siteid) fetch first 1 rows only*

> *Oracle assetnum = :assetnum and siteid = :siteid and status = 'ACTIVE'*
> *and nextdate = (select min(nextdate) from pm where assetnum = :assetnum and siteid = :siteid and status =*

'ACTIVE' and group by assetnum, siteid) and rownum = 1

NOTE: There can be multiple PMs for one asset, and it is possible that the next due date could be the same for more than one PM. Therefore, the number of records returned needs to be limited to just one.

So far, we have used the relationships to return the information which is already provided in a database column: a description, a date, or any other value, but... this is not the end. We can use the power of SQL to return also calculated values.
This trick requires using a small Maximo table which will be used as a foundation for our query. Pick any table with relatively small number of columns (because you will need to provide a dummy value for each column) that have the type and length you need to present the information. For example, if you need to present text, you can use an **ALN** column; for numeric values column of **DECIMAL** or **AMOUNT** type will be suitable.

Below you can find just one example but the possibilities are endless:

I want to place in ***Assets*** application a text field with information on how many Work Orders were created for this asset and how many of them are already closed. This text field must be read-only as this information is calculated. The field will display **DESCRIPTION** attribute from **ACTIONSCFG** table.
I will create a new relationship between **ASSET** and **ACTIONSCFG** objects:

DB2
1 = 2 union
select
2 as actionscfgid,
'x' as optionname,
'WARCTRGRP' as app,

```
0 as ordernum,
1 as layoutid,
'This asset has ' concat to_char(count(1)) concat ' WOs, '
concat to_char(count(case when status = 'CLOSE' then 1
end)) concat ' are closed' as description,
'3333' as contentuid,
'2345' as rowstamp,
' ' as templateid
from workorder where assetnum = :assetnum and siteid =
:siteid

Oracle
1 = 2 union
select
2 as actionscfgid,
'x' as optionname,
'WARCTRGRP' as app,
0 as ordernum,
1 as layoutid,
'This asset has ' || to_char(count(1)) || ' WOs, ' ||
to_char(count(case when status = 'CLOSE' then 1 end)) ||
' are closed' as description,
'3333' as contentuid,
'2345' as rowstamp,
' ' as templateid
from workorder where assetnum = :assetnum and siteid =
:siteid
```

The relationship consists of two parts joined by *UNION* operator:

- *1=2*—this is to ignore the actual content of **ACTIONSCFG** table. All we need from it is **DESCRIPTION** column which will be calculated in the second part.
- The second part contains *SELECT FROM WORKORDER* command—please review this carefully. Theoretically, I have a relationship between **ASSET** and **ACTIONSCFG**

objects but actually, **ACTIONSCFG** table is only used as a medium for calculation.

- In *WHERE* clause I refer to the current **ASSET** record, so the second part of the query processes all the Work Orders related to it.
- You need to provide dummy values for all the columns other than **DESCRIPTION,** and here is *0* for **ORDERNUM**, *2345* for **ROWSTAMP**, etc. This is required by *UNION* operator; we need to provide all the columns from **ACTIONSCFG** table.
- The most important is the line calculating the content of **DESCRIPTION** column. *SELECT* command will calculate the number of all the WOs for this asset: *count(1)* and also the ones which are closed already: *count(case when status = 'CLOSE' then 1 end)*. Both the values are converted to text afterwards and returned as a sentence. You can also use here any subquery or database function to perform the calculations needed.

This is the result of the configuration:

WOs: This asset has 1 WOs, 1 are closed

Figure 168 Calculated Field

NOTE: Be careful while designing the relationships as you should always define how many records the relationship can return—just one row or multiple rows. Save this information in **Remarks** field.

Database Formulas

IBM has introduced a new feature to automate the Maximo applications: database formulas. You can create formulas and functions used by them using the following actions:

- Add/Modify Function
- Add/Modify Formula for Attributes
- Add/Modify Formula for Object

You can use the formulas to count records, calculate total values or dates. You can also write your own functions to perform more sophisticated actions.

NOTE: Please be aware, that formulas for the persistent fields are only executed during add and save events i.e. when the main record is created or updated. Let's take an example: you have a formula, which counts the Work Order tasks *count$woactivity*. Then, you add a new task, but the field with the number of tasks will not change unless you update any field in the Work Order. The non-persistent attributes will be updated immediately after any change.

e-Audit

One of my customers wanted to put into the history ALL the fields from an application. From a security point of view, it may sound like a good idea but it may affect the database performance. Whenever the user adds a record to the application with e-Audit or modifies it, a copy of the record will be saved in **A_** table. If there are hundreds of users, this may be a considerable performance limitation. So, you should agree upon a balance between security and performance.
E-Audit can be used to track the changes in Maximo system. It is enough to enable e-Audit for **MAXATTRIBUTECFG** object to track the changes made to the database and for **MAXPRESENTATION** to track screen changes.

e-Signature for applying configuration changes

You can switch off e-Signature (**Manage eSig Actions** option) for *Database Configuration* application but I suggest not doing so. I know that this may be annoying, but the comments entered in **Reason For Change** field in **Electronic Signature Authentication** dialog while approving the database changes can help resolve potential issues. I suggest describing briefly the introduced changes and (if possible) including the reference to the originating requirement(s). This can be useful to determine not only what was changed but also why the database changes were made in the past. You can review this information in ***Login Tracking*** application using the saved query.

Auto-numbering

There are a few considerations while setting up the auto-numbering mechanism:

- At which level should the numbering work: site, system?
- Agree with the customer upon prefixes because this is the buyer who will be using the system, so this is them who should confirm what is better for locations: *L* or *LOC*. Do not use hyphens in prefixes.
- Define the start number. Remember that the initial import of the data will consume some numbers. Thus, it may be wise to change the starting value for manually entered data after the migration is finished. For example, the imported data can start at 1000 and the manual one at 2000.
- Do not forget to add *&AUTOKEY&* default value in database.
- ***Crafts*** application requires a little different treatment because there is no entry in ***Organizations*** application to set auto-numbering for Crafts. Also, **CRAFT** attribute has the check box **Can Autonumber** unchecked and read-only. You have to run the following SQL commands to enable auto-numbering for this application:
  - *DB2 insert into autokey (prefix, seed, orgid, siteid, autokeyname, setid, langcode, autokeyid) values ('C', 1000, 'SITE', null, 'CRAFT', null, 'EN', nextval for autokeyseq);*
  - *update maxattributecfg set canautonum=1, autokeyname = 'CRAFT' where attributename='CRAFT' and objectname ='CRAFT';*

- *update maxattribute set canautonum=1, autokeyname = 'CRAFT' where attributename='CRAFT' and objectname ='CRAFT';*
- and then add *&AUTOKEY&* as a default value for **CRAFT**, apply the database configuration changes and re-start Maximo.

Make the attachments visible in other applications

Applications with attachment control always have **DOCLINKS** relationship, which defines the attachments that are visible. For example, the below query defines the attachments for ***Assets*** application.

> *(ownertable = 'ASSET' and ownerid = :assetuid) or (ownertable = 'LOCATIONS' and ownerid = (select locationsid from locations where location = :location and siteid = :siteid)) or (ownertable = 'ITEM' and ownerid = (select itemid from item where itemnum = :itemnum and itemsetid = :itemsetid and itemtype in (select value from synonymdomain where maxvalue ='ITEM' and domainid='ITEMTYPE'))) or (ownertable = 'TOOLITEM' and ownerid = (select itemid from item where itemnum = :itemnum and itemsetid = :itemsetid and itemtype in (select value from synonymdomain where maxvalue ='TOOL' and domainid='ITEMTYPE')))*

As you can see, the clauses responsible for displaying attachments from other applications are separated by *OR* operator, and you can easily add other conditions to display the attachments, for example, from the related purchase orders or from the parent asset.

NOTE: These queries can heavily affect performance so test them in the database tool first. Moreover, the query presented in the example is not very efficient. You can rewrite it using *UNION* operator to increase the speed:

> *doclinksid in (select doclinksid from doclinks where ownertable = 'FINCNTRL' and ownerid = :fincntrluid union select doclinksid from doclinks where ownertable*

= 'WORKORDER' and ownerid in (select workorderid from workorder where orgid = :orgid and fincntrlid in (select fincntrlid from fincntrl where projectid = :projectid))

Cannot turn off admin mode

If you cannot disable Admin Mode, run the below query in the database tool.

*select * from maxvars where varname = 'CONFIGURING'*

If the returned value is equal to 1, then change it using an update command:

update MAXVARS set varvalue='0' where varname = 'CONFIGURING'

This should resolve the issue.

Saved Queries

It is good to have the query presented below. You can change the *FIELDNAME* to the required value and check where it is used.

objectname in (select objectname from maxattributecfg where attributename like '%FIELDNAME%')

All the objects with the domain *DOMAINNAME*:

objectname in (select objectname from maxattributecfg where domainid = 'DOMAINNAME')

Application E-mail Listener

Maximo can send email notifications as well as connect to the mailbox (or even multiple mailboxes) and process the incoming email.

This message can either trigger a workflow or another interaction, for example, to change the status in ***Purchase***

Orders application simply by replying to the email (see, ***Email Interaction Setup*** application for details—not described here). The standard workflow used by E-mail Listener is *LSNRBP*, which can create or update Service Requests, or change their statuses.
This can be used as a very simple integration between systems; for example, SCADA system can send the alerts to the mailbox *failures@company.com*—they will be saved as Service Requests.
You can also create your own workflows to create other objects, such as, Work Orders.
As mentioned before, Maximo can parse messages from different mailboxes, so you can have multiple listeners defined, each with a different workflow and functionality.

While configuring the listener, please remember about a few details:

- Maximo can process messages only from the senders who have a person record in the system. If the sender does not exist in the system, the e-mail is ignored.
- Enable auto-delete in the listener definition. This will ensure that once the message is processed, it will be deleted from the inbox.
- Also, while enabling the listener, make sure the inbox is either empty or contains only messages that should be processed. A common mistake is that before, the inbox has been used for manual message processing, which means someone has entered its content into the system, but the messages have still been kept in the inbox. If you enable the listener, it will process ALL the messages in the inbox again, which can potentially duplicate the requests.
- Make sure that the email server supports *POP3/IMAP* protocols.
- The dedicated email address for the mailbox must be different from *maxadmin* address.

- The email account should be excluded from all the company notifications. Otherwise, you will have SRs with holiday wishes, policy changes, welcoming new employees, etc.
- The mailbox should also be secured against spam.
- The mailbox has no size limit so the email listener could be used, for example, to create a Service Request by SCADA systems, which may send large log files as attachments).

Known Issues and Initial Changes

E-mail Listener requires cron task: *LSNRCRON* to be enabled.

Module Work Orders

The Work Order is the main object in the system: it is the result of the PM schedule or a Service Request, it is the cost collector and the scheduling tool, all in one.

The first thing you should explain to the customer is the Work Order life cycle.

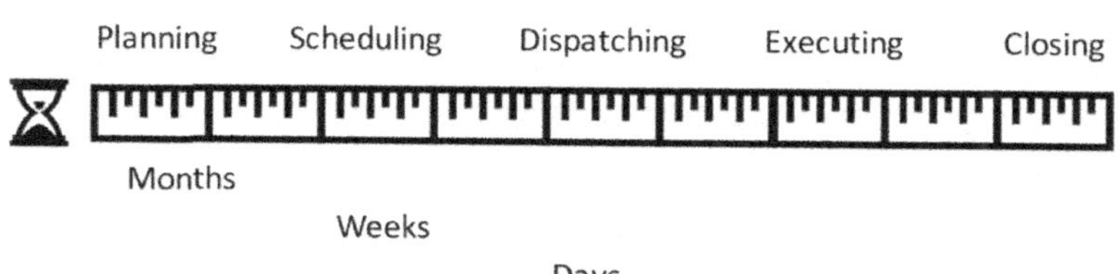

Figure 169 Work Order Life Cycle

Not all Work Orders will go through all the phases—above is a generic diagram. For example, failures usually do not have planning phases and the Work Orders generated from PM do not have the planning and scheduling phases. Please pay attention to the diminishing time perspective.

Planning more considerable work can take weeks or months and includes defining a list of tasks to be performed, creating a list of the required materials and necessary skills (at this moment in time, the planner operates at the skill level, not with the names of the laborers). The planned materials can trigger purchase requests or reservations. Once the work is planned, it can be scheduled (target dates should be defined) and assigned to the right owner group; again, this step can take weeks to finish. When the target date is drawing closer, the dispatcher will assign the actual workers for the skills based on the information about the work. This can be done a day before the target date or in the morning on this day. Work execution can take days or weeks. Once the work is done, it is time for quality checks, completing the tasks list, sorting out the inventory, reporting all the labor time, and waiting for the invoices for the external services. This is also the moment to generate any follow-up work if needed. Then the Work Order can be closed.

Application Work Order Tracking

Work Orders can be created:

- from a Service Request,
- manually on a desktop computer:
    - in ***Work Order Tracking*** application as new ones,
    - in ***Work Order Tracking*** application from other Work Orders (Follow-Up work),
    - in ***Quick Reporting*** application,
    - in ***Assets/Locations*** application,
- manually on a mobile device:
    - as new WOs,
    - from other Work Orders (Follow-Up work),
- from PM,
- from Condition Monitoring,
- from Purchase Order (application ***Job Plans***, **Work Assets** tab, checkbox **Create WO When Purchasing This Item**),
- from SCADA system as a result of events/alarms,
- from Predictive Maintenance system.

Why have I listed all the methods? Because the customer should understand that there are multiple ways a Work Order can be created, and they should consider introducing the missing ones. For example, Follow-Up work functionality should be a common practice for inspection Work Orders.

This book has no specific chapter about mobile technologies but if the customer decides to use mobile devices, you should carefully plan the workflow for Work Orders (as well as for other applications used on mobiles). This means the Work Order that should be processed on a mobile device requires a special workflow. For example, this record should become read-only for all the desktop users.

Known Issues and Initial Changes

Maximo's focus on the *1:1* relation between the functional location and asset has an unexpected result. You may have not a functional location but a physical one—a room with only *1* asset installed. And you may want to create a Work Order to paint this room but then suddenly, the asset will be included in the WO, too. Fortunately, the asset information can be deleted from the Work Order to indicate this is a task only for the Location.

The **Target Start** and **Target Finish** fields define the time limits for the work order, set by a PM or an SLA. Those fields should be read-only to avoid their content being updated by the users. This configuration will keep the data accurate and consistent.

Because I have listed different ways to create a WO, the customer may think about analyzing the sources of the work. To fulfill this requirement, you will need to add a new field **Source** and a mechanism (e.g. escalation, script…) that will enter the value there, see below:
Source: *PREVENTIVE* (from PM) – when: *pmnum is not null and pointnum is null*
Source: *CONDMON* (from Condition Monitoring) – when: *pointnum is not null*
Source: *PURCHASE* (from PO) – when: *generatedforpo is not null*
Source: *MANUAL* – when: *generatedforpo is null and pointnum is null and pmnum is null*
Feel free to change the descriptions or to add more sources.

You can use this information to create a Result Set on the Start Center to present a pie chart with a number of WOs by **Source**.

The customer may want to use the **Owner Group** and **Owner** fields, but then it is always confusing to see what happens when you choose first a Person Group, e.g. *ELEC*, and then a person:

John Doe. First, **Owner Group** field gets populated with *ELEC* but then suddenly, it will be cleared and **Owner** field is populated with *John Doe*. The users expect that the group will not remain empty, indicating we have chosen *John Doe* from *ELEC* group. You can fix that by using a new field introduced in version 7.5, **Assigned Owner Group (ASSIGNEDOWNERGROUP)**, which will keep the chosen person's group name. What you need to do is changing the fields on the screen: Remove **Owner Group** and add **Owner Group Assign**. From now on, the correct information will be visible: *ELEC* and *John Doe*.

There is a slight discrepancy between how **Work Log** and **Communication Log** tabs work. **Work Log** is by default sorted in descending order, i.e. the latest entry is first on the list, but communication log is sorted in ascending order, which is surprising. The only way to fix that is to edit **LIBRARY.XML** file and change the table **commlog** adding:

orderby="createdate desc"

to the table 'definition' (server restart is required).

If the customer decides to use Cost Management projects with a Work Order (for example, to determine the budget for work), then you need to add the fields related to projects. They already exist in the database: **FCPROJECTID** and **FCTASKID**. For **FCPROJECTID** attribute you must specify **PARENTPROJECT** as the lookup; for **FCTASKID** attribute, the lookup is **PARENTTASK.**

A common request is to send email notifications to selected users after the following events:

- owner change,
- New Work Log entry.

To fulfill it you will need to create new escalations and communication templates based on the following objects, respectively:

- WOOWNERHISTORY,
- WORKLOG.

You will need to mark the above tables as **Main Object?** in *Database Configuration* application first.

While planning or reporting the actual usage of materials, or while planning the services, the user has the option either to choose the material/service from the list or enter it as free text.

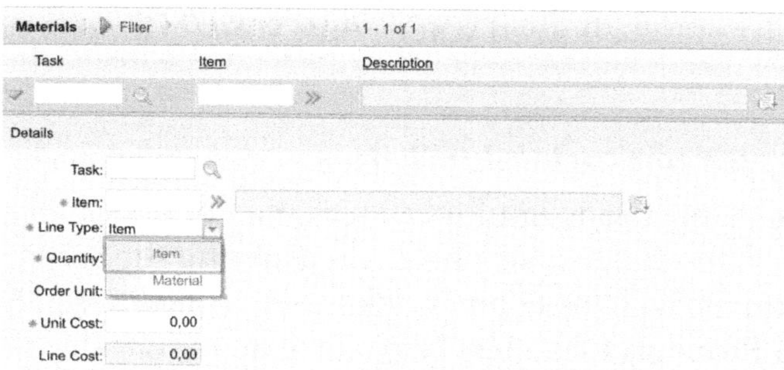

Figure 170 Catalog Selection or Free Text

The customer's business rules may exclude this type of free entry—everything must be chosen only from the approved catalogs. You will need to add the default value and make the following fields read-only:

- Plans tab:
    - **WPSERVICE.LINETYPE**, default value: *STDSERVICE*,
    - **WPMATERIAL.LINETYPE**, default value: *ITEM*,
- Actuals tab:
    - **MATUSETRANS.LINETYPE**, default value: *ITEM*.

NOTE: The same principle applies to the *Purchase Requisitions* and *Purchase Orders* applications.

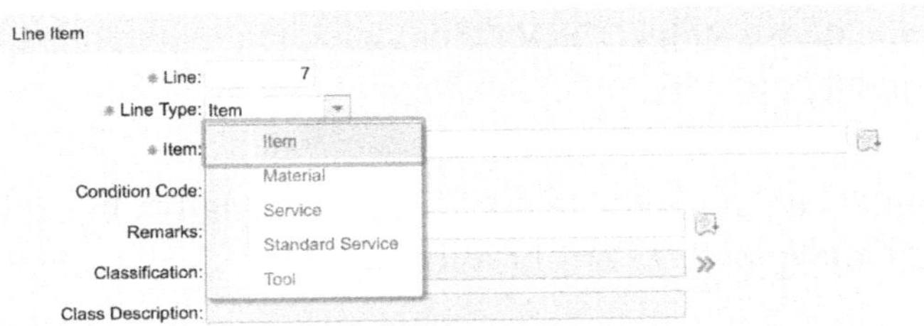

Figure 171 PR/PO Line Type

However, in this case, the Java class behind the fields: **PRLINE.LINETYPE** and **POLINE.LINETYPE** must be modified to limit the list of the allowed values only to *Item Standard Service* and *Tool*.

Checking for potential duplicates

In larger organizations, multiple users may occasionally try to report the same failure. To prevent registering the same event multiple times, Maximo can check for you if the same **Failure Class** and **Problem Code** has been already reported for the current asset/location. You can enable this verification in *Organizations* application, action **Work Order Options/Other Organization Options, Display Duplicate Problem Warning**. This feature will display the following dialog while trying to save a new Work Order:

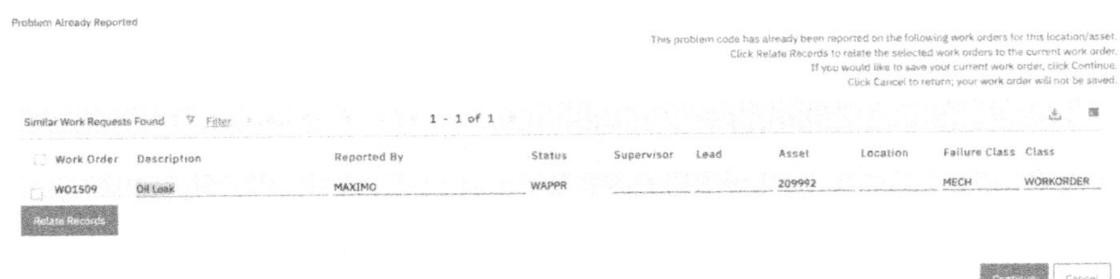

Figure 172 Problem Already Reported Dialog

The user can then decide not to save the new Work Order because it is an obvious duplicate, or to relate it to an already existing WO, or to save it anyway because this is a different issue.

Work Priority

A lot of companies have not enough resources and too many work orders to be executed. The only method to manage such a situation is prioritizing the work: what should be done now, what can wait? You could use Maximo to determine the right order of the work.

The first step is to define the Asset/Location priority: how critical is this equipment? This is a separate, important topic, which requires an analysis among of, among others the impact of failures on safety, environment and production.

In the second step, you can assign priority to the Job Plan or Preventive Maintenance. Not every work is equally important—please compare an internal visual inspection and an ultrasound inspection, when you need to order some external services.
In the *Work Order Tracking* application, you will find both the priorities: **Asset/Location Priority** and **Priority** (of the work).
NOTE: The Asset's value supersedes the value from the Location.

Now, you can ask Maximo to calculate the resulting priority for the Work Order. There is a hidden field **Calculated Priority** (**WORKORDER.CALCPRIORITY**), which is calculated based on the two above priorities. The calculation method is defined in *Assignment Manager* application, action **Set Preferences/Set Priority Preferences**.

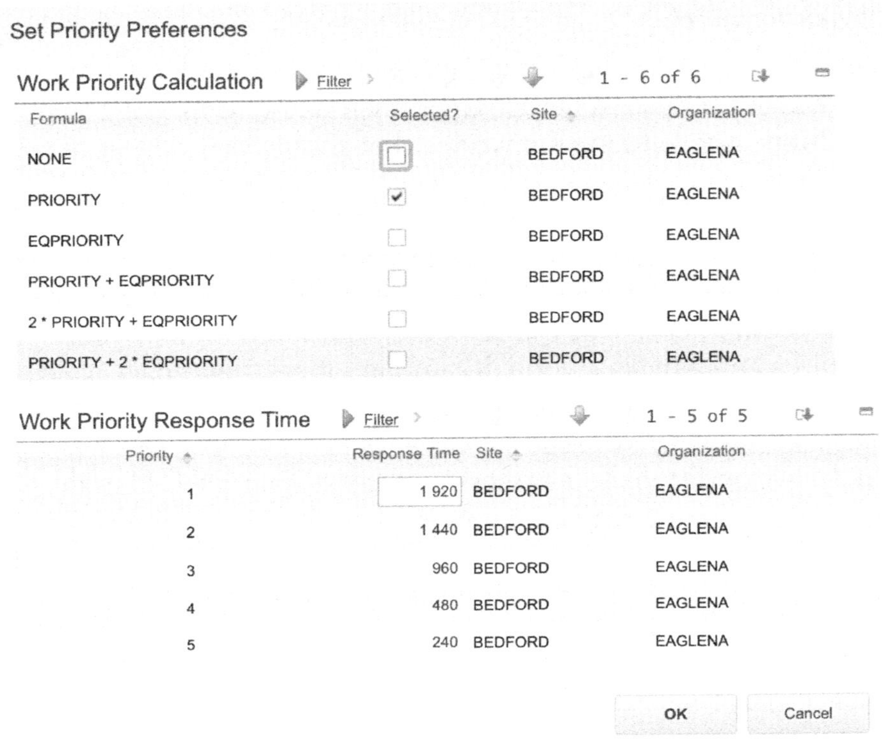

Figure 173 Set Priority Preferences

NOTE: The response times are defined in minutes.

You will need to add this **Calculated Priority** field to the *Work Order Tracking* application (best as a read only attribute). Additionally, the priority calculation will update another hidden field **Respond By** (**WORKORDER.RESPONDBY**). It determines the expected response time for this work order. You can also add it to the application to help the workers know how much time they have to respond to this issue.
The standard range for priority values is between *0* (lowest) and *999* (highest). Numerous maintenance professionals suggest, using only values from *1* to *4*. While defining your own values, bear in mind that the result may be a multiplication of the input values e.g. *4 x 2*, thus the **Calculated Priority** result must be within range *0-8*.

Repair Facilities

Fleet companies usually have the assets associated to one site but because they are moving, they can be overhauled or repaired in another site. Maximo's answer to this requirement is the concept of Repair Facilities. These are locations marked as Repair Facility, which can be assigned to the Work Order.
Let us take an example: there is a truck *1002,* which is owned and managed by *Location D* (*Site 3*), but it is moving and needs to be repaired in *Site 1*.

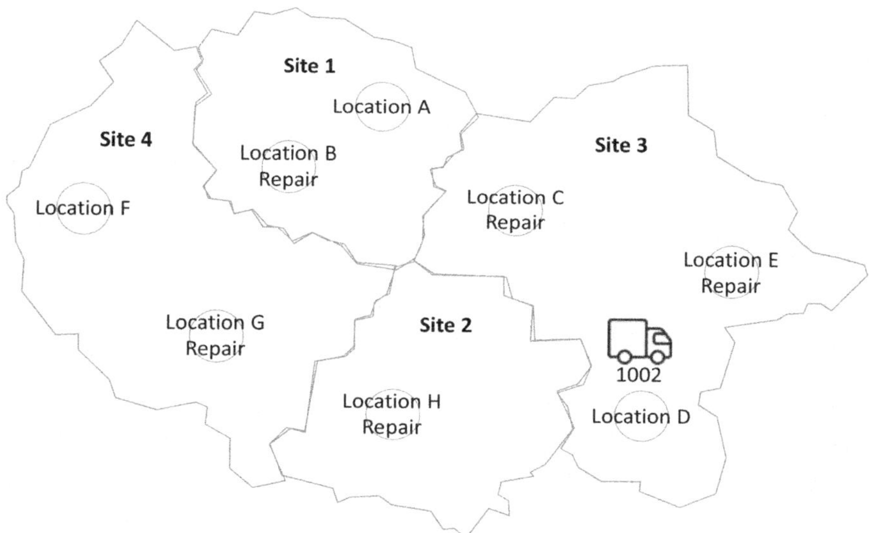

Figure 174 Repair Facilities

I can create a Work Order in *Site 3* for the truck and assign the repair location. Normally, when I work in Site 3, I can only see the locations from this site: *Location C, Location D* and *Location E.* But in Repair Facilities lookup, all of the repair locations in my organization will be visible: *Location B, Location C, Location E, Location G* and *Location H.* This will allow me to create the WO with the following details:

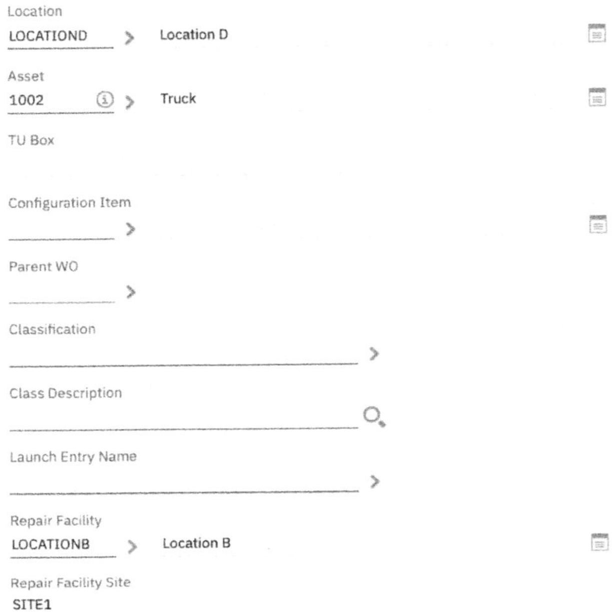

Figure 175 A Work Order with Repair Facility

To use Repair Locations, you must first enable it in *Organizations* application, action **Work Order Options/Other Organization Options, Enable Repair Facilities.**

Then, the repair locations must be defined (**Type:** *REPAIR*), just check **Is a Repair Facility** checkbox. A repair facility can have its own structure; for example, the truck workshop can be divided into bays. Each of the child locations can be also a Repair Facility. This will help schedule the work to avoid planning two Work Orders for the same time for the same bay.

You can also assign a default repair facility to the asset—this information will be used to generate PM Work Orders.

Finally, you must ensure that the security groups involved in the repair process have an access to the required repair facilities. In

Security Groups application, on **Repair Facilities** tab, you will either authorize this group to all the locations or to the specific ones. In the above example, the group must be authorized to access *Site 3* (where the asset is) and Repair Facility *Location B*.

In *Users* application there is **Default Repair Facility** field, which will be used to populate the **Repair Facility** field on the Work Order record.

Edit History Work Order

Sometimes, the customer will say, "I want to be able to edit the closed Work Orders." When you hear that, it means the Work Order process is wrong as why would one need to edit a Work Order that is already closed? Go back and verify the workflow—there should be enough time before closing the WO to report the time of labor, to add the invoices and to enter all the work-related comments. You can also create a special role (or leave it to *maxadmin*) which will have the authorization to open a closed WO but it must be an exception and not a rule. Also, the customer must understand that the number of actions available while editing the closed WOs is very limited:

- you can change the description and long description of the Work Order;
- you can and log entries;
- you can add new labor transactions but not modify the existing ones;
- you can add new material transactions but not modify the existing ones;
- you can attach new documents;
- you can add or delete Parent Work Order and/or child Work Orders (they must not be closed);
- you can report failure codes.

You cannot modify:

- Asset, Location, Status, GL Account,
- the planned labor, materials, tools,

- safety information.

Multiple Assets, Locations and CIs

Customers tend to think they may have their cakes and eat them. They want to have one Work Order for multiple assets to avoid creating a separate WO for each asset, and at the same time, to have the cost of this WO allocated to each of these assets. You cannot do it in Maximo without non-trivial customization, and in my opinion, you should not do it. Instead, you should explain how the table **Multiple Assets, Locations and CIs** works. It allows for creating just one Work Order with the same task for multiple assets (for example, inspection of fire extinguishers) but there is a price for doing so: you cannot distribute the costs of doing it. Instead, the cost should be allocated to the GL Account specified on the Work Order. This is a good compromise: the customer should have an account for collecting such costs, which are by definition indirect costs. In numerous cases, you cannot just say that the cost $100 for five assets should be allocated as $20/each because there might be some deviations. To illustrate, one of my customers wanted to collect all the costs for the so-called 'first aid' Work Order—small jobs, like changing light bulbs, greasing machines, etc. The Work Order was created for all the machines in the specific area but the cost was allocated to a designated GL Account. This is the best practice that may be suggested.

Projects and Investments

Work Orders can be used not only for failures and preventive actions. Maximo offers powerful mechanisms in the form of a Work Order hierarchy. It does not sound remarkable but actually, it offers the same options as project management tools do. The customer can plan a complicated turnaround or investment process by creating one 'big' task and then splitting it into some smaller steps—first, Work Orders; next, tasks. The hierarchy allows for gathering costs to the top; the target, scheduled and actual dates represent the progress. If you add the relation to the Cost Management project, the customer will have a full picture of the project. You can also assign Project Managers to each of the major steps (in **Supervisor** field). They can then monitor the progress of the sub-Work Orders and react accordingly.

The existing hierarchy can be easily copied to a new Work Order because **Duplicate Work Order** action has an option to copy not only the current Work Order but also the whole hierarchy. Some customers may use this feature to create a dummy Work Order with a hierarchy of child Work Orders for the repeating projects and copy it whenever a new project is opened.

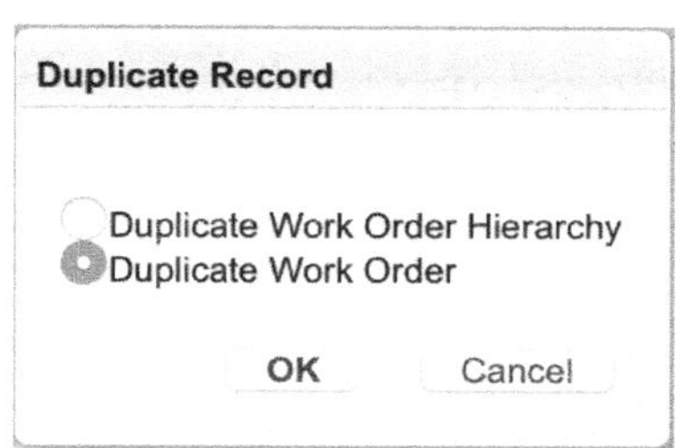

Figure 176 Duplicate Work Order Options

Elaborate tasks may also require reporting work progress: *15%, 33%, 60%,* etc. However, the progress may be reported not only in percentages but also in other units. For example, a work order could be created to replace *100* valves, so the progress will be reported in the number of valves repaired: *10, 25, 40...*

To monitor the progress, you will need to add several fields: units of measure, planned value, actual value. You may also build a more sophisticated mechanism and, instead of the actual value, you may add the two following fields:

- Reported value, which will be stored in e-Audit giving the insight into who and when reported this value;
- Total progress, which will be calculated by the script as the sum of all the reported values.

Closing Work Order

The last phase of the Work Order is its closure. In other words, this is the confirmation that all the labor transactions, all the issues and returns, all the invoices for the external services, failure codes, etc. have been entered and the Work Order has been completed.

But this is also a good moment that can be used for some automation; I will give you one example. My customer has (as part of his service organization) a small production team. They produce assets, which are then installed as part of their services. They use Work Orders to monitor the production process; also, they use classifications in WOs that describe the features of the produced assets. The classifications are shared with *Assets* application, and there is a mechanism based on Java classes that automatically generates (when a WO is closed) a new asset with the same classification and attributes copied from the originating WO.

Work Order Meter Readings

Customers responsible for fleet or rolling stock maintenance may ask you how they can check at what mileage the tires or brake pads for a particular vehicle have been changed. The information about mileage is entered for an asset in *Work Order Tracking* application using **Enter Meter Readings** option. However, this reading cannot be found anywhere in the work order—you can only check it in the asset record (**Manage Meter Reading History** option). Even then, the reading history dialog does not contain the information whether the reading was associated with the work order or not.

You can fix it by adding a new tab in *Work Order Tracking* application which will contain the meter readings (there could be more than one value, for example: the initial mileage and another one after the test drive). You have to use **WOMETER** object in this table and additionally, a new relationship to **METERREADING** object should be defined to display the reading value (Where Clause: *:meterreadingid = meterreadingid*).

Meter Readings | Filter | 1 - 2 of 2 | Download

Reading Date	Meter	Reading	Status
03.06.16 11:06	PRZEB	594,00	INPRG
18.04.16 20:23	PRZEB	100,00	WOGEN

Figure 177 A Sample Meter Readings Table

But the configuration is not finished yet—to make our work consistent you have to update the reading history dialog in ***Assets*** (and/or ***Locations***) application and add columns with the work order number and its description. This will help the user to answer the initial question. This dialog is based on **METERREADING** object and now we need to add the relationship to **WOMETER** table (Where Clause: *:meterreadingid = meterreadingid*).

Continuous Meter Readings | Characteristic and Gauge Meter Readings

Meter Readings | Filter | 1 - 5 of 5

Meter	Description	Enter as Delta?	Rollover?	Modified Reading	Modified Delta	Reading	Delta	Work Order	Description
PRZEB	Przebieg	☐	☐			594,00	104,00	ZP6020	Przegląd techniczny
PRZEB	Przebieg	☐	☐			490,00	170,00		
PRZEB	Przebieg	☐	☐			320,00	120,00		
PRZEB	Przebieg	☐	☐			200,00	100,00		

Figure 178 A Sample Reading History Dialog

The above setup opens new ways of data analyzing, for example:

- What is the average mileage between failures for the vehicles (similar to MTBF KPI)?
- Who in the company is actually a rally driver—calculate the average mileage between the brake pads change (based on the failure code) for each vehicle and add the username to the data sheet.

Service Addresses

Utility or Service Provider companies use the work addresses every day to know where technicians have to go to do their job. Maximo has a dedicated application to add and edit addresses:

Service Address. The options of addresses can be found in *Organizations* application, action **Service Address Options**. They can be created directly in the *Assets* or *Locations* applications, or integrated with an external GIS system. An address consists of a postal address and/or geographical coordinates—it can be associated to an Asset, Location, Service Request or Work Order.
NOTE: The above objects can have single addresses only. Addresses can be inherited by child Assets and Locations, and are copied over to SR or WO record.

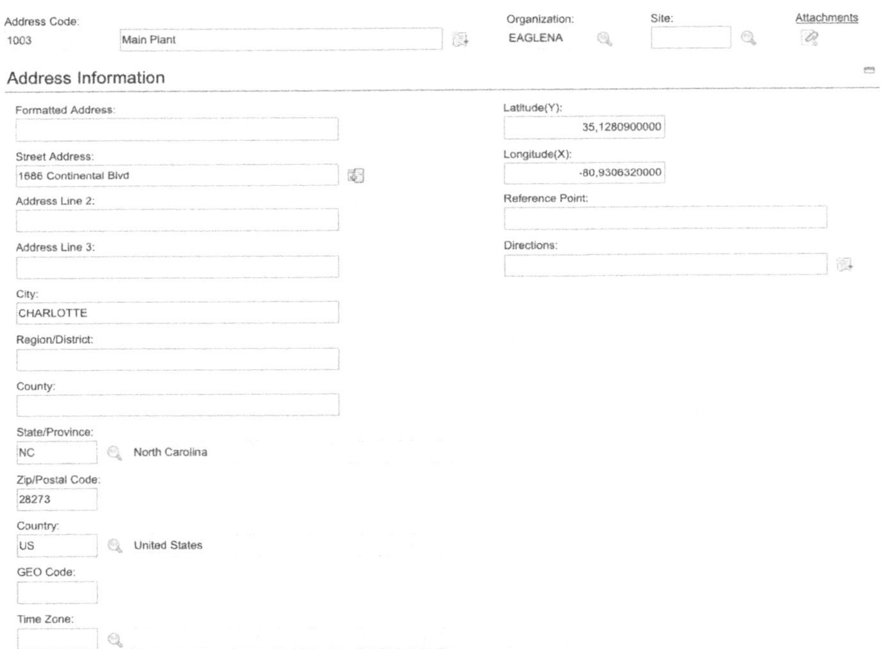

Figure 179 A Sample Service Address

There is another potential area of application for addresses. The customer may own a fleet of cars, buses or locomotives. Once they are equipped with GPS trackers, you may introduce an interface to upload the current position of those assets to Maximo. Each position will be saved as a new Service Address with latitude and longitude.

If e-Audit function for **Service Address** field is enabled, you will be able to observe the history of movement of this asset.

Saved Queries

Below are a few exemplary queries to find specific Work Orders.

WOs delayed:

targcompdate is not null and actfinish > targcompdate

WOs with Work Log or Communication Log entries:

exists (select 1 from worklog where recordkey = wonum and class = woclass) or exists (select 1 from commlog where ownerid = workorderid and ownertable = woclass)

WOs with safety information:

wonum in (select distinct wonum from wosafetylink)

WOs with SLAs:

exists (select 1 from slarecords where ownerid = workorderid and ownertable = 'WORKORDER')

Application Quick Reporting

My understanding of the purpose of *Quick Reporting* application is to allow quick entering of smaller tasks which have already been done. These tasks do not require any planning and are mostly related to failures. This kind of post factum reporting can increase the number of events reported because users do not need to enter tons of information. However, before you allow them to access *Quick Reporting*, you should at least answer the below questions because this application will be part of a bigger workflow:

- Is it needed to use *Quick Reporting* in this implementation?
- What kind of failures will be entered in *Quick Reporting*?

- Have you implemented in ***Quick Reporting*** all the interface changes made in ***Work Order Tracking*** application: the new fields, removed fields, mandatory information?
- Should the access to this application be restricted to the selected users only?
- How will you know that a particular work order has been reported in ***Quick Reporting*** application?
- How does ***Quick Reporting*** fit into the existing work orders workflow?
    - What should be the default status of the work orders reported there: *INPRG, COMP*?
    - Which information should be required for these work orders?
    - Maybe some fields should be already populated?

Application Labor Reporting

This application supports only one dimension of the Work Order—reporting labor time spent on doing the work. Some customers do not use this application at all while other ones want it to be extended. For example, a common request is to allow not only reporting time spent but also the number of miles driven (for drivers).

Interestingly, you can make corrections to the work time. Just create a new transaction with a negative value, e.g. *-0:35* = subtract *35* minutes of work.

In most cases only the worked hours (from the past) can be reported, but in ***Organizations*** application in **Labor Options** there is a setting which allows entering work time also for future: **Future Labor Transaction Tolerance in Hours**.

The action **Daily Attendance** allows for entering information about Labor attendance. This information can be either entered manually or better, through an integration from the HR system.

NOTE: Please make sure that collecting this information and using it (for example, to determine the utilization levels) is allowed by the local law.

Known Issues and Initial Changes

Depending on the option **Automatically approve labor?** in ***Organizations*** application, the records on the list in ***Labor Reporting*** may be approved or not. In the latter case, your customer may ask you to show only the unapproved records on the list. This will help the person (manager) who will approve the transactions. To do this, you have to edit the application definition in ***Application Designer*** and add the below condition to filter out the records (as I mention here: Application Designer—there are multiple ways of doing it):

genapprservreceipt = 0.

Now only the unapproved transactions will be visible.

You can also sort the table by date and Labor code—this will ensure that all the daily transactions are grouped together.

Finally, you can define Conditional UI to color the transactions with the number of hours greater than the daily norm, for example. Use the condition:

:regularhrs > 8.0

and **Property**: *cssclass = bgyellow.*

Start Date	Regular Hours	Premium Pay Hours
24.04.20	**8:00**	
27.04.20	8:00	
28.04.20	8:00	
29.04.20	8:00	
04.05.20	8:00	
05.05.20	8:00	
06.05.20	8:00	
07.05.20	8:00	
08.05.20	11:30	
11.05.20	8:00	
12.05.20	8:00	
13.05.20	8:00	
14.05.20	12:00	
15.05.20	8:00	
18.05.20	8:00	

Figure 180 Transactions Above the Daily Limit

Such a small feature can greatly improve the approval of hours.

Saved Queries

The below query searches for any potential mismatched crafts.

craft not in (select craft from laborcraftrate where laborcr aftrate.laborcode = labtrans.laborcode)

The below clause can be added to your query to show only the transactions for the work done on Saturday on Sunday.

DB2 dayofweek_iso(startdate) > 6

Application Service Requests

This is an application that enables to communicate between departments or groups of people. It is most often used to connect the worlds of maintenance and production department (operators). Usually, you will not allow the operators to use

Work Orders to report issues (there are exceptions to that rule, for example, the operations manager). The main reason is that the licensing model *Service Requests* or, more precisely, *SELF-SERVICE* module, is free for all users, while the access to *Work Order Tracking* requires a paid license. Service Requests are important because they give the company the opportunity not only to improve the communication between the production and maintenance but also to increase the awareness of the joint responsibility for the assets. This is something you should emphasize—it is the idea of registering all (or almost all) the issues related to a specific machine. Having a full history of the problems allows for a better diagnosis and informed decisions. Service Requests are easy to use and they encourage users to share their observations.
But this is not the only potential use of Service Requests. Technicians can use it to report issues or the ideas for improving preventive maintenance plans. They can also request a training if they need it. A Service Request can be also used by planners to inform storeroom managers about new Kits, which should be prepared for planned activities...

Service Requests can be generated by *SELF-SERVICE* module but they can also come from other systems. For example, many machines have their own operating panels that are in fact computers. They may have already built-in applications for reporting downtime, changeovers and failures. You may need to integrate with such applications and generate Service Requests based on this input. This will be another step in making closer the communication between the production and maintenance groups.

Adding Activities Tab

You may have already discovered the application *Ticket Templates*. You can define there a list of activities and other attributes for **Class** *SR*; then, in *Service Requests* application, you can select the action **Apply Service Request Template**. Some information from the Ticket Template will be visible, like

Internal Priority, but where are the activities? By default, there is no **Activities** tab in ***Service Requests*** application, but you can create it.
Add a new tab to the application and name it: **Activities**, insert there a table with the following parameters:

- Bean Class: *psdi.webclient.beans.servicedesk.ActivitiesBean,*
- Relationship: *WOACTIVITY.*

Add some columns to the table, for example, **TICKETID**, **DESCRIPTION**. Now, you will be able to see the list of activities from the Ticket Template.
NOTE: Service Requests can have only activities, labor, materials; other resources are not supported.

Known Issues and Initial Changes

Please check the comment about **Site** field in Application Create Service Request.
NOTE: **Asset Site** field is filled in automatically based on **Person's Site** field from either **Reported By** or **Affected By** person record.

There is a small difference between the ***Work Order Tracking*** and ***Service Requests*** applications. Closed Work Orders are by default filtered out, while you can still see closed Service Requests on the list. You should add similar filtering (*historyflag = 0*) to SR application but remember two of them should be modified: ***Service Requests*** and ***View Service Requests***.

As I mention earlier, it will be perfect if Service Requests are used to report all the asset-related issues. But there is a price for encouraging people to report everything—some requests might not require any action from the maintenance side. Such requests must be rejected or canceled. Therefore, you should provide a means to do that by adding a new status: *REJECTED* or *CAN* (it should be a synonym of *CLOSED*).

Saved Queries

The below query will find all the SRs with SLA agreement.

exists (select 1 from slarecords where ownerid = ticketuid and ownertable = 'TICKET')

SRs with Work Log or Communication Log entries:

exists (select 1 from worklog where recordkey = ticketid and class = 'SR') or exists (select 1 from commlog where ownerid = ticketuid and ownertable = 'SR')

Other topics

Login Page and Logos

Some companies have strong visual identification guidelines. They may request adding to Maximo their logos, colors and sometimes, even special fonts to make the software look like any other application.
The logo is usually added:

- to the menu bar (sometimes, you have to replace the vendor's logo),
- to the log-in page (but only when the customer does not use SSO, in which case this screen will not be used),
- to the reports (or report templates, to be precise).

Colors and fonts can be changed in Maximo CSS files.

While talking about the menu bar, I recommend replacing a standard graphic file with a colored version depending on the system environment:

- development environment—a red menu bar,
- test environment—a green menu bar,
- production—a standard menu bar or company colors.

This visual signal tells the user where they are and what they can do. Once, I have had a user who worked very diligently but—in the test environment!

The menu bar is a place where you can also add information about the user's default insert site (importantly, in the previous Maximo versions this information was visible). Quite often, the users who have an access to numerous sites forget what their current insert site is and start entering information that is not intended for this place. You can add site information in **TITLEBAR.JSP** file, it does not require restarting or rebuilding. Insert the below line at the beginning of the script.

<%@ page contentType="text/html;charset=UTF-8" buffer="none" import="psdi.server.MXServer,psdi.security.UserInfo"%>

Then add these lines:

String definssite = "";
MXServer mxServer = MXServer.getMXServer();
UserInfo userInfo = mxServer.getSystemUserInfo();
definssite = control.getWebClientSession().getUserInfo().getInsertSite();

And, finally, add: *+" @" + definssite* at the end of the following lines:

apptitle = control.getWebClientSession().getMessage("login","welcomeusername",new String[]{userFullName});
and
apptitle=docTitle;

Refresh the screen and you will see the application name (or username), followed by *@SITE* information.

None of my customers uses the self-registration feature, so removing that link from the screen is recommended, I think. You can comment out the whole section in **LOGIN.JSP** file (which requires rebuilding Maximo) but there is a quicker and simpler way (I have found it on maximotimes.com).
In ***Database Configuration*** application, choose the action **Messages** and find the records with **Message Group**: *login*, **Message Key**: *newuserlink* and *newuserlabel*, replace the existing values with:

<script type="text/javascript"> var e = document.getElementById("otherlinks"); e.parentNode.removeChild(e); </script>.

Remember to repeat these steps for all the installed languages. Make sure to deactivate and disable the standard workflow for self-registration: *SELFREG*.

Choosing a skin for a session

IBM is constantly re-designing the Maximo look & feel and introduces new skins. Although the new skins follow Web design trends, not every user is satisfied with these changes. Therefore, you may give the users freedom to choose their preferred skin for a session. You need to define multiple links to Maximo system on the landing page with the reference to all the available skins. The link looks like this:

https://<server>/maximo/ui/?skin=<skin>

Today you have the following options (in the order from the newest):

- iot18,
- tivoli13,
- tivoli09,
- classic.

NOTE: Please verify this list after each major upgrade as IBM may decide not to support older skin(s).

Maximo in Multiple Browser Tabs

The configuration of the application layout will be easier if you are able to immediately check the results of your work, without the need to go back and forth to ***Application Designer*** application. You can log into Maximo in two browsers or simply open a new tab in the browser and enter the URL:

https://server/maximo

This will open another window with Maximo. You can then do the changes in the application in one tab, and open the modified application in another.

The same trick can be used for other use cases, such as, reviewing asset records and job plans.

Attachments

Known Issues and Initial Changes

Maximo has a very powerful security mechanism that defines the access to applications, data and reports but does not cover attachments. The result is that everybody with the access to *Work Order Tracking* application can see all the attachments saved with Work Orders as well as all the files attached to the related objects, like Assets or Locations. There is no easy way in Maximo to configure that but you can rely on external DMS to define visibility rules.

Some users may complain that their URLs are not entirely saved. This is because the length of the URL is limited to 250 characters (**DOCLINKS.URLNAME**) while some Intranet links are longer. You can extend the length of this field or teach users to use one of the available URL shorteners and save only the shorter forms.

Saved Queries

The below query will identify the attachments (it should be run in the database tool) that are no longer used and potentially, can be deleted.

> *select urlname from docinfo where not exists (select 1 from doclinks where doclinks.docinfoid = docinfo.docinfoid)*

Start Centers

You should design Start Centers to help users answer three basic questions:

- What should I do next?
- What is important for me?
- Where can I find the information I need?

To answer the first question, you should use Inbox and/or Result Sets. They should display only the records that require action from the user: the list of work orders waiting for the approval or the list of PMs with some missing information. By default, you should not display the records which are processed normally (management by exception).

The second question is answered with the help of KPIs or charts that describe the performance of the user, their group or the process.

The answer to the third question is Favorites portlet with links to the applications used by each role.

Known Issues and Initial Changes

In Result Set portlets, you cannot use queries which include the following clauses:

- rownum > 2,
- group by.

Very often, during Start Centers configuration, you will find that the saved query from the application must be amended. If this is the query you have defined, there is no problem; however, if the query has been prepared by someone else, you will not be able to edit it. From the user interface's point of view, you cannot even identify the owner of this query. The only method to check this is to display the content of **QUERY** table in the database. You can then ask the query's owner to change it or you can modify it in the database (be careful!). You can also take ownership of this query by updating the owner information.

My standard approach to designing Start Centers is not to give to users an access to changing their dashboard layout. This is to ensure the consistency of the view. However, they should be granted an access to *Favorite Applications Setup* application to manage this list freely. Of course, in *Start Center* application, all the users should have an access to the option **Can Update Start Center** to refresh the dashboard's definition. If the users have more than one Start Center, it is advised to give them an access to **Display Settings** option, which allows rearranging the tabs (normally, they are sorted alphabetically, but the user may want to make one of them default). This option is defined as a read access to *Layout and Configuration* application.

Whenever an update in the Start Center is made available for the users, they must be informed about this to refresh their dashboards. I suggest using a Bulletin Board for that purpose.

By default, Result Sets display only the fields from the current object, e.g. from Assets. However, you may also want to include the Location's description in the Result Set. Normally, you would use the relationship between the asset and location (or a dot notation): *LOCATION.DESCRIPTION*. To achieve the same effect in the Result Set (applies to version 7.6 and above) use the Report Object Structures (ROS). In Object Structures application, create a new record with the field **Consumed By** equal to *REPORTING*, **Application**: *ASSET*. Add *ASSET* as the main object, then the related object *LOCATIONS* with **Parent Object**: *ASSET* and **Relationship**: *LOCATION*. **Cardinality** must be *SINGLE*! Save the new object structure. You can add another related object, for example, to include the fields from the *Companies* or *Item Master* applications.
NOTE: The relationship between the objects must be defined in advance.

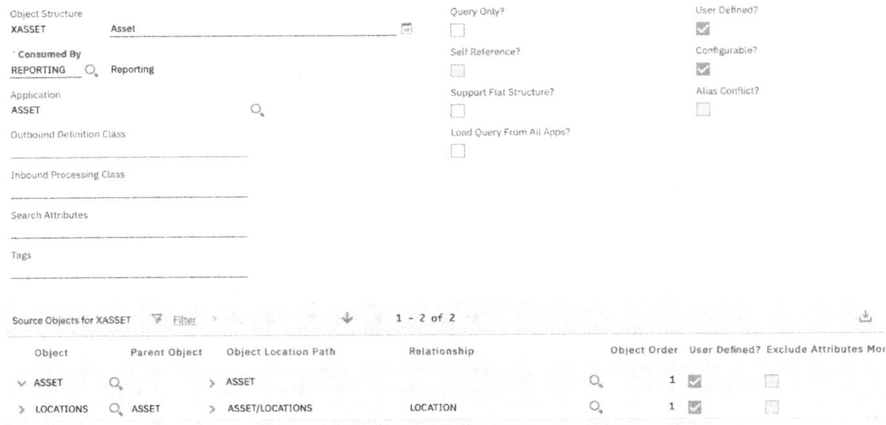

Figure 181 The Object Structure for Result Set

In the next step, you must authorize a group to have an access to this ROS. In *Report Administration* application, use the action **Set Report Object Structure Security**. Find your new object structure and assign a security group to it (at least *MAXADMIN*). NOTE: This security group must be authorized to access the Signature Option: **Create Report** in the application with which ROS is associated, in this case it was **ASSET**.

Report Object Structure Security

Report Object Structures — Filter — 6 - 10 of 32

Object Structure	Description	Application
REP_ASSETSCHED	Asset Schedule Details	Assets
XASSET	Asset	Assets
REP_CLASS	Classification Details	Classifications
REP_CONDM	Condition Monitoring Details	Condition Monitoring
REP_DMCOMPRESULT	Migration Manager comparison results	Migration Manager

Report Object Structure Security — 1 - 1 of 1

Group	Description
MAXADMIN	Maximo Administrators (Super Users)

New Row

Cancel OK

Figure 182 Set Report Object Structure Security

Now, in Result Set window, choose the application *ASSET* and a query, and when you click on *Location* position in **Object List** section, you will have an access to all the locations fields, including **Description**, which you can now use in your Result Set.

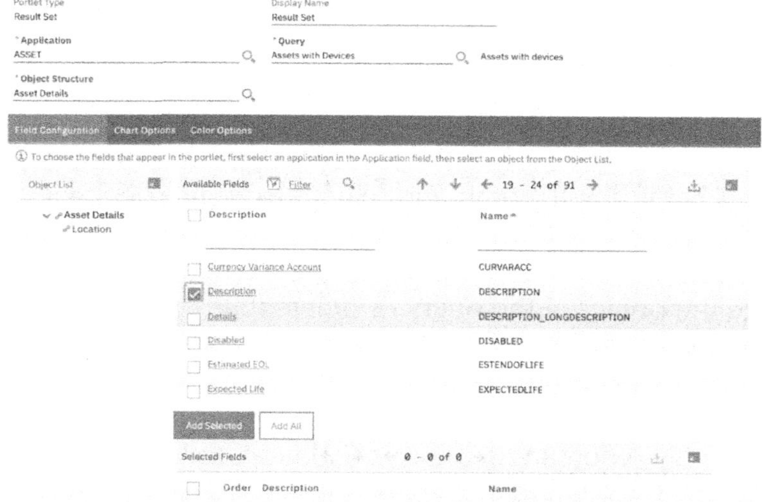

Figure 183 A Result Set

Object Structures can have multiple levels, e.g. WO—Asset—Meter, and you can refer to all of them on the Start Center. However, there is also a limitation: only 1 relation between the same objects is allowed. For example, the customer wants to see two PM meters on a Start Center: mileage and hours worked (**Next Meter Reading** information). We can define two relationships between **PM** and **PMMETER** objects:

pmnum = :pmnum and siteid = :siteid and metername = 'MI'

pmnum = :pmnum and siteid = :siteid and metername = 'HRS'

but only one of them can be used in the Object Structure and in the Result Set.

Finally, as a reminder: Do you know what **Open Result Set in the Application** button in the Result Set does?

Saved Queries

You may sometimes need to quickly edit a Start Center but then you will find that someone else is doing that. The below query (to be run in the database tool) will help identifying the current editor.

> *select userid, description from scconfig where groupname is null*

Another helpful SQL command may help you to deal with queries that belong to inactive users (as mentioned before, you cannot edit them). If you find any such record, you can either change the owner of the query or delete it:

> *select * from query where not exists (select 1 from maxuser where owner = userid and status = 'ACTIVE')*

Alternatively, you can create an escalation, for example, to automatically assign the orphaned queries to *maxadmin* user. Remember to make **QUERY** table the main object in ***Database Configuration*** application first.

Summary

This was the last part of my book. In the first part, I described my vision of the Maximo implementation project. I have presented the necessary organization as well as the tools and products that need to be delivered. This is critical knowledge each functional consultant should possess and use on daily basis because it helps to deliver successful solutions.

The second part was dedicated to the functionality of Maximo. My goal was to give as much useful information about the implemented processes as possible, but also to show what can be improved in Maximo to deliver better solutions. It is nearly impossible to describe and comment on each and every screen and dialog. My book should be rather treated as a guide of how to look at applications and consider reflecting a business process using standard applications.

But one thing should be clear: Maximo is a highly integrated maintenance system. After reading this book, one should have a better picture of how its main components work together. Let us take a look at this summary diagram with all major applications:

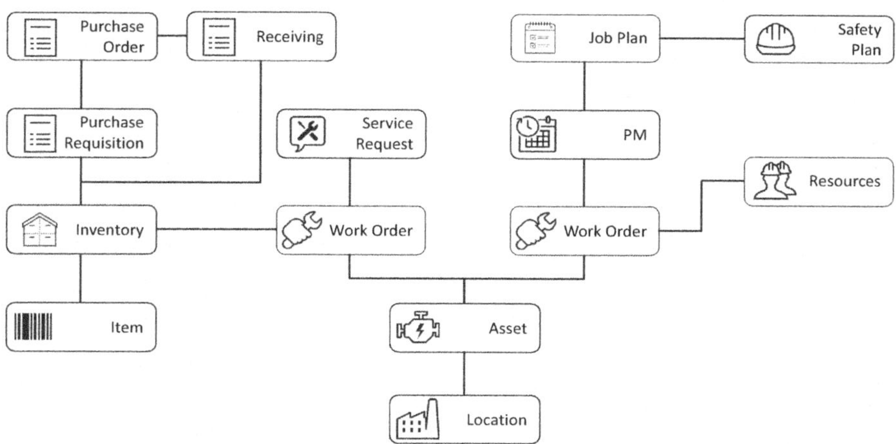

Figure 184 Integrated System

I am sure my book will help you to describe the role of each application and the main concepts and processes like functional locations, cost roll-up, work planning, material ordering.

Where can you go from here?
This should not be the last step in your Maximo education. Please play as much as possible with the system and check the online Help. Thanks to that, you will better understand how Maximo works. Read the system documentation provided by IBM, among others:

- Administering Maximo Asset Management;
- Developing Applications;
- Implementing Workflow Processes;
- there is also an interesting Finance Manager Guide, but from Version 7.1.

Check also other IBM resources:

- sign up to *Maximo IoT Community* https://www.ibm.com/community/iot/maximo;
- enroll to Maximo training on *Watson Internet of Things Academy* https://www.ibm.com/services/learning;
- view *IBM IoT Support* channel on YouTube http://www.youtube.com/c/IBMIoTSupportVideos.

If possible, participate in IBM events, especially the ones about new version announcements, but also about End of Support (EOS) announcements.

You can also join a Maximo User Group (MUG)—the local one, e.g. African, Australian, Canadian, UK & Ireland, or the one with a focus on specific industries, like transportation or utilities.

There are also other valuable resources on the Internet that are worth checking, such as Stack Overflow, Maximo groups on LinkedIn or numerous blogs. Also, IBM Partners publish very interesting articles.

During your projects, you may find a feature missing from Maximo or not working the way users expect. You should then submit an enhancement request for a new feature (or modify an existing one)—IBM now calls these requests: Ideas. You can register them at: https://ideas.ibm.com. The proposal itself does not have much clout, so you need to get support for it (Votes) using your network of professional contacts. The more votes a proposal gets, the more likely it is to be implemented in the next version of Maximo.

Please contact me on LinkedIn:
https://www.linkedin.com/in/robert-zientara or via e-mail: rgzientara@gmail.com if you have any suggestions, questions or comments.

Thank you!

Author

Appendixes

Team roles

This chapter contains descriptions of the critical skills for each role in your team.

Project manager:

- experience in Maximo or ERP projects,
- PMP or PRINCE2 certification,
- a senior position,
- strong communication skills.

Solution architect/lead consultant:

- a very deep knowledge of Maximo,
- business skills,
- listening skills.

Industry consultant:

- real-life experience in the industry,
- CMMS/EAM knowledge.

System architect:

- the knowledge of industry standards,
- the knowledge of Maximo compatibility matrix.

System engineer:

- the application server knowledge,
- the database knowledge,
- the operating system knowledge,
- the knowledge of Maximo installation.

Maximo consultants:

- Maximo knowledge,
- business skills,

- at least a medium SQL knowledge,
- the knowledge of office tools.

Java programmer:
- a deep Java knowledge,
- a deep SQL knowledge,
- a basic knowledge of the application server,
- a deep knowledge of Maximo MBO.

Mobile programmer:
- good UI/UX skills,
- a deep SQL knowledge,
- a deep knowledge of mobile programming.

MIF specialist:
- a deep Java knowledge,
- a deep SQL knowledge,
- a deep knowledge of Maximo MBO.

Data migration consultant:
- a deep SQL knowledge,
- good ETL skills.

Release manager:
- the knowledge of a Migration Manager,
- a deep SQL knowledge,
- good spreadsheet skills.

Report writer:
- a deep SQL knowledge,
- good graphic design skills,
- a deep knowledge of the report engine (including multi-language reports).

Technical writer:
- fast typing skills,

- good editing skills,
- a deep knowledge of the text editor.

Tester:

- experience in testing,
- the knowledge of the testing tool or good spreadsheet skills (depending on the test method).

Trainer:

- good presentation skills,
- a deep knowledge of the presentation software,
- high training skills.

Support Analyst:

- a general knowledge of Maximo,
- the ability to diagnose problems,
- communication skills,
- stress resistance.

Database tables

This chapter contains a list of the selected database tables—Maximo has over 1000 tables! They are divided by application but this structure is not equal to the services defined in Maximo. This is not by any means an official Entity Relationship Diagram (ERD) of a Maximo database, but rather a list of useful tables which can be used to prepare queries or reports.

Assets:
ASSET—the main table,
ASSETTRANS—the history of the asset movements,
ASSETLOCRELATION—the relations between the assets,
ASSETLOCRELHIST—the history of relation changes,
ASSETLOCUSERCUST—the information about the users and custodians,
ASSETHIERARCHY—the hierarchy of the assets,
ASSETANCESTOR—a flattened hierarchical structure; you can quickly find all children for a parent,
ASSETSTATUS—downtime information,
PLUSCASSETSTATUS—the history of status changes,
PLUSCTEMPLATE—Asset Template table.

Attachments:
DOCLINKS—the links between the documents and objects,
DOCINFO—information about the documents.

Bulletin Board:
BULLETINBOARD—the main table,
BBOARDMSGSTATUS—the information on whether the user has viewed the message.

Classifications:
CLASSSTRUCTURE—the main table,
CLASSANCESTOR—a flattened hierarchical structure; you can quickly find all children for a parent,

CLASSUSEWITH—the links between a classification and objects,
CLASSSPEC—the list of classification attributes,
ASSETSPEC—the list of classification attributes for a specific asset,
ASSETSPECHIST—the history of asset attribute changes,
ITEMSPEC—the list of classification attributes for a specific item,
JOBPLANSPEC—the list of classification attributes for a specific job plan,
JOBTASKSPEC—the list of classification attributes for a specific job task,
LOCATIONSPEC—the list of classification attributes for a specific location,
PDSPEC— the list of classification attributes for a Purchase Requisition/Purchase Order/Request for Quotation,
TICKETSPEC—the list of classification attributes for a specific Service Request,
WORKORDERSPEC—the list of classification attributes for a specific work order.

Communication Log:
COMMLOG—the main table.

Condition Monitoring:
MEASUREPOINT—the main table,
MEASUREMENT—the list of historical values,
CHARPOINTACTION—the list of actions for characteristic meters,
POINTWO—the list of generated Work Orders.

Crafts:
CRAFT—the main table,
CRAFTRATE—craft rates,
CRAFTSKILL—craft skill levels.

Cron Tasks:
CRONTASKDEF—the main table,

CRONTASKINSTANCE—instances of cron tasks,
CRONTASKPARAM—the parameters of cron tasks,
CRONTASKHISTORY—the history of actions,
TASKSCHEDULER—the last run of cron tasks.

Escalations:
ESCALATION—the main table,
ESCREFPOINT—escalation points with actions,
ESCNOTIFICATION—mapping between escalation points and notifications,
ESCREPEATTRACK—the list of the processed records,
ESCCOMMLOG—Communication Log,
ESCSTATUS—the status of escalations with the list of emails not sent.

Failure Codes:
FAILURECODE—the main table,
FAILURELIST—the hierarchy of problems, causes and remedies,
FAILUREREMARK—the remarks from Work Orders,
FAILUREREPORT—the hierarchy of the problems, causes and remedies from Work Orders or Service Requests.

Financial Management:
FINCNTRL—cost management projects, the main table.

Inventory:
INVENTORY—the main table,
INVBALANCES—item balances,
INVRESERVE—item reservations,
INVTRANS—inventory transactions,
MATRECTRANS—material receipt, transfer and return transactions.

Inventory Usage:
INVUSE—the main table,
INVUSELINE—inventory usage lines,
INVUSESTATUS—status history.

Invoices:
INVOICE—the main table,
INVOICELINE—invoice lines,
INVOICECOST—distributed costs information,
INVOICESTATUS—the history of status changes,
INVOICEMATCH—the invoice matching information,
INVOICETRANS—cost and currency differences.

Items:
ITEM—the main table,
ITEMSTRUCT—Item Assembly Structure details,
ITEMSTATUS—status history.

Job Plans:
JOBPLAN— the main table,
JOBTASK—the list of tasks in a plan,
JOBLABOR— the planned labor,
JOBMATERIAL— the planned materials,
JOBSERVICE— the planned services,
JOBTOOL— the planned tools.

KPIs:
KPIMAIN—the main table,
KPIHISTORY—the history of readings.

Labor:
LABOR—the main table,
LABORCRAFTRATE—labor craft rates,
LABORQUAL—the connections between a person and qualification,
LABORCERTHIST—the history of certifications,
ATTENDANCE—daily attendance entries.

Locations:
LOCATION—the main table,
LOCSYSTEM—the list of location systems,
LOCHIERARCHY—the hierarchy of the locations,

LOCANCESTOR—a flattened hierarchical structure; you can quickly find all the children for a parent.

Login Tracking:
LOGINTRACKING—the main table.

Long Descriptions:
LONGDESCRIPTION—the main table.

Meters:
METER—the main table,
METERGROUP—meter group definition,
METERINGROUP—the relation between the meters and meter group,
ASSETMETER—the relation between the assets and meters,
LOCATIONMETER—the relation between the locations and meters,
PMMETER—the relation between the PMs and meters,
MASTERPMMETER—the relation between the Master PMs and meters,
WOMETER—the relation between the work orders and meters,
METERREADING—asset readings for continuous meters,
LOCMETERREADING—location readings for continuous meters,
MEASUREMENT—asset and location readings for characteristic and gauge meters.

Material Requests:
MR—the main table,
MRLINE—Material Request lines,
MRSTATUS—the history of status changes,
MRCOST—distributed costs information.

Person:
PERSONANCESTOR—a flattened hierarchical structure; you can quickly find all the children for a parent.

Pictures:
IMGLIB—the main table.

PMs:
PM—the main table,
MASTERPM—Master PMs,
PMANCESTOR—a flattened hierarchical structure; you can quickly find all the children for a parent,
PMSEQUENCE—PM Job Plan Sequence,
MASTERPMSEQ—Master PM Job Plan Sequence,
PMFORECAST—PM Forecast information,
PMFORECASTLABOR—PM Forecast Labor Costs,
PMFORECASTMATERIAL—PM Forecast Material Costs,
PMFORECASTSERVICE—PM Forecast Service Costs,
PMFORECASTTOOL—PM Forecast Tool Costs.

Purchase Orders:
PO—the main table,
POLINE—Purchase Order lines,
POSTATUS— the history of status changes,
POCOST—distributed costs information.

Purchase Requisitions:
PR—the main table,
PRLINE—Purchase Requisitions lines,
PRSTATUS— the history of status changes,
PRCOST—distributed costs information.

Queries:
QUERY—the main table,
DEFAULTQUERY—default queries for a specific user for an application.

Relationships:
RELATION—the main table,
RELATIONRULES—the list of relationship rules,

ASSETLOCRELATION—the links between the assets and relations.

Reports:
REPORT—the main table,
REPORTADHOC—QBR reports,
REPORTDESIGN—XMLs of the reports,
REPORTJOB—the currently running reports,
REPORTSCHED—the planned reports,
REPORTUSAGELOG—the list of report executions (cleared by the cron task *REPORTUSAGECLEANUP*),
REPORTLABEL—the labels on the report,
REPORTLOOKUP—the list of report lookups,
REPORTAUTH— Report authorization for security groups.

Requests for Quotations:
RFQ—the main table,
RFQLINE—Requests for Quotation lines,
RFQSTATUS— the history of status changes,
RFQVENDOR—the list of vendors.

Routes:
ROUTES—the main table,
ROUTE_STOP—the route's elements with the information about the Job Plan.

Safety:
HAZARD—the list of hazards,
HAZARDPREC—the precautions associated with the hazard,
LOCKOUT—lockout procedures,
PRECAUTION—the list of precautions,
SAFETYPLAN—the list of safety plans,
TAGOUT—the tagout procedure for asset/location,
TAGLOCK—a step in the tagout procedure.

Security:
APPLICATIONAUTH—group authorization for the application,

SIGOPTION—the list of Signature Options,
MAXGROUP—the list of Security Groups,
MAXUSER—the list of users,
GROUPUSER— the assignment of the users to the security groups.

Service Addresses:
SERVICEADDRESS—the main table,
TKSERVICEADDRESS—the addresses associated with Service Requests,
WOSERVICEADDRESS—the addresses associated with Work Orders.

Service Requests:
TICKET—the main table,
SR—the main view (TICKET),
TKOWNERHISTORY—the history of the ownership,
TKSTATUS—the history of status changes,
RELATEDRECORD—the list of related Service Requests/Work Orders.

Shipment:
SHIPMENT—the main table,
SHIPMENTLINE—shipment lines.

Start Centers:
ACTIONCFG—configuration of Quick Insert portlet,
FACONFIG—configuration of Favorite applications portlet,
INBXCONFIG—configuration of Inbox/Assignments portlet,
KPIGCONFIG—configuration of KPI Graph portlet,
KPILCONFIG—configuration of KPI List portlet,
LAYOUT—configuration of a given Start Center,
PORTLET—portlet definitions,
REPORTLISTCFG—configuration of Report List portlet,
RESULTSETCOLS—configuration of the columns in Result Sets,
RSCONFIG—configuration of Result Set portlet,
SCCONFIG—the layout of Start Centers for each user,

SCTEMPLATE—Start Center templates and XMLs with presentation definitions.

Terms and Conditions:
TERM—the main table with the definition of terms and conditions,
CONTRACTTERM—terms for contracts,
INVOICETERM—terms for invoices,
POTERM—terms for Purchase Orders,
PRTERM—terms for Purchase Requisitions,
RFQTERM—terms for Requests for Quotation.

Workflow:
WFPROCESS—the main table,
WFTRANSACTION—the history of workflow actions,
WFACTION—the actions used in the workflow,
WFNODE—the list of nodes,
WFASSIGNMENT—the assignment of the records (used in Inbox/Assignments),
WFINSTANCE—a workflow instance information,
EVENTRESPONSE—the records with a disabled status change.

Work Log:
WORKLOG—the main table.

Work Orders:
WORKORDER—the main table,
WOSAFETYLINK—work-related hazards,
WOHAZARDPREC—precautions to mitigate above hazards,
WOHAZARD—detailed information about work-related hazards,
WOPRECAUTION—detailed information about work-related precautions,
WOANCESTOR—a flattened hierarchical structure; you can quickly find all the children for a parent,
WOOWNERHISTORY—the history of the ownership,
WOSTATUS—the history of status changes,

RELATEDRECORD—the list of related Service Requests/Work Orders,
WPLABOR—the planned labor (tab: **Plans**),
WPMATERIAL—the planned materials (tab: **Plans**),
WPSERVICE—the planned services (tab: **Plans**),
WPTOOL—the planned tools (tab: **Plans**),
PRICALC—priority calculation,
ASSIGNMENT—the list of assigned labor,
LABTRANS—labor transactions (tab: **Actuals**),
MATUSETRANS—the materials used (tab: **Actuals**),
SERVRECTRANS—service transactions (tab: **Actuals**),
TOOLTRANS—the tools used (tab: **Actuals**).

Data types

This is a list of the most-used data types in Maximo:

- ALN—alphanumeric, lower- and uppercase,
- AMOUNT—decimal numbers, used for currency representation,
- DATE—date only, no time,
- DATETIME—date and time,
- DECIMAL—decimal numbers,
- DURATION—duration; for example, 0:30 is half an hour,
- FLOAT—floating numbers,
- GL—general Ledger account,
- INTEGER—integer numbers,
- LOWER—lowercase characters,
- TIME—time only, no date,
- UPPER—uppercase characters,
- YORN—Yes or No, the database contains 1 or 0.

Variables

This is a list of the variables you can use in Maximo, for example in queries, conditional expressions or relationships:

- :&APPNAME&—the application name, used to access the current MBO,
- :&DATE&—the current date e.g. *installdate = :&date&,*
- :&DATETIME&—the current date and time e.g. *reportdate = :&datetime&,*
- :&HOSTNAME&—the URL of Maximo server,
- :&MBONAME&—the name of the current business object,
- :NO—False value e.g. *rotating = :no,*
- :&OWNER&—the name of the current MBO's owner,
- :&OWNERNAME&—the name of the current MBO's owner,
- :&PERSONID&—person ID of the logged-in user,
- :&UNIQUEID&—unique ID of the current object,
- :&USERNAME&—logged-in user e.g. *reportedby = :&username&,*
- :YES—True value e.g. *istask = :yes.*

NOTE: The variable can return an empty string.

Project Deliverables—sample content

This chapter contains sample structures of different documents (products) to be delivered during the project.

Initial Presentation

There is always an official presentation at the beginning of the project with the introduction of the team, Project Management methodology, project phases, etc.
Then follows your presentation about Maximo. Start with the system navigation and afterwards, elaborate on the purpose of Maximo modules.
Next, explain how the major applications work, show some data models in Assets and Locations, and finally, go through some scenarios, for example: ordering materials for a Work Order.
It is important to include some slides about the integrations between Maximo and other systems to confirm that data will be entered only once (numerous customers are very concerned about this issue).
During your presentation, use some examples from other projects to explain the possible solutions (if applicable).

Final Presentation

Importantly, to get the approval of your work you must explain what you have done and how this fits the customer requirements.
First, explain what the drivers are to introduce the system, who will be using it and what for. Above all, present the expected benefits!
Next, recap the workshops, thank for the participation and contribution. Remind about some interesting facts you may have learned during the workshops.
Then explain how Maximo will fulfill the customer's requirements. Show some slides about data models and how the business processes will be supported. Do not forget about the

integrations with other systems and how they will support the processes.
Finally, describe the documents which have been delivered and how to read them. If in the documents you use any notation, like BPMN, to describe the processes, this is the moment to explain it, too. This is also the moment to present how the users should provide their comments—in a spreadsheet, with references to the chapters and page numbers, etc.

Spreadsheets for Homework

This is not an official product. The content provided by the customer will be part of your Functional Specification but having these files prepared earlier will shorten the discussion. Use colors to indicate the mandatory and optional columns, and provide a few lines of sample data to help the customer understand what is required and in what form.

ASSETNUM	PARENT	SERIALNUM	ASSETTAG	AS_LOCATION	AS_DESCRIPTION	VENDOR	FAILURECODE	AS_MANUFACTURER
unique id leave it empty for Maximo to generate it					description of the asset eg. Industrial Robot XYZ	requires a vendor dictionary		
A-1000		45544			Transformer	ABB		
A-1001	A-1000	233490113			Oil Tank	ABB		

Figure 185 An Example of an Import Spreadsheet

- List of system languages (English must be installed as the base language)
- List of GL Accounts (segments, allowed segment values, allowed segment combinations)
- List of fiscal periods
- List of currencies
- List of hazards and precautions
- Calendar definition with shifts and holidays
- List of crafts
- List of qualifications
- List of labor
- List of person groups
- List of measure units
- List of technical attributes
- List of classifications

- Mapping classification—attributes
- List of companies
- List of items
- List of tools
- List of company addresses
- Auto-numbering prefixes for assets, locations, Job Plans, Work Orders

Migration Templates

They should be prepared for all the information to be imported into the system. It should include at least the following information:

- the source system,
- the list of the data to be imported; for example, inventory balances, the list of labor,
- the format of extracted data,
- the cleansing procedure,
- data mapping,
- the importing method:
    - using MBO or direct database import,
    - disabling standard functionality, for example, to import historical data,
- the testing procedure,
- metrics.

Configuration Document

This is a summary of the installation phase. It should cover both hardware and software.

- Architecture of the system:
    - the list of the environments and for each of them:
        - VLANs, firewalls, load balancers,
        - servers—addresses, names, users (logins, passwords—probably, delivered in a sealed envelope),
        - the installed software: its version and patches,

        - JVMs installed,
        - transmission protocols and the ports used.
- Maximo configuration files
- The scripts used during the installation
- DB/OS/application server configuration

Functional Specification

Here you can find a sample structure of the functional specification document. It is based on the business processes that will be supported by Maximo and describes the necessary configuration to tailor Maximo to the customer's needs. This is one of the methods to prepare this document. Another approach would be to describe the modules and applications including the processes when applicable.

- Implementation team members (name, company, department, role in the project)—you can also include a photo of the whole team if the customer agrees.
- Glossary of terms
- Basic procedures (this should be also the first chapter of your user manuals, described in End User Manuals). The purpose of repeating this chapter is to minimize the risk of the specifications being not approved by the customer. Remember that the customer knows nothing about Maximo; therefore, they will need a reference to understand your writing.
- General settings:
    - the organization/site structure:
        - General Ledger structure,
        - calendars,
        - currencies,
    - the basic settings:
        - Tax options,
        - Inventory options,
        - WO options,
    - the layout of the screen and reports (logos, specific colors),

    - the expected data volume,
    - the languages installed,
    - specific security measures.
- The planned configuration of the system:
    - the data model—this should cover in detail how the customer's data will be represented in Maximo: what will be an asset and what will be a location, etc.; include diagrams and screenshots with sample data, for example, with hierarchies to help the users visualize their data,
    - processes grouped by Maximo modules (Work Orders, Assets, Inventory, etc.):
        - BPMN diagram of the process,
        - the process flow description (including notifications and escalations) and how it will be supported by Maximo: a workflow or status changes,
        - a state transition diagram— I include it to verify the completeness of the transitions,
        - RACI table—to describe the roles in the process,
        - the application(s) required by the process:
            - a screenshot of the application and its tabs (include main dialog windows and **Advanced Search** window), and a short description: what it is for, what its main functions are, how it works; the good thing is that you can prepare this information once and use it later as a template; of course, you must revisit it after a new Maximo version is released to change the screenshots and the functionality description,

        - for each tab/dialog prepare a description of the required changes in terms of removing/adding/changing fields; use mock-ups to present the future layout of the screen or new screens; use the descriptions such as:
            - a new field 'Fixed Asset Number' will be added (alphanumeric, length 25),
            - the field 'Priority' will be removed,
            - the tab 'Topology' will be removed,
- data migration (major information only):
    - the source system,
    - which data will be migrated,
    - the expected data volume,
- the integration:
    - the target system,
    - which data will be exchanged,
    - the direction of data exchange,
    - frequency,
- mobile application(s):
    - the use of mobile devices to support the process,
- KPIs,
- reports:
    - security,
    - performance limitations,
    - the hours of execution,
    - include a mock-up—for reports, a spreadsheet form is the best,
- a reference to the customer's requirements (how they will be implemented).

- Security Profiles and Start Centers design—at least basic information: which group will have an access to which applications, the type of the access: read, save, insert.

Technical Specification

This is not an official product but an internal guide for your consultants and developers of how to implement the configuration described in Functional Specification. In smaller projects, it may be skipped but it is extremely useful if you are cooperating with offshore developers. Usually, it is built around Maximo applications. Here is a sample structure:

- Maximo module:
    - Maximo application:
        - form changes (mock-ups for layout changes, data filtering, sorting, signature options),
        - Saved Queries,
        - database changes (tables and attributes but also, relationships and indexes),
        - domains,
        - Workflows,
        - Actions,
        - Escalations,
        - communication templates,
        - roles,
        - Cron tasks,
        - the e-mail listener,
        - interfaces (Integrations),
        - automation scripts,
        - conditional expressions,
        - Security Groups,
        - Start Centers,
        - KPIs,
        - Java classes,
        - reports.

Technical Documentation

This is the other side of the Technical Specification document. The previous one describes the planned changes in Maximo; this one summarizes the actual changes made in an out-of-the-box system. The structure will be similar to Technical Specification and will reflect all the configuration objects:

- forms (screenshots of all the changed tabs and dialogs, data filtering, sorting, changed/new signature options),
- Saved Queries,
- database changes (new tables, changed/new columns, changed domains/Java classes, changed/new relationships and indexes),
- the system properties,
- domains,
- Workflows,
- Actions,
- Escalations,
- communication templates,
- roles,
- Cron tasks,
- e-mail configuration, including the e-mail listener,
- interfaces (Integrations, including Java classes),
- automation scripts,
- conditional expressions,
- translation,
- Security Groups (with the detailed descriptions of the access and options, data restrictions; they should rather have a form of an additional document because of their size),
- Start Centers,
- KPIs,
- reports,
- attachments,
- patches/fixes files,
- the code of Java classes,

- report files,
- TDToolkit XLIFF files.

Maintenance Procedures

If you want the project to be successful and ensure that Maximo will work properly, you have to think about the time when you will leave the customer alone with the system. These procedures will ensure the system will be up and running. Usually, they are part of the documentation for system administrators. In most cases, they refer only to the production environment, not to tests or QA.

- System start/stop procedure.
- The backup of the system.
- Restore from the backup.
- Switching between the production and backup environment (for High Availability setup).
- The installation of a software fix:
    - the installation of a hot fix can remove custom class mapping, so they must be reviewed and fixed when necessary after the fix is installed.
- Change the procedure:
    - how to report a change,
    - the evaluation of the change's impact on the existing functionality: applications, mobile application, report,
    - change the approval process,
    - the implementation of the planning change (including translations of new objects),
    - configuration of the system,
    - saving new/changed files in the software repository,
    - updating Technical Documentation,
    - updating the End User Manuals.
- Release the procedure:
    - version management (this should be related to development procedure),

- the procedure of how to translate files using TDToolkit
- the process of migrating the application between the development, test and production servers:
  - the migration of configuration using Migration Manager/manual work (or a third-party product),
  - the migration of data (Calendars, Security Groups, Reports, Start Centers, Person Groups),
- rebuild applications,
- re-deploy applications,
- adding a new or updated report (request page generation),
- provide training for end users and administrators,
- make a copy of the production environment and move it to the test and development environments.

- The rollout procedure (adding a new site, country):
  - the procedure of adding a new language to translation files,
  - creating a new organization, new sites or system parameters:
    - creating/adding Company and Item Set,
    - defining new limits and tolerances in Security Groups,
    - importing new GL Account structures,
    - a new site may require specific local information, e.g. there must be created a new Person Group for each site with at least one person,
    - defining standard calendars, e.g. *24H* and custom calendars for the new site/country,
    - defining financial periods,
  - the migration of new data for new sites:

        - before importing, there might be a need to temporarily disable some functionalities, e.g. site restriction,
        - after migration, make a copy of the production environment and move it to the test and development environments.
- The upgrade procedure:
    - install a new version,
    - remove the unnecessary new fields introduced by the new version,
    - check if critical attributes, like RMI port, have not changed,
    - rename applications/fields if needed,
    - make sure the changed logos and menu bar graphics are not affected by the upgrade,
    - check if the new version have not added some new values to the domains, for example, Work Types,
    - check the path to the attachments (DOCLINKS).
- Periodical maintenance
    - Daily maintenance:
        - review logs,
        - check the scheduled reports,
        - check the email errors,
        - check the escalation errors,
        - check the number of the users logged in and compare with JVM allowed users,
        - monitor CPU/RAM/processes/network,
        - monitor the disk space of attachments,
        - monitor the size of the database; add additional disk space if required,
        - check integration queues,
        - User management:
            - a new user:
                - create a new person (define default insert site, language, locale),

            - create a new user,
            - add to Security Groups,
            - add to Person Groups,
            - check whether the user desktop matches the minimal system requirements,
        - a changed user/user deactivation:
            - change person details,
            - change/deactivate the user login,
            - change/remove Security Groups.
            - change/remove Person Groups,
    - processing user requests (Service Desk for users):
        - ensure proper end user communication,
        - investigate the issue and check the issue's impact on the existing functionality,
        - when debugging is required, disable it after the work is done,
        - prepare the fix or report a PMR with IBM Technical Support,
        - implement the fix,
        - test the fix,
        - update the Technical Documentation,
        - release the fix using the Release procedure,
    - create the backup.
- Weekly maintenance:
    - run Database Integrity Check,
    - reorganize the database (update statistics),
    - rebuild indexes.
- Monthly maintenance:
    - report on Maximo performance and issues to SLA Manager,
    - ensure time synchronization between all the servers and clients, including mobile devices,
    - optimize the system (delete obsolete data, including unused workflow data),
    - remove the unnecessary files, such as:

        - orphaned attachments,
        - old log files,
        - the files from incoming emails processing (start with LSNR...),
        - the files generated by the cost rollup report,
    - test the procedure "Restore from the backup",
    - periodically, refresh the test/training environment with a copy of the production (NOTE: Observe the security policy and personal data protection requirements. Data anonymization may be required as described earlier),
    - check the PMs for errors,
    - monitor PMR progress,
    - check the security bulletins that regard Maximo,
    - check for new fixes/upgrades.
- Yearly maintenance (or End-of-year tasks):
    - update calendars (holidays),
    - update financial periods,
    - set to zero the following values:
        - Assets: Year to Date Costs,
        - Inventory: Year to Date, Last Year, 2 Years Ago, 3 Years Ago quantities,
        - Labor: Year to Date Hours,
        - Stocked Tools: Year to Date, Last Year, 2 Years Ago quantities,
    - change the Auto-numbering prefixes (in case they are year specific),
    - update exchange rates (this can be done also daily or monthly),
    - release the unused material reservations,
    - run the *Report Usage* report to determine which reports are no longer used.
- Non-scheduled maintenance:
    - site deactivation:
        - complete all the open SRs and WOs,
        - deactivate all PMs,

- deactivate the users.

End User Manuals

This is some proposed content of the end user manuals:

- basic procedures—the introduction to the user interface: elements of the screen, system navigation, how to sort tables, how to search, how to print and export data, etc.; you should include screenshots and describe each element and function thoroughly (this part can be prepared once and used as a template but, of course, you must revisit it after a new Maximo version is released);
- for each role, create a manual: a list of the use cases with detailed instructions and screenshots, e.g. how to create a purchase requisition, how to approve it; this should include a list of the reports available for this role and the information on which application to find them in;
- sometimes, the customer will ask you to prepare manual procedures for the time when Maximo is down—this should include not only a description of the manual work and paper forms but also the procedure for entering this information into the system once it is the back up;
- think about sharing the manuals under system menu: **Help**; you can create the documentation using Maximo Help Customization Toolkit—**Help** menu automatically distributes the manuals to all the users; all the documentation updates will be also immediately made available for them.

Training for end users

Sometimes, this is a tricky task because these people might be extremely busy and inviting them for a long training session is not possible. Try to make it short and productive.

Sample topics to be presented:

- Introduction to the project by customer managers: this is a good opportunity to present the internal project goal and invite the users to use the system.

- Basic procedures.
- Process flow and participation in the process of each of the roles: my approach is to explain to the end users how the whole process works in Maximo, even if they will play different roles in the system—this is to ensure that they will perform their duties bearing in mind that their output is important for the next step in the process.
- Exercises: you should avoid having only a lecture—hands-on exercises are the best education tool, even if it takes time to prepare student materials with tasks.
- Training materials can be delivered in the form of presentation files, audio/video files or e-learning.

Training for administrators

System administrators can participate in end user training, too, to gain knowledge about the system functionality, but during a dedicated training, you will teach them the following:

- the system architecture (logical and physical),
- the modules and applications,
- User management (Security Groups and Person Groups),
- troubleshooting (checking logs),
- the system configuration:
    - modifying the database structure (new columns, relationships, indexes),
    - modifying forms (adding controls, dialogs, signature options),
    - system properties,
    - domains,
    - Cron tasks and Escalations (roles, actions),
    - Workflow modifications,
- reports:
    - setting up a development environment,
    - creating simple reports,
    - sub-reports,
    - managing the reports in Maximo.

A training for administrators can be prepared just once and used numerous times. Of course, you must revisit it after a new Maximo version is released to update the screenshots and content.

Unfortunately, most of these documents have to be prepared manually during the project (you can have a library of empty documents with at least predefined structure) but there are exceptions.

The first one is a document called Basic Procedures (mentioned in Functional Specification, End User Manuals and Training for end users). You can prepare it once and re-use it in all the projects because it is all about Maximo's basic features without referencing to changes made during implementation. You may have to update it when a new Maximo version is released because there might be some changes in navigation and other mechanisms.

Another exception is Technical Documentation. This has to be prepared for each project but you can automate its preparation using Maximo features. To do it, you have to design several Maximo reports that will generate chapters for this document:

- the system configuration (with sub-reports for each configuration area),
- new reports in the system,
- Security Groups,
- Start Centers.

In fact, preparing these reports can be very easy assuming you are going to use the naming convention that I described in Part I (using prefix *X* for new objects). You can use the below queries to find the updated objects.

New tables:

- *select * from maxobjectcfg where upper(objectname) like 'X%'*

New attributes:

- *select * from maxattribute where upper(attributename) like 'X%'*

New relationships:

- *select * from maxrelationship where upper(name) like 'X%'*

New applications:

- *select * from maxapps where upper(app) like 'X%'*

New modules:

- *select * from maxmodules where upper(module) like 'X%'*

New Signature Options:

- *select * from sigoption where upper(optionname) like 'X%'*

New saved queries:

- *select * from query where upper(clausename) like 'X%'*

New system properties:

- *select * from maxprop where upper(propname) like 'X%'*

New domains:

- *select * from maxdomain where upper(domainid) like 'X%'*
- *select * from alndomain where upper(domainid) like 'X%'*
- *select * from numericdomain where upper(domainid) like 'X%'*

New conditions:

- *select * from condition where upper(conditionnum) like 'X%'*

New automation scripts:

- *select * from autoscript where upper(autoscript) like 'X%' and status = 'Active'*

New actions:

- *select * from action where upper(action) like 'X%'*

New workflows:

- *select * from wfprocess where upper(processname) like 'X%' and active = 1*

New roles:

- *select * from maxrole where upper(maxrole) like 'X%'*

New escalations:

- *select * from escalation where upper(escalation) like 'X%' and active = 1*

New communication templates:

- *select * from commtemplate where upper(templateid) like 'X%' and status = 'ACTIVE'*

New KPIs:

- *select * from kpimain where upper(kpiname) like 'X%' and realtime = 1*

New object structures (integration):

- *select * from maxintobject where upper(intobjectname) like 'X%'*

New publish channels (integration):

- *select * from maxifaceout where upper(ifacename) like 'X%'*

New service buses (integration):

- *select * from maxifacein where upper(ifacename) like 'X%'*

New external systems (integrations):

- *select * from maxextsystem where upper(extsysname) like 'X%'*

New reports:

- *select * from report where upper(reportname) like 'X%'*

New security groups:

- *select * from maxgroup where upper(groupname) like 'X%'*

Cron Tasks:

- *select * from crontaskdef*
- *select * from crontaskinstance where active = 1*
- *select * from crontaskparam*

Restrictions:

- *select * from securityrestrict*

You can also have a section in the report about organizations and sites:

- *select * from organization where active = 1*
- *select * from site where active = 1*

And about the auto-numbering schema:

- *select autokeyname, seed, prefix from autokey*

You may not always add new system properties but you will often modify the standard ones. Then the question arises: How do you find the changed values? The below query will find all the system properties modified after a specific date.

- *select p.propname, p.description, p.maximodefault, v.propvalue from maxprop p left join maxpropvalue v on p.propnmae = v.propname where v.changedate >= '01-01-2016'*

You can replace the static date information with this query, which will return the approximate Maximo installation date:

- *DB2 select starttime from crontaskhistory order by starttime fetch first 1 rows only*
- *MS SQL Server select top 1 starttime from crontaskhistory order by starttime*
- *Oracle select starttime from crontaskhistory where rowid = (select min(rowid) from crontaskhistory)*

Your query will then look like this:

- *DB2 select p.propname, p.description, p.maximodefault, v.propvalue from maxprop p left join maxpropvalue v on p.propnmae = v.propname where v.changedate > (select starttime from crontaskhistory order by starttime fetch first 1 rows only)*

Of course, these reports will not contain changes to standard objects, such as, extending the length of the login name or modified Java classes, but I estimate that over 80% of the technical documentation can be automatically generated, which saves your precious time. Just find a good report writer and tell them to prepare the above reports.

Index

Notes

Made in United States
Orlando, FL
10 May 2022

17727269R00222